W9-AFE-383

$55.00

1-2-96

3539450

STATISTICS ON

STATISTICS ON

Crime& PUniShmeNt

A Selection of Statistical Charts, Graphs and Tables
About Crime and Punishment
From a Variety of Published Sources
with Explanatory Comments

Timothy L. Gall and
Daniel M. Lucas, *Editors*

Peter C. Kratcoski, Ph.D.
Professor of Criminal Justice Studies and Sociology
Kent State University
and
Lucille Dunn Kratcoski, M.A.
Research Associate,
Contributing Editors

GALE

DETROIT · NEW YORK · TORONTO · LONDON

Eastword Publications Development Inc. Staff
Timothy L. Gall and Daniel M. Lucas, *Editors*

Gale Research Inc. Staff
Donna Wood, *Coordinating Editor*

Mary Beth Trimper, *Production Manager*
Shanna Heilveil, *Production Assistant*
Cynthia D. Baldwin, *Product Design Manager*
Michelle DiMercurio, *Art Director*

∞™ The paper used in this publication meets the minimum requirements of American National Standard for Information Sciences-Permanence Paper for Printed Library Materials, ANSI Z39.48-1984.

How to use this book

This book presents statistics on crime and punishment in the United States. Each of the statistical presentations appears on a two-page spread. The table or graphic containing the statistics is presented on a left-hand page and the explanatory text, the source citation, and contact information appears on the facing right-hand page. Also included in this volume is a general introduction to the problems concerning crime and punishment and a glossary of related terminology. Finally, a thorough index facilitates ease of use.

A tabular or graphical representation of the data

Title

A summary analysis of the data

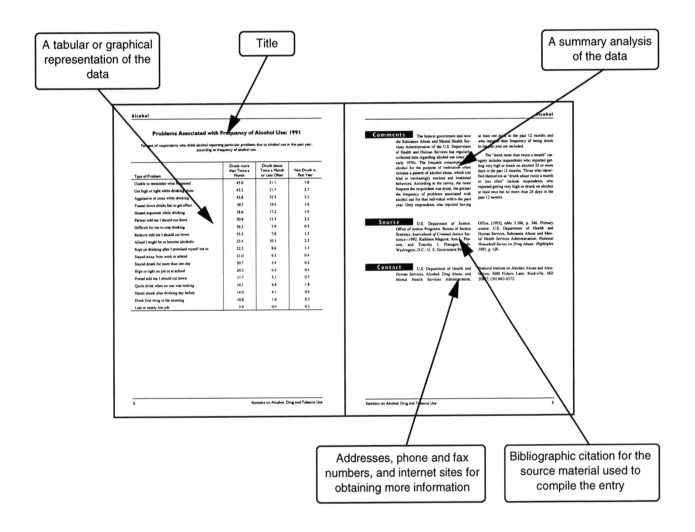

Addresses, phone and fax numbers, and internet sites for obtaining more information

Bibliographic citation for the source material used to compile the entry

Advisory Board

Table of Contents

How to Use this Book v

Advisory Board vi

Introduction xi

Acknowledgments, Sources and Contacts xxi

CRIME

Historical trends
How many crimes are committed per police officer? 2
How many law enforcement officers are protecting us? 4
How often is a victimization reported to the police? 6
How often are thefts and household crimes reported? 8
How often are crimes of violence reported? 10
At what time of day are most crimes committed? 12
At what time of year do violent and property crimes occur most frequently? 14
Does more poverty lead to more crime? 16

Demographic trends
How often are men and women victims of violent crimes? 18
How old are crime victims? 20
How old are murder victims? 22
What is the racial diversity of murder victims and murderers? 24
Personal crime victimization rates by race 26
What is the annual family income of crime victims? 28
What is the annual family income of household property crime victims? 30
How often does the victim of a violent crime know the offender? 32

Geographic trends
Crime rates for cities, suburban, and rural areas 34
Urban, suburban, and rural crime victims 36
Crime in metropolitan areas 38
How frequent is violent crime among the states? 40
How frequent is property crime among the states? 42
Residential and nonresidential burglaries, 1988–94 44
Where do robberies happen most often? 46

Personal (violent) crime
How many murders are committed in the U.S. each year? 48
Why do murders happen? 50
How many victims of rape and sexual assault are there, and how many of them report
   the crime to the police? 52
How many rapes are committed in the U.S. each year? 54
How many victims of robbery are there, and how many of them report the crime to the police? 56
How many robberies are committed in the U.S. each year? 58

How often does aggravated assault occur in the U.S. each year? 60
How often do assaults occur in each state? 62

Property and household crime
How many U.S. households are affected by a crime? 64
How often are households victimized by thieves each year? 66
How much do criminals in the U.S. steal, and how much of that stolen property is recovered? 68
How often are burglaries taking place? 70
How often are thefts taking place? 72
What type of larceny-thefts are reported most often? 74
In which states is the problem of motor vehicle theft most severe? 76
How many motor vehicles are reported stolen each year? 78
How much shoplifting takes place? 80
What types of property are torched by arsonists? 82
How big is the arson problem? 84
How many bombings are taking place in the U.S.? 86

Organized crime, drugs, and vice
How common are drug trafficking arrests? 88
How many people are arrested for prostitution each year? 90

Financial and electronic crime
Counterfeiting trends, 1985–94 92
How much money is counterfeited? 94
What kinds of electronic crimes are committed? 96

Hate crimes
Hate crimes in 1994 98
Hate crimes and race 100
What kinds of violent hate crimes are most common? 102

Profile of a perpetrator
What was the racial composition of robbers in 1992? 104
How old are violent offenders? 106
How common is juvenile delinquency? 108
How frequently is a child murdered, and how frequently is a child the murderer? 110
Juveniles and gang-related killings 112
For what crimes are minors usually arrested? 114

PUNISHMENT

Criminal Arrests
What portion of all arrests are from cities or rural areas? 118
How often are arrests made for crimes that are reported? 120
Which regions have the highest arrest rates for aggravated assault? 122
How often are minors arrested for certain offenses compared to adults? 124
Male and female arrests for violent and property offenses 126
What is the racial diversity of arrested persons? 128
Arrests in the U.S., 1990–94 130
Arrests in the U.S. during 1993 132
Arrests for economic crimes 134

Convictions of criminals
How often does a crime result in an arrest? 136
How often do economically-motivated crimes result in prison sentences? 138
During one year, how many people are convicted of felonies by state courts? 140

Sentencing and Corrections
How many adults are part of the correctional population? 142
What proportion of the adult correctional population is on probation, in jail or prison, or on parole? 144
How many adults are on probation? 146
Who is on probation? 148
What proportion of the population is in prison? 150
What type of criminals are in state prisons? 152
State and federal prisoners in 1994 154
How fast are the numbers of state and federal prisoners growing? 156
How many people are in local jails? 158
Which states have the highest concentrations of jail inmates? 160
How frequently does someone convicted of a homicide receive a life in prison or death sentence? . . . 162
How often do murderers receive a life sentence or death sentence? 164
How many people enter and leave prison within a year? 166
Annual turnover of state prisoners 168
Admissions and first releases of violent prisoners. 170
What happens to those leaving parole? 172
How long does a criminal usually stay in prison before receiving a parole? 174
Historical trends in U.S. executions from the 1890s to the mid-1990s 176
How many prisoners have been executed in the U.S.? 178
How frequently are persons serving a death sentence executed? 180
Which states executed prisoners most frequently in 1994? 182

Prior Arrests & Recidivism
How often does someone accused of a felony have a prior conviction? 184

Civil (non-criminal) cases
What types of civil cases are most common? 186
How much money is usually awarded to civil lawsuit winners? 188

Economic costs of crime and justice
The costs of crime to victims. 190
Average amounts stolen during economically-motivated crimes 192
How much is stolen in a typical robbery? 194
How much is stolen in a typical burglary? 196
How much is stolen in a typical larceny-theft? 198
Property damages from arson 200
How much has been spent on the justice system in recent years? 202
How much is the justice system costing each of us? 204
How much does government spend on the criminal justice system? 206
How much tax money is spent on police protection and on corrections during a year? 208

Glossary 211

Index 221

Introduction

by
Peter C. Kratcoski, Ph.D., Chairperson
Department of Criminal Justice Studies
Kent State University, Kent, Ohio
and
Lucille Dunn Kratcoski, M.A.
Research Associate

Statistics on Crime and Punishment presents three phases of the criminal justice process in sequence: crime, justice, and punishment. When a crime is reported, law enforcement personnel work to apprehend the offender, the judicial process is then initiated, and, if the offender is convicted, some form of punishment will normally follow. However, the path from commission of a crime to justice and punishment is not always a direct one. The actual amount of crime in the United States is far greater than that presented in any statistical report. Crimes may not be reported to the police for various reasons, including the victim's fear of reprisal by the offender or the beliefs that the police will take no action; or that there is little hope of apprehending the offender, recovering stolen property or receiving compensation for injuries or damages.

Many crimes are never cleared through arrests, and not all arrested offenders are convicted of the crimes with which they are charged. Some are diverted out of the justice system, others are found not guilty, or, very frequently, plea bargaining (an agreement between the prosecutor and the defense attorney) results in some of the charges being dropped or reduced in severity in exchange for a guilty plea by the defendant. Punishment is dependent on practical considerations. Many offenders who do not have extensive records of previous offenses and are not viewed as dangerous are given community sanctions such as probation (supervision by officers employed by the court), community service, or house arrest. If a sentence of incarceration is given, few offenders serve the total sentence they receive. A sentence to jail or prison may be suspended, and the offender placed on probation, with the condition that the original sentence will be imposed if the rules of probation are violated. Some offenders receive "shock probation." After serving a short portion of the sentence, they may apply to the sentencing judge for release from incarceration and placement on probation. Because of jail and prison overcrowding, some offenders are released after serving only a portion of their sentences, to make room for newly sentenced offenders. The "punishment" established for other offenders may actually be some type of treatment. This occurs most frequently in cases involving alcohol or drug abuse or sex offenses. Convicted offenders are placed under supervision and required to take part in treatment for a specific period of time.

Crime Trends and Criminal Justice System Responses

This volume contains statistical material on the number and types of crimes reported, the times of day and locations where crimes are most likely to occur, the personal characteristics of offenders, and the amount of violent and property crime, organized crime, hate crime (offenses that target specific persons because of their race or ethnic origins), and juvenile crime. In the first line of defense against all of these crimes are police officers, who are faced with the formidable task of investigating reported crimes and apprehending offenders, either while the criminal act is in progress or as a result of investigative activity.

One trend in policing the United States that is having an effect in increasing police efficiency and protecting citizens is *community policing*. This implies a partnership between the police and citizens that stresses involvement in services and programs that are needed to improve the standard of life in the community. These may include crime watch programs, neighborhood patrol by residents, and crime prevention education. Officers are seen more frequently in face-to-face contact with citizens than in the past. Changes to bring this about include use of foot or bicycle patrol and the establishment of police substations in neighborhoods. These stations give residents a heightened sense of security and also serve as dialogue points between the persons living there and the police. This contact may result in quick reporting of crime or suspicious activity and tips to the police on the identity of persons who have committed crimes in that area. The interaction with officers as role models may also have positive effects on young people.

Although the total amount of recorded crime has stabilized in recent years, violent crime has continued to increase. The easy availability of firearms is closely tied to this trend. An ever increasing percentage of violent crime involves use of firearms, chiefly handguns, in assaults and robberies. There has been strong debate over gun control, culminating in the passage of the federal legislation called the Brady Bill (named for James Brady, former president Ronald Reagan's press secretary who was wounded during an attempt on the president's life). This bill provides for a background check on applicants for purchase of handguns, and a five-day waiting period for such purchases. Although these controls may have some deterrent effect on purchase of handguns for criminal purposes, there still are opportunities for obtaining guns through illegal means. In addition, there are already many firearms in the possession of persons who acquired them before these controls were initiated.

The violent crime increases are also related to gang activity. In the 1990s, criminal gangs have been identified as operating in all 50 states, and the age range of gang members has expanded, with extreme gang violence concentrated in the older teen and young adult ages. The average age of arrested gang offenders is now 18 to 19, but gangs are recruiting members at very early ages. Gangs have become increasingly involved in drug trafficking, which is closely related to gang violence. Drive-by shootings and assassinations are another manifestation of this violence.

To deal with gang problems, many cities have established police gang control units, which gather intelligence on the gangs and their leaders and work to control gang violence. Some states have increased the criminal penalties for gang involvement, and have revised their criminal codes to provide for automatic transfer to adult criminal court for juveniles who are involved in violent crimes and determinate (set length) sentences for certain violent crimes. This is a way of isolating and institutionalizing the gangs' leaders. Other efforts to reduce gang activity involve community and school programs to provide alternative activities for youths who might be attracted by the lure of gang involvement.

The increases in violent juvenile crime have also been addressed by other changes in the juvenile justice system. Holding habitual and violent delinquents until their court hearings take place, rather than releasing them into the community, was upheld in the U.S. Supreme Court decision, *Schall v Martin* (1984). The cases of serious juvenile offenders may also be transferred (waived) to criminal court for trial, and the number of transfers has steadily increased. Some states have reduced the age for adult court jurisdiction over serious offenders. For example, in New York State 13 to 15 year olds charged with murder, rape, robbery, or arson are now sent directly to adult courts. The State of Washington has determinate sentencing based on a point system, with serious, violent, repeat offenders virtually certain to be institutionalized.

Historical Trends in Punishment

Opinions on the appropriate punishment for crimes have swung back and forth from confidence that severe punishment is the most effective deterrent to the belief that most criminal offenders are disturbed individuals who must receive some sort of treatment if they are to change their behavior.

In the sixteenth and seventeenth centuries, imprisonment was rarely used as a punishment for the common criminal. Those incarcerated were political prisoners or persons awaiting trial. Convicted offenders were given harsh punishment, such as mutilation of the offending body member (cutting off the hand of a thief, for example) or were put to death. In seventeenth century England, more than 200 offenses were punishable by death. These punishments were carried out in public, to maximize their effects as deterrent to criminal behavior by those who observed them.

In the eighteenth century, Cesare Beccaria, writing in Italy, developed the "pleasure-pain" principle—the belief that the punishment for an unlawful act should be just severe enough to deter a person from committing it. In England, Jeremy Bentham set forth the theory of "utilitarianism," which agreed with Beccaria's idea on many points. Specific punishments were to be set for all offenses. He also suggested the use of prisons as correctional institutions and proposed that they be located in the center of the community, so that the citizens would be constantly reminded of the penalties for crime.

During the nineteenth century and the early twentieth century, *punishment* was viewed as an important element in crime control, both for its deterrent effects and as a means of retribution for the offenses committed. However, in the twentieth century, particularly in the years following World War II (1945–1975), *rehabilitation* came to be viewed as an important function of the correctional process. There was a search for the underlying causes of criminal behavior, and attempts were made to change offenders by identifying their problems and "treating" them, This treatment often took the form of psychological counseling, academic and vocational education, and treatment for substance abuse. *Indeterminate* sentences were used, that is, the amount of time the offenders spent under supervision, within the broad ranges of maximum and minimum periods of confinement, was based on the judgment of those supervising them regarding the progress of their rehabilitation and their readiness for release. Community corrections also developed during this period, with offenders being sent to halfway houses, given *work release*, granted furloughs from institutions (short periods in the community), or placed on probation as their rehabilitation progressed.

In the 1970s, the place of rehabilitation and treatment in the correctional process came under strong criticism. Studies of recidivism (reoffending) by those who had received rehabilitative treatment revealed that these efforts appeared to have minimal effects in changing unlawful behavior. As crime rates rose and the seriousness of the crime problem increased, particularly in large cities, there were pressures to adopt a new approach to punishment. This came in the form of the *justice model,* under which the offense itself, not the background of the offender, is the focus of action, and just punishment is applied. This is carried out by the implementation of *determinate sentences* (specific penalties that must be applied for certain offenses). The decisions on release from incarceration or supervision

are no longer based on judgments as to the rehabilitation of the offender. With the exception of some reduction in the length of the sentence for good behavior while incarcerated, the offenders receive specific length sentences.

Currently, predominantly as a result of the sharp increases in violent offenses, there is strong public pressure to increase the severity of these determinate sentences and to keep repeat offenders incarcerated. Criminal codes of many states require mandatory prison sentences if firearms are used in the commission of crimes, and mandatory life sentences for repeat serious offenders are based on a "three strikes and you're out" philosophy. Drug trafficking offenses, viewed as closely related to the increases in violent crime, also carry mandatory prison terms for those convicted. The death penalty was not used between 1968 and 1976 as a result of challenges to its constitutionality. It was declared constitutional in 1976 by the U.S. Supreme Court. However, few executions were carried out until the mid 1980s. In the 1990s, they are taking place with increasing frequency. The pendulum has definitely swung away from the idea of punishment as an opportunity for rehabilitation and toward punishment as a means of retribution and deterrence.

The trend toward longer sentences has created its own set of problems. In 1993, the average state prison system was operating with more than 15% more inmates than its rated capacity, even though more than 13,000 beds had been added to state institutions in 1992. The longer, mandatory sentences have caused the prison population to increasingly be made up of hardcore offenders, who pose ever escalating security problems. Some less serious offenders, as we noted earlier, are being released before completion of their sentences to make room for newly sentenced offenders. Treatment or counseling is limited to those with mental health problems or substance addictions.

As a result of prison overcrowding, there has been a resurgence of interest in community corrections, especially for nonviolent offenders. Some state departments of correction have developed statistically tested risk instruments to evaluate the potential dangerousness of convicted offenders and help determine whether they can be assigned to residential community corrections facilities such as halfway houses or live in the community under probation or parole supervision. Using a point system, such factors as the age of the offender, the number and types of previous offenses, the current offense, substance abuse history, and other factors are considered in determining the risk levels.

Statistics on Crime and Punishment

The material presented in this book allows us to examine various factors related to crime, justice and punishment. We can explore such questions as the time of day or month of the year when various types of crimes most often occur, the age, sex, and racial distributions of offenders and their victims, the differences in the amount and types of urban, suburban, and rural crime, the characteristics of the victims and offenders in violent personal crime cases, and the locations and amounts of property crime. We can discover which types of crimes are most frequently cleared by arrests, how many persons are under correctional supervision each year, the characteristics of the prison population, and trends in the use of life sentences and the death penalty. However, in reading and interpreting this information, it is very important to be aware of the sources of the information, how it is presented in the tables, charts and graphs, and whether the findings apply only to a specific, small segment of the population or can be generalized to a broader group.

This information has been collected for various reasons. The statistics related to numbers and types of reported crimes and arrests, characteristics of offenders, and geographic trends are important to local, state and federal law enforcement agencies. They are used to assess the efficiency and effectiveness of operations, and as the basis for future allocation of personnel and resources. The data on dispositions of cases in the courts and jail and prison inmate numbers and characteristics are vital to those responsible for administering those agencies. Because the expenditures for the criminal justice system are so high, it is important that local, state and federal government agencies have accurate information as the basis for decision making.

Methods of Obtaining Information

Many of the statistics reported in this volume are taken from the Federal Bureau of Investigation's *Uniform Crime Reports* (*Crime in the United States*).

Another major reference is the *Sourcebook of Criminal Justice Statistics,* a publication of the U.S. Department of Justice's Bureau of Justice Statistics, which contains information gathered from a wide variety of public and private agencies, research organizations and academic institutions, and from public opinion polls. Other major references cited in this book include *Statistical Abstracts* developed by the U.S. Bureau of the Census, *Juvenile Court Statistics* compiled by the U.S. Office of Juvenile Justice and Delinquency Prevention, reports by the U.S. Secret Service Office of Government Liaison and Public Affairs, and by the U.S. Department of Transportation, and U.S. Department of Justice reports on jails and jail inmates and correctional populations.

All of the researchers involved in compiling these statistics sought to provide accurate information, but used varying methods to collect the data. For example, the *Uniform Crime Reports* prepared by the FBI are summaries of yearly crime statistics provided by local, state, and federal law enforcement agencies. All types of crimes are listed, but the most serious offenses are grouped as "index crimes," subdivided into violent crimes (murder, forcible rape, robbery, and aggravated assault) and property crimes (burglary, larceny-theft, motor vehicle theft, and arson). Information on the number of crimes reported to police and the number cleared by arrests is given, and there are many statistical breakdowns in terms of age, sex, race, and geographic locations. Trends in criminal behavior are also shown, through five and ten year comparisons. The *Uniform Crime Reports* are the most frequently used and quoted sources for crime statistics. However, it is important to realize that they contain information only on crimes that have been reported to the police, and that not all police jurisdictions in the United States submit their statistics for inclusion in the reports. *Juvenile Court Statistics*, prepared by the National Center for Juvenile Justice, has similar limitations. Only offenses by juveniles that reached the point of formal referral to juvenile courts are included. Many incidents involving juveniles are handled in other ways, without court involvement. In addition, not all juvenile courts in the United States report their statistics to the National Center.

While the many types of official reports are compiled on the basis of offenses that have come to the attention of law enforcement personnel or are summaries of information on persons who have come into contact with some facet of the criminal or juvenile justice systems, information for another major source of statistics in this book, the National Crime Victimization Survey (*Criminal Victimization in the United States*) is collected in a different way. Each year, the Bureau of Justice Statistics asks a sample of more than 100,000 U.S. residents to respond to a questionnaire about their experiences or lack of experience as victims of crime during a specific year, and the circumstances surrounding such criminal events. The incidents may or may not have been reported to the police. These victimization surveys include incidents that did not result in arrests. For example, a potential victim may have been able to flee from or ward off a person who was trying to commit a criminal act. In addition, the victims of certain offenses may never have contacted the police to report crimes that were committed. A rape victim might fear the embarrassment or trauma of describing the assault, a victim who could identify the perpetrator of some type of crime might fear retaliation, and victims of burglaries or robberies might not report the occurrences because they felt that there was little hope of recovering their property. The households included in the National Crime Victimization Survey are chosen in such a way that they form a "representative sample." Because of this scientific method of selection, findings from the survey can be regarded with a high degree of certainty as representative of the entire U.S. population.

Government agencies are not the only sources of information on crime, justice, and punishment. Colleges and universities are frequently involved in research on these topics, assisted by funding from government agencies, such as the National Institute of Justice, or from private groups or foundations. For example, the University of Michigan's Institute for Social Research has conducted nationwide surveys of high school seniors each year since 1975. The high school students are asked to anonymously report their involvement in delinquent activities, including use of drugs and alcohol and traffic violations and accidents, and their victimization experiences in school and elsewhere. The findings from such research are called "self-report" data. Much of this information may be unknown to anyone but the person involved in the activity. Self-report studies are valuable, since they can reveal data that would otherwise be undetected. However, the accuracy of the findings is dependent upon the truthfulness of the respondents. Some participants in the

research might exaggerate their experiences, others might purposely understate them, or may forget to mention incidents that occurred. One method of checking the validity of such information is to compare the response with official reports, but this is time consuming and difficult to accomplish.

Forms In Which Statistics Are Presented

When examining the statistical information presented in this book, it is highly important to be aware of the form in which the material is presented. The easiest figures to understand are those that state the total number of times a particular thing occurred. In a table or graph, total numbers will have some reference point. For example, the table on victimizations reported to the police included in this volume shows the total number of victimizations and the total number reported to the police for each type of crime. Another commonly used reference point is the year in which a total number of offenses occurred. If we compare the total number of offenses year by year, increases or decreases become apparent.

Percentages are also useful in helping us understand what the figures presented mean. For example, in the table that reports the times of day when most crimes are committed, total numbers are given for specific types of crimes. To report and compare the times of day when each offense was committed, three time categories were established, and the percentage of total incidents that occurred during each time period is provided. This enables us to immediately see that robberies occurred most often between 6 p.m. and midnight, while assaults happened most frequently between the hours of 6 a.m. and 6 p.m., and motor vehicle thefts were most frequent between midnight and 6 a.m.

Another factor that must be understood is the use of *rates*. In the table that gives the total number of reported rapes each year for the years 1960 through 1994, we see that there were only 17,190 reported rapes in 1960, compared to 102,100 in 1994. On the basis of total offenses alone, there were nearly six times as many rapes reported in 1994 as in 1960. However, since the population of the United States increased considerably from 1960 to 1994, the *percentage* of rape victims in the total population may not have increased as greatly. To determine the *rate*, the number of offenses is compared with the total number of persons in the population that year, using 100,000 persons as a dividing point. The rate per 100,000 persons is given in the same table, and we find that the rate was 9.6 rapes per 100,000 persons in 1960, and 39.2 per 100,000 in 1994. The rate in 1994 was slightly more than 4 times the rate in 1960. Through this comparison, we see that the increase in the rate was not as great as the increase in the total number.

When reading the tables, look for such qualifying explanations as rate per 100 families, rate per 1,000 persons, or victimizations per 1,000 persons age 12 or over. If the *mean* (average) number is presented, that is arrived at by dividing the total number of offenses by the number of persons involved. If the *median* number is given, this means that this number is the midpoint, with half of the figures falling above this point and half of them below it. For example, in the table on the amount of money awarded in civil lawsuits, the *mean* (average) award for professional malpractice cases was $1,057,000, while the *median* award was $356,000.

When quoting statistics, it is vital to:

- identify the source of the material;

- understand the method used to obtain the information;

- mention the population to which the findings can be applied (adults, juveniles, convicted offenders, persons with a specific income level or place of residence);

- be aware of the limitations of the application of the findings (for example, were the subjects all males, were only some of the eligible participants surveyed, have criminal or juvenile codes changed since the statistics were originally corrected);

- clearly state the form in which the statistics are being presented (total numbers, rates, percentages).

Perspectives in Crime in the United States

The amount and nature of crime in the United States can be viewed from various perspectives. For those concerned with planning for crime control and deployment of law enforcement officers, information about the number and locations of reported crime is vital. They are also interested in the times of day and of the year when crimes occur most frequently, and in the relation of age, gender, race, or ethnic background, socio-economic status, and place of residence to criminal activity. The most serious crimes recorded by the FBI each year in its *Uniform Crime Reports* are categorized as violent (involving force or the threat of force), or property crimes. The violent crimes in the index include murder and non-negligent manslaughter, rape, robbery, and aggravated assault. The index property crimes are burglary, larceny-theft, motor vehicle theft, and arson. In addition to these, information on certain other types of crime is vital. Drug trafficking, frequently related to organized crime or gang activity, is sometimes investigated by special local, state, or federal task forces, formed to gather and exchange information. Counterfeiting and electronic crimes pose special problems in the 1990s. These are investigated by the U.S. Secret Service, an agency of the U.S. Department of the Treasury. Hate crimes, committed to harm or intimidate members of certain racial or ethnic groups, must be carefully monitored. These are investigated by local agencies, and the FBI frequently becomes involved, because the civil rights of the victims may have been violated. By analyzing the available data, law enforcement officials are able to develop profiles of the types of persons most likely to be involved in specific types of crimes.

Serious offenses by juveniles are also increasing, *Juvenile Court Statistics* show substantial increases in the number of juvenile delinquency cases, and violent offenses are increasing at a faster rate than property offenses.

- The National Crime Victimization survey revealed that, in 1993, only about one-third of the victimizations that occurred in the U.S. were reported to police. Motor vehicle thefts were the offenses most likely to be reported, while thefts were the least likely to be reported. Violent crimes occur most frequently during the summer months, while property crimes like shoplifting, burglary, and thefts are more common in November and December. The victims of violent crimes are most likely to be black males, under age 25. Members of families that earn less than $7,500 per year are the most frequent victims of assaults and thefts, but persons in higher income categories ($50,000 and above) are the most frequent victims of motor vehicle theft. In 1992, 60% of all nonfatal violent victimizations were committed by persons who were strangers to the victims.

- According to the FBI's *Uniform Crime Reports,* crime occurred more frequently in cities in 1993 than in suburbs or rural counties, and the amount of crime increased with the size of the cities. Burglaries are twice as likely to occur at a private residence than on commercial property. Robberies are most likely to happen on the street or highway, but those that occur in places of business frequently involve multiple victims. Of stolen items, nearly two-thirds of motor vehicles are recovered, while less than 20% of other stolen property is ever recovered. Rates of larceny-theft, which includes shoplifting, pocket-picking, purse-snatching, and theft of motor vehicle parts, remained fairly stable from 1979 through 1994. Shoplifting makes up about 15% of all thefts. The number of arson offenses and the number of deaths from arson have shown a pattern of decline since the 1970s. The total number of murders committed steadily increased from 1960 to 1993, and the rate per 100,000 persons increased by 86% in that time period. More than half of the murders in 1994 resulted from some type of personal dispute, but the numbers of gang style and juvenile gang killings have been increasing. Rates of aggravated assault more than doubled in the period from 1973 to 1993.

- More than 1 million drug-related arrests were made in 1993, and more than 85,000 arrests for prostitution and commercialized vice occurred each year from 1992 through 1994.

- Counterfeiting activity has steadily increased since 1985, as a result of advances in computer and photocopying technology that make it much easier to produce counterfeit paper money. New technology has also resulted in increases in electronic crimes (computer fraud, illegal electronic fund transfers, or accessing of corporate or personal records or accounts).

- Hate crimes (acts motivated by the racial or ethnic characteristics of the victims) are crimes against persons in almost three-fourths of the cases, with intimidation and assault being the most common.

- Total arrests of juveniles for serious delinquency offenses increased more than 16% in the years 1984 to 1993. In the same period, violent crime by juveniles increased 68%, led by murder and nonnegligent manslaughter, which increased more than 168%, and aggravated assault (98% increase). Use of handguns in homicides committed by juveniles has grown sharply. Total delinquency offenses referred to the juvenile courts from 1983 through 1991 showed a steady pattern of escalation led by increases in violent offenses.

- According to the FBI, gang related killings rose from 353 in 1987 to 1,268 in 1994, an increase of 250%. Ninety percent of these killings were juvenile gang killings, and gang related murders accounted for nearly 6% of all murders reported in 1994.

- Persons under age 18 were arrested for 17% of all crimes in 1993. More than 40% of all arson, vandalism, and motor vehicle theft arrests, more than 30% of burglary and larceny-theft arrests, and more than 25% of robbery and buying, receiving, or selling stolen properly arrests in that year were of persons under age 18.

Criminal Justice Responses to Crime Through Arrests, Court Processing, and Sentencing

Arrest is the first step in the process of holding offenders accountable for their actions. Geographic location and density of population are important factors related to the types of crimes committed and the arrests accomplished. In 1993, more than 75% of all arrests took place in cities. The factors that contribute to urban crime include poverty, crowded living conditions, unemployment, gangs, and drug related activity. Certain offenses, such as prostitution and robbery, are closely associated with city life, while offenses like driving under the influence of alcohol or drugs and offenses against family and children occur rather frequently in rural areas. The vast majority of all arrested offenders are males, and blacks are overrepresented in the arrest statistics. Persons under age 18 are most likely to be arrested for property crimes than for violent crimes, but violent crimes by juveniles have been increasing at a faster rate than violent crimes by adults. Violent crimes are much more likely than property crimes to result in arrests.

Nearly 900,000 persons were convicted of felony offenses in l993. Of these, over 90% pleaded guilty, and the remainder were found guilty by a judge or a jury. We noted earlier that many guilty pleas are the result of plea bargaining, which may have reduced the severity or number of charges and resulted in a shorter prison sentence or probation instead of prison. Since incarcerated offenders are being held for longer periods of time because of changes in the criminal codes that call for determinate sentences, the large number of persons convicted poses enormous problems for corrections. More prisoners are entering state and federal prisons each year than are being paroled or released as a result of completion of their sentences. In addition, the seriousness of the offenses of many paroled offenders make them strong candidates for recidivism (reoffending) and return to prison as parole violators. Currently, those released on parole for the first time have served about one-fourth of their actual sentences, while violent offenders are serving about half of their maximum sentences before being paroled.

The number of persons under correctional supervision increased nearly 150% from 1980 to 1992. This number includes persons placed on probation, those held in jails, either awaiting trial or serving sentences, prisoners held in federal or state institutions, those placed on parole, and persons held in private or public community based facilities. Those held in federal or state prisons are most likely to be serious violent offenders, but the number of drug offenders imprisoned has also escalated, due in part to mandatory prison sentences for drug related offenses. Authorities report that a large proportion of those imprisoned for violent offenses were also involved in drug related criminal activity. Local jails hold about one-third of all incarcerated offenders. Although many of these inmates are persons awaiting trial or serving short sentences, prison overcrowding at the state and federal facilities has resulted in some serious offenders now being held in local jails.

The most severe and controversial form of punishment in the United States is the death penalty. Fourteen states still do not allow it. One factor contributing to the controversy is the allegation that it has not been equally applied to all racial and ethnic groups. African-Americans, in particular, have been given death sentences for offenses for which other ethnicities received less harsh forms of punishment. For example, from 1930 through 1991 more than 50% of the 4,016 persons legally executed in the United States for the crime of rape during those years were African-Americans.

More than 15,000 legal executions have been conducted in this country. The vast majority of those executed have been adult males, but youths under the age of 13 account for approximately 2% of the executions. The youngest person ever executed (recorded in 1786) was 12 years old.

Currently, 36 states and the federal government allow capital punishment for specific offenses. The method used varies, with the most common being lethal injection. Other methods include electrocution, hanging, lethal gas, and a firing squad.

The death sentence or life imprisonment is given in more than 25% of homicide cases. Those convicted of murder are the most likely to receive life sentences or the death penalty, and murderers convicted in jury trials are more likely to receive such sentences than those convicted by judges. Since some states do not have a death penalty, life in prison without parole or life plus added years sentences are given for persons who are repeat offenders or have been involved in particularly brutal or multiple murders.

The total cost of crime to victimized persons and to local, state, and federal governments is enormous. The cost to crime victims was estimated at more than $18 billion in 1992 alone. Victims may seek redress for damages in civil courts, which can order financial judgments but do not impose criminal penalties. In the years 1982 to 1992, the amount spent on the justice system increased over 160%. Operation of the justice system costs each citizen more than $360 per year, with a total of nearly $5 billion being spent annually.

- More than 75% of all arrests take place in cities. Males are arrested more often than females in every offense category. In 1993, blacks were arrested for more than 30% of all offenses, more than double their percentage in the total population. Blacks accounted for more than half of all murder and non-negligent manslaughter and robbery arrests that year.

- In 1993, 83% of the arrests of persons under age 18 were for property crimes, and 17% were for violent crimes. For those over age 18, 69% of the arrests were for property crimes, and 31% for violent crimes.

- Arrests for property crimes and other crimes decreased from 1990 to 1994, but violent crime increased about 7%.

- Arrests for forgery and counterfeiting and fraud increased substantially from 1990 to 1994.

- In 1992, 31 of every 100 persons convicted of robbery, 21 of every 100 convicted of burglary, and 26 of every 100 convicted of drug trafficking received prison sentences.

- Every year, from 1900 through 1993, approximately 20% of all offenses reported to the police were cleared by arrests. Reported violent offenses were more than twice as likely as property offenses to result in arrests.

- In 1992, of the nearly 5,000,000 persons under correctional supervision, 59% were on probation, 9% were held in jails, 18% were in prisons, and 14% were on parole.

- During the 1990s, state prisons released about 60,000 violent offenders per year, but they admitted over 80,000 violent offenders per year, for a yearly gain of over 20,000 violent offenders. The average sentence for a violent crime is eight years, and the average time served is less than four years.

- Of the adult offenders who left parole supervision in 1992, 40% were returned to incarceration because of parole revocation or sentencing for a new offense. The majority of those paroled for the first time were male minority group members in their late twenties.

- In 1993, 2,716 persons were under sentence of death and 38 were executed. This is the highest number of executions carried out since 1962.

Summary

The statistics presented in this volume reveal that serious problems exist for those concerned with protecting citizens and administering justice. Even though many offenses reported to the police are never cleared by arrests, the number of offenders processed by the criminal justice system has become so great that justice and correctional agencies are strained to keep up with the volume of cases and to provide dispositions for convicted offenders. The cost to the public, in terms of criminal victimization and tax dollars spent to support this activity, is very great.

The trends in crime presented here have brought about some changes in law enforcement and correctional approaches. Special task forces are being formed to investigate such offenses as drug trafficking and gang violence. Criminal code revisions have provided more severe penalties for serious offenders, and efforts are being made to develop community corrections options for less serious offenders. The deterrent effects of the death penalty are being tested by the carrying out of executions.

Other efforts to reduce and control crime are taking place. In-school programs are being used to attempt to keep youths away from the lure of gang membership, and to inform them of the problems associated with substance abuse. Community policing has emerged as a cooperative venture between law enforcement personnel and citizens, which can result in mutual benefits. In many areas, public concern about crime has resulted in efforts to increase the number of police officers and to demolish buildings that are locations for drug dealing or gang activities. There is a growing realization that crime control and public safety are major concerns.

Acknowledgments, Sources and Contacts

ACKNOWLEDGMENTS

Laurence J. Stewart, Fire Analysis and Research Division, National Fire Protection Association (Quincy, MA).

James J. Stephan, Statistician, U.S. Department of Justice, Bureau of Justice Statistics (Washington, DC).

Eric Harnischfeger, Office of Government Liaison and Public Affairs, United States Secret Service (Washington, DC).

USE OF SOURCES

The procedures for gathering statistics about crime, justice, and punishment differ widely from state to state, and even from city to city. For this reason, this volume includes a significant portion of source material from various branches of the U.S. Department of Justice (USDJ).

Details about reported crimes and arrests in this volume are often taken from tabulations compiled by the Federal Bureau of Investigation (FBI). The FBI uses standardized definitions and reporting procedures that make it possible to adequately compare information from across the country. In particular, the FBI's Uniform Crime Reports (UCR) program serves as a national primary resource for statistics on reported crime data, and is often used as a starting point by researchers interested in a more detailed topic. Many of the tables in this volume taken from FBI data have been clarified through summing together the statistics from separate categories, tables, and totals.

Much of the information concerning victimizations, sentencing, and corrections comes from the Bureau of Justice Statistics (BJS). The BJS also uses standardized definitions and procedures that make comparisons between different areas of the country possible. One particular BJS source mentioned often in this volume is the National Crime Victimization Survey (NCVS). The NCVS is a national primary statistical resource used by the USDJ, and often forms the foundation for other,

more specialized crime surveys. Many of the tables included in this volume taken from NCVS data have been simplified from the originals by combining or summing categories and by limiting the time series under analysis. However, care was taken to maintain the statistical credibility of the original data tables. The NCVS underwent a major redesign overhaul in 1993. The NCVS information from the older survey design used during 1973–92 is often utilized in this text in order to show trends in victimizations that took place over several years. Results from the redesigned 1993 NCVS were first made available in mid-1995. The numbers for the 1993 NCVS are not compatible with the 1973–92 numbers. The BJS has indexed some of the 1993 NCVS results to the older 1992 NCVS, but an index for comparison to other years is not yet available.

This volume concentrates only on the general aspects of crime, justice, and punishment. For this reason, space devoted to specific types of crime is limited. Also, social issues that involve the influence of crime as a factor are not covered in this volume. Another volume of this series, however, contains statistics about the role of crime in substance abuse and drug trafficking, and still another volume has some criminal statistics about weapons and violent incidents. Students interested in these specific topics should consult either the *Alcohol, Drug, and Tobacco Use* volume or the *Weapons and Violence* volume.

DESCRIPTION OF SOURCES

Correctional Populations in the U.S.

Correctional Populations in the United States (CPUS) presents a tabulation of persons under some form of correctional supervision. Since 1926, the Bureau of the Census has compiled detailed prisoner statistics. The U.S. Department of Justice, Office of Justice Programs maintains the CPUS program, which collects questionnaires from correctional facility authorities from across the U.S. The CPUS series has detailed information on admissions, releases, sentences and time served, inmates under sentence of death, recidivism, and crowding. The CPUS makes possible general comparisons between the different correctional institutions in each state, as well as general year-to-year comparisons.

Juvenile Court Statistics

The Office of Juvenile Justice and Delinquency Prevention (OJJDP), a branch of the U.S. Department of Justice, annually gathers statistics regarding juvenile delinquency cases. The National Center for Juvenile Justice prepares this information for the OJJDP through the Juvenile Court Statistics (JCS) annual series.

The JCS series measures juvenile delinquency using "disposed" cases. A disposed case is one in which a definite action took place or is currently underway. It does not necessarily mean that the case is closed. Violent offenses are measured as "person offenses" and include: criminal homicide, forcible rape, robbery, aggravated assault, simple assault, other violent sex offenses, and other person offenses.

National Corrections Reporting Program

The National Corrections Reporting Program (NCRP), initiated in 1983, is administered by the U.S. Department of Justice's Bureau of Justice Statistics. The NCRP collects individual-level data on all prison admissions and releases and on parole entries and discharges, with multiple admissions or releases per person during the year counted as separate events. The NCRP covers prisoners admitted to or released from custody regardless of the jurisdiction where the prisoner was sentenced. The 1992 report used here included only inmates with a sentence of more than one year, except where noted. Information on all inmates, including those with a sentence of one year or less, is contained in the public-use data tape that may be obtained from the National Archive of Criminal Justice Data at the University of Michigan.

National Crime Victimization Survey

The National Crime Victimization Survey (NCVS) is sponsored by the U.S. Department of Justice's Bureau of Justice Statistics. The NCVS measures aspects of crime at the national level. Over 100,000 randomly selected persons age 12 and older from about 49,000 households are given questionnaires that ask about personal and household experiences with crime. House-

holds stay in the sample for 3 years and interviews occur at 6-month intervals. New households rotate into the sample on an ongoing basis. The NCVS has used this stable data collection method since 1973, making it possible to estimate national proportions of crime.

The NCVS is especially useful in measuring unreported crimes. This is accomplished through asking about information on crimes suffered by individuals and households, regardless of whether or not an incident was ever reported to the police. Since the NCVS measures both reported and unreported crime, any changes in the hesitance to report crime or in technological improvements in keeping records do not affect the results.

The NCVS collects detailed information about victims of crime. Characteristics of victims in the NCVS include: demographic description, relationship with the offender, whether or not the crime was part of a series of crimes over a six-month period, self-protective measures used and assessment of their effectiveness, and what the victim was doing when victimized. The NCVS occasionally includes special supplements about particular topics such as school crime or violence against women.

The NCVS also is useful because it collects information that is not available or unknown in the initial police report. This follow-up information includes contacts the victim has made with the criminal justice system after the crime, extent and costs of medical treatment, and recovery of property.

The NCVS, however, does not measure homicides because it is impossible to survey murder victims. It also does not measure any crimes that happen to children under 12 years of age, since they are omitted from the survey.

Starting in 1993, the NCVS was changed and redesigned to include sexual assault in the types of sexual crimes counted. Other improvements and enhancements were added as well, making direct comparisons of 1993 information with estimates from 1992 and previous years incompatible. For this reason, data from both the 1992 and 1993 NCVS are included in this volume.

National Jail Census & Annual Survey of Jails

The National Jail Census (NJC) is a data collection study by the U.S. Department of Justice's Bureau of Justice Statistics that focuses on the nation's locally administered jails. The NJC, taken every fifth year since 1983, was conducted in 1970, 1972, 1978, 1983, 1988, and 1993. The information presented here is from the 1993 NJC, and included all 3,287 locally administered confinement facilities in the U.S. that hold inmates beyond arraignment and were staffed by municipal or county employees. Also included in the 1993 NJC were 17 jails that were privately operated under contract for local governments and 7 facilities maintained by the Bureau of Prisons and functioning as jails. Excluded from the census were temporary holding facilities (such as drunk tanks and police lockups) that do not hold persons after they are formally charged in court. Also excluded were state-operated facilities in Alaska, Connecticut, Delaware, Hawaii, Rhode Island, and Vermont, which have combined jail-prison systems.

The Annual Survey of Jails (ASJ) is conducted in each of the four years between the full censuses. The ASJ is conducted to estimate baseline characteristics of the nation's jails and the inmates housed in these jails.

National Judicial Reporting Program

The National Judicial Reporting Program (NJRP) compiles detailed information on the sentences and characteristics of convicted felons, and provides the only nationwide detailed description of the sentences that felons receive in state courts. Surveys of felony sentencing were conducted in 1986, 1988, 1990, and 1992. The 1992 survey cited here was based on a sample of 300 counties selected to be nationally representative. The 300 counties include the District of Columbia and at least one county from every state except, by chance, Vermont. The 1992 survey excluded federal courts and those state or local courts that did not adjudicate adult felony cases.

National Pretrial Reporting Program

The Bureau of Justice Statistics began the National Pretrial Reporting Program (NPRP) in February 1988 to collect demographic, criminal history, pretrial processing, adjudication, and sentencing information on felony defendants in state courts of the nation's 75 most populous counties. The NPRP does not include federal defendants. The 1992 NPRP collected data for 13,206 felony cases filed during May 1992 in 40 of the nation's largest counties. These cases, which were tracked up to a full year, were part of a two-stage sample that was representative of the estimated 55,513 felony cases filed in the nation's 75 most populous counties during that month.

National Prisoner Statistics

The National Prisoner Statistics program (NPS) conducts an advanced count of prisoners immediately after the end of each calendar year. A detailed, final count containing any revisions to the jurisdictions' advanced count is published later. Most states provide a count of the number of inmates under their jurisdiction as of December 31, regardless of the location of their inmates. These counts do not include inmates housed for other jurisdictions, such as other states' inmates and pretrial detainees who are housed in another jurisdiction's facilities. Some states provide custody counts, that is, the number of inmates housed in state facilities regardless of jurisdiction. These counts exclude inmates housed outside of each state's prison facilities, such as inmates housed in local jails. Custody counts are used to calculate the total number of inmates in prisons and jails.

Uniform Crime Reports

The Federal Bureau of Investigation (FBI) maintains the Uniform Crime Reports (UCR) program. The UCR program, which began in 1929, measures police workload and activity. Local police departments, which represent about 95% of the U.S. population, voluntarily report information to the FBI. The information includes details on the following crimes reported to police: homicide, forcible rape, robbery, aggravated assault, burglary, larceny-theft, motor vehicle theft, and arson. In recent years, a special report of UCR data tabulating bias-motivated "hate crimes" has also been made available.

The UCR data consist of monthly law enforcement reports made directly to the FBI or to centralized state agencies that then report to the FBI. Each report submitted to the UCR program is examined thoroughly for reasonableness, accuracy, and deviations that may indicate errors. Large variations in crime levels may indicate a change in record-keeping procedures, incomplete reporting, or changes in a jurisdiction's boundaries. Monthly reports are compared with previous submissions and with those of similar agencies to identify any unusual changes in an agency's crime counts.

The UCR, unlike the NCVS, can provide local data about states, counties, cities, and towns. It also measures crimes affecting children under 12 years of age. Experts agree that the NCVS can not provide reliable information about this segment of the population. The UCR program also counts the number of arrests and details on arrested persons. The UCR also collects information on the number of homicides (murders and nonnegligent manslaughters), crimes that are uncounted in a survey that interviews victims. The UCR also gathers data on the circumstances surrounding homicide and the characteristics of homicide victims.

The UCR program, unlike the NCVS, relies on reported information and cannot address the hidden problem of unreported crimes. The UCR also utilizes information from initial police reports, even though the information on such reports often changes later. Inconsistency in reporting among the thousands of law enforcement agencies that submit reports also affects the UCR program.

United States Secret Service

The United States Secret Service (USSS), a branch of the U.S. Department of the Treasury, is responsible for detecting and arresting any person committing an offense relating to the fraudulent negotiation, forgery, or counterfeiting of currency, coins, obligations, and securities of the United States and foreign governments. The USSS also is responsible for detecting and arresting persons involved in specific types of fraud, including: electronic funds transfer fraud, credit and debit card fraud, computer access fraud, food stamp fraud, and fraud dealing with false identification documents or devises.

After the end of each fiscal year, the USSS compiles a record of its investigative activity from over 100 field offices across the U.S. and abroad. Each case is classified as one of five types: counterfeiting, forgery, financial crime/fraud, protective intelligence, or other. The

USSS gathers detailed information about criminal activity trends, offenses, arrests, and convictions relating to these crimes.

PRIMARY SOURCES

Fire Analysis and Research Division, National Fire Protection Association.

U.S. Bureau of the Census, *Statistical Abstract of the United States: 1995* (Washington, D.C.: U.S. Government Printing Office, 1995).

U.S. Department of Commerce, Economics and Statistics Administration, *Poverty in the United States: 1992* (Washington, D.C.: U.S. Government Printing Office, 1993).

U.S. Department of Justice, Bureau of Justice Statistics, "Capital Punishment 1993" (Washington, D.C.: U.S. Government Printing Office, December 1994).

U.S. Department of Justice, Bureau of Justice Statistics, "Capital Punishment 1994" (Washington, D.C.: U.S. Government Printing Office, February 1996).

U.S. Department of Justice, Bureau of Justice Statistics, "Civil Jury Cases and Verdicts in Large Counties" (Washington, D.C.: U.S. Government Printing Office, July 1995).

U.S. Department of Justice, Bureau of Justice Statistics, *Correctional Populations in the United States, 1992* (Washington, D.C.: U.S. Government Printing Office, 1995).

U.S. Department of Justice, Bureau of Justice Statistics, "The Costs of Crime to Victims" (Washington, D.C.: U.S. Government Printing Office, February 1994).

U.S. Department of Justice, Bureau of Justice Statistics, "Crime and the Nation's Households, 1992" (Washington, D.C.: U.S. Government Printing Office, August 1993).

U.S. Department of Justice, Bureau of Justice Statistics, "Criminal Victimization 1993" (Washington, D.C.: U.S. Government Printing Office, May 1995).

U.S. Department of Justice, Bureau of Justice Statistics, *Criminal Victimization in the United States, 1992* (Washington, D.C.: U.S. Government Printing Office, 1994).

U.S. Department of Justice, Bureau of Justice Statistics, *Drug and Crime Facts, 1994* (Washington, D.C.: U.S. Government Printing Office, June 1995).

U.S. Department of Justice, Bureau of Justice Statistics, *Felony Defendants in Large Urban Counties, 1992* (Washington, D.C.: U.S. Government Printing Office, 1995).

U.S. Department of Justice, Bureau of Justice Statistics, "Felony Sentences in State Courts, 1992" (Washington, D.C.: U.S. Government Printing Office, January 1995).

U.S. Department of Justice, Bureau of Justice Statistics, *Historical Corrections Statistics in the United States, 1850–1984* (Washington, D.C.: U.S. Government Printing Office, 1986).

U.S. Department of Justice, Bureau of Justice Statistics, "Jails and Jail Inmates, 1993–94" (Washington, D.C.: U.S. Government Printing Office, April 1995).

U.S. Department of Justice, Bureau of Justice Statistics, *National Corrections Reporting Program, 1992* (Washington, D.C.: U.S. Government Printing Office, 1994).

U.S. Department of Justice, Bureau of Justice Statistics, "Prisoners in 1993" (Washington, D.C.: U.S. Government Printing Office, June 1994).

U.S. Department of Justice, Bureau of Justice Statistics, "Prisoners in 1994" (Washington, D.C.: U.S. Government Printing Office, August 1995).

U.S. Department of Justice, Bureau of Justice Statistics, *Sourcebook of Criminal Justice Statistics—1992* (Washington, D.C.: U.S. Government Printing Office, 1993).

U.S. Department of Justice, Bureau of Justice Statistics, *Sourcebook of Criminal Justice Statistics—1994* (Washington, D.C.: U.S. Government Printing Office, 1995).

U.S. Department of Justice, Bureau of Justice Statistics, *Report to the Nation on Crime and Justice* (Washington, D.C.: U.S. Government Printing Office, 1988).

U.S. Department of Justice, Bureau of Justice Statistics, "Violent Offenders in State Prison: Sentences and Time Served" (Washington, D.C.: U.S. Government Printing Office, July 1995).

U.S. Department of Justice, Federal Bureau of Investigation, Criminal Justice Information Services, Uniform Crime Reports, "Hate Crime—1993" (Washington, D.C.: U.S. Government Printing Office, June 1994).

U.S. Department of Justice, Federal Bureau of Investigation, Criminal Justice Information Services, Uniform Crime Reports, "Hate Crime—1994" (Washington, D.C.: U.S. Government Printing Office, 1995).

U.S. Department of Justice, Federal Bureau of Investigation, *Crime in the United States, 1994* (Washington, D.C.: U.S. Government Printing Office, 1995).

U.S. Department of Justice, Federal Bureau of Investigation, *Crime in the United States, 1993* (Washington, D.C.: U.S. Government Printing Office, 1994).

U.S. Department of Justice, Federal Bureau of Investigation, *Crime in the United States, 1992* (Washington, D.C.: U.S. Government Printing Office, 1993).

U.S. Department of Justice, Federal Bureau of Investigation, *Crime in the United States, 1991* (Washington, D.C.: U.S. Government Printing Office, 1992).

U.S. Department of Justice, Federal Bureau of Investigation, *Crime in the United States, 1990* (Washington, D.C.: U.S. Government Printing Office, 1991).

U.S. Department of Justice, Office of Juvenile Justice and Delinquency Programs, *Juvenile Court Statistics, 1991* (Washington, D.C.: U.S. Government Printing Office, 1994)

U.S. Department of Transportation, Federal Highway Administration, *Highway Statistics 1993* (Washington, D.C: U.S. Government Printing Office, 1994).

U.S. Department of Transportation, Federal Highway Administration, *Highway Statistics 1992* (Washington, D.C: U.S. Government Printing Office, 1993).

United States Secret Service, Office of Government Liaison and Public Affairs.

OTHER SOURCES CONSULTED

Gibbons, Don C. *Talking About Crime and Criminals.* Englewood Cliffs, CA: Wadsworth Publishing Co., 1996.

McShane, Marilyn D. and Frank P. Williams, eds. *The Encyclopedia of American Prisons.* New York: Garland Publishing, 1996.

U.S. Department of Justice, Bureau of Justice Statistics. "Child Victimizers: Violent Offenders and Their Victims." Washington, D.C.: U.S. Government Printing Office, March 1996.

U.S. Department of Justice, National Institute of Justice. "Victim Costs and Consequences: A New Look." Washington, D.C.: U.S. Government Printing Office, February 1996.

U.S. Department of Justice, National Institute of Justice. "Violence by Young People: Why The Deadly Nexus?" in *National Institute of Justice Journal,* August 1995.

U.S. Department of Justice, Office of Juvenile Justice and Delinquency Programs. *Juvenile Offenders and Victims: A National Report.* Washington, D.C.: U.S. Government Printing Office, 1995.

CONTACTS

National Fire Protection Association, 1 Batterymarch Park, Quincy, MA 02269-9101. (617) 770-3000.

Shoplifters Alternative, 380 North Broadway, Suite 206, Jericho, NY 11753. (800) 848-9595.

U.S. Department of Commerce, Bureau of the Census, Washington, D.C., 20233. (301) 457-2800. The Bureau of the Census also maintains a World Wide Web server at http://www.census.gov.

U.S. Department of Justice, Bureau of Justice Statistics Clearinghouse, Box 6000, Rockville, MD 20850. (800) 732-3277. A World Wide Web server is operated at http://ncjrs.aspensys.com:81/ncjrshome.html. Inquiries can also be sent by e-mail to askncjrs@aspensys.com.

U.S. Department of Justice, Federal Bureau of Investigation, Uniform Crime Reports, Criminal Justice Information Services Division, Washington, D.C. 20535. Information Dissemination: (202) 324-5015.

U.S. Department of Justice, Juvenile Justice Clearinghouse, P.O. Box 6000, Rockville MD 20849. (800) 638-8736. A World Wide Web server is operated at http://ncjrs.aspensys.com:81/ncjrshome.html. Inquiries can also be sent by e-mail to askncjrs@aspensys.com.

U.S. Department of Justice, National Institute of Justice, National Criminal Justice Reference Service, Box 6000, Rockville, MD 20849. (800) 851-3420. A World Wide Web server is operated at http://ncjrs.aspensys.com:81/ncjrshome.html. Inquiries can also be sent by e-mail to askncjrs@aspensys.com.

U.S. Department of Transportation, Federal Highway Administration, 400 7th St. SW, Washington, D.C. 20590. Public Affairs: (202) 366-0660.

United States Secret Service, Office of Government Liaison and Public Affairs, 1800 G St. NW, Washington, D.C. 20223. (202) 435-5708.

CrIme

How many crimes are committed per police officer?

The number of reported crimes and full-time law enforcement officers per 100,000 inhabitants in 1993 for the fifty states, the District of Columbia, and Puerto Rico.

State	Crimes per 100,000 Inhabitants	Officers per 100,000 Inhabitants	Crimes per Officer
Alabama	4,878.8	205.3	23.8
Alaska	5,567.9	174.1	32.0
Arizona	7,431.7	200.6	37.0
Arkansas	4,810.7	139.4	34.5
California	6,456.9	210.2	30.7
Colorado	5,526.8	232.9	23.7
Connecticut	4,650.4	257.2	18.1
Delaware	4,872.1	296.5	16.4
District of Columbia	11,761.1	759.5	15.5
Florida	8,351.0	243.2	34.3
Georgia	6,193.0	281.2	22.0
Hawaii	6,277.0	230.6	27.2
Idaho	3,845.1	183.6	20.9
Illinois	5,617.9	257.0	21.9
Indiana	4,465.1	159.0	28.1
Iowa	3,846.4	159.2	24.2
Kansas	4,975.3	238.6	20.9
Kentucky	3,259.7	183.1	17.8
Louisiana	6,846.6	314.7	21.8
Maine	3,153.9	161.5	19.5
Maryland	6,106.5	262.7	23.2
Massachusetts	4,893.9	246.0	19.9
Michigan	5,452.5	197.9	27.6
Minnesota	4,386.2	159.4	27.5
Mississippi	4,418.3	176.8	25.0
Missouri	5,095.4	196.5	25.9
Montana	4,790.0	159.4	30.1
Nebraska	4,117.1	180.7	22.8
Nevada	6,180.1	240.4	25.7
New Hampshire	2,905.0	204.6	14.2
New Jersey	4,800.8	357.4	13.4
New Mexico	6,266.1	212.8	29.4
New York	5,551.3	316.6	17.5
North Carolina	5,652.3	227.4	24.9
North Dakota	2,820.3	156.9	18.0
Ohio	4,485.3	179.2	25.0
Oklahoma	5,294.3	190.9	27.7

[Continued]

How many crimes are committed per police officer?

[Continued]

State	Crimes per 100,000 Inhabitants	Officers per 100,000 Inhabitants	Crimes per Officer
Oregon	5,765.6	157.3	36.7
Pennsylvania	3,271.4	238.0	13.7
Puerto Rico	3,341.4	363.2	9.2
Rhode Island	4,499.0	224.3	20.0
South Carolina	5,903.4	205.5	28.7
South Dakota	2,958.2	132.3	22.4
Tennessee	5,239.5	205.0	25.6
Texas	6,439.1	215.9	29.8
Utah	5,237.4	185.8	28.2
Vermont	3,972.4	145.0	27.4
Virginia	4,115.5	208.9	19.7
Washington	5,952.3	159.2	37.4
West Virginia	2,532.6	170.7	14.8
Wisconsin	4,054.1	225.7	18.0
Wyoming	4,163.0	236.5	17.6
U.S. Total	5,482.9	226.7	24.2

Comments The FBI annually compiles statistics on the amounts of crime reported throughout the U.S., and also on the number of full-time police officers on duty.

The District of Columbia, Florida, and Arizona led the nation in crimes reported per inhabitant in 1993. New Hampshire, North Dakota, and West Virginia had the lowest.

D.C. also had the largest number of police officers per inhabitant, followed by Puerto Rico and New Jersey. South Dakota, Arkansas, and Vermont had the fewest.

By combining these two sets of statistics, we can see the number of reported crimes per officer in 1993. This can somewhat indicate police workload and activity per state. Washington, Arizona, and Oregon led the nation in crimes reported per police officer. Pennsylvania, New Jersey, and Puerto Rico had the fewest.

Source U.S. Department of Justice, Federal Bureau of Investigation, *Crime in the United States, 1993* (Washington, D.C.: U.S. Government Printing Office, 1994), pp. 68–78, 295, 373.

Contact U.S. Department of Justice, Federal Bureau of Investigation, Uniform Crime Reports, Criminal Justice Information Services Division, Washington, D.C. 20535. Information Dissemination: (202) 324-5015.

How many law enforcement officers are protecting us?

State and local sworn police protection (full-time equivalent employment),
and the ratio of officers to population, 1980–92.

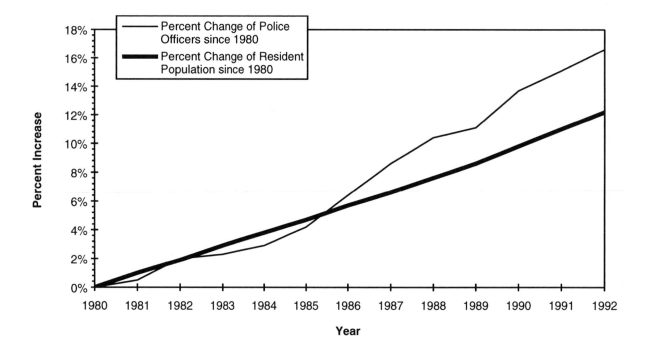

Year	State and Local Police Officers (Full-time Equivalent, Sworn Protection)	Resident Population of the U.S.	Percent Change of Police Officers Since 1980	Percent Change of Resident Population since 1980	Police Officers (Full-Time Equivalent, Sworn Protection) per 10,000 Population
1980	461,810	227,225,000	0.0	0.0	20.3
1981	464,141	229,466,000	0.5	1.0	20.2
1982	470,909	231,664,000	2.0	1.9	20.3
1983	472,459	233,792,000	2.3	2.9	20.2
1984	475,124	235,825,000	2.9	3.8	20.1
1985	481,146	237,924,000	4.2	4.7	20.2
1986	491,276	240,133,000	6.4	5.7	20.5
1987	501,440	242,289,000	8.6	6.6	20.7
1988	509,619	244,499,000	10.4	7.6	20.8
1989	513,242	246,819,000	11.1	8.6	20.8
1990	525,075	249,402,000	13.7	9.8	21.1
1991	531,706	252,131,000	15.1	11.0	21.1
1992	538,510	255,028,000	16.6	12.2	21.1

Comments From 1980 to 1992, the total number of state and local police officers rose from 461,810 to 538,510, an increase of 16.6%. This is the number of sworn police officers who were actually involved in protection services and is counted on a full-time equivalent basis (e.g., two half-time officers would count as one full-time officer).

Although the number of officers grew by 16.6%, the population of the U.S. grew from 227,225,000 to 255,028,000—an increase of 12.2%. Therefore, the number of police officers in relation to the population grew by just 4.4% during those years.

Another way to compare the number of police officers and the population would be through a ratio. In 1980, there were about 20.3 police officers per 10,000 residents. By 1992, that ratio had grown to 21.1 officers per 10,000 residents. The increase in the ratio from 20.3 in 1980 to 21.1 in 1992 was 4.4%, the same 4.4% as mentioned above. Both ways of looking at the figures measure the same increase, but slightly differently.

Source U.S. Department of Justice, Bureau of Justice Statistics, *Sourcebook of Criminal Justice Statistics—1994* (Washington, D.C.: U.S. Government Printing Office, 1995), p. 39, table 1.29.

U.S. Bureau of the Census, *Statistical Abstract of the United States: 1995* (Washington, D.C.: U.S. Government Printing Office, 1995), p. 8, table 2.

Contact U.S. Department of Justice, Bureau of Justice Statistics Clearinghouse, Box 6000, Rockville, MD 20850. (800) 732-3277. A World Wide Web server is operated at

http://ncjrs.aspensys.com:81/ncjrshome.html. Inquiries can also be sent by e-mail to askncjrs@aspensys.com.

How often is a victimization reported to the police?

A comparison of the numbers of victimizations experienced and reported to the police in the U.S. during 1993.

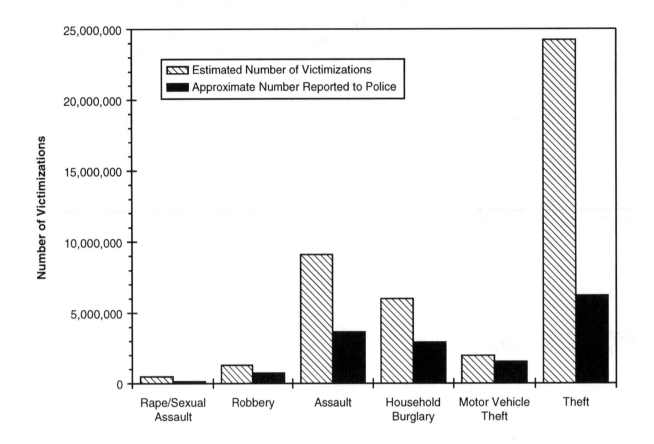

Type of Crime	Estimated Number of Victimizations	Percent Reported to Police	Approximate Number Reported to Police
Rape/Sexual assault	485,000	28.8%	140,000
Robbery	1,307,000	56.1%	733,000
Assault	9,104,000	40.2%	3,660,000
Household burglary	5,995,000	48.9%	2,932,000
Motor vehicle theft	1,967,000	77.8%	1,530,000
Theft	24,250,000	25.6%	6,208,000
All crimes	43,622,000	35.2%	15,355,000

Comments   In 1993, only about 35.2% of all criminal victimizations in the U.S. were reported to the police, according to the National Crime Victimization Survey (NCVS). This means that of the 43.6 million criminal victimizations that occurred in 1993, less than 15.4 million were reported.

The estimated 24.2 million thefts occurring in 1993 accounted for 56.2% of all victimizations, but theft victims reported the incident the least often (only 25.6% of the time). On the other hand, motor vehicle thefts accounted for only 8% of all victimizations, yet those victims reported the incident 77.8% of the time. Perhaps the reason motor vehicle thefts are reported more often than other crimes is in order to satisfy insurance company requirements.

The NCVS annually collects information on experiences with crime from over 100,000 people, regardless of whether or not the incident was reported to the police. Murder statistics are not included because the victims cannot be surveyed.

Source   U.S. Department of Justice, Bureau of Justice Statistics, "Criminal Victimization 1993" (Washington, D.C.: U.S. Government Printing Office, May 1995).

Contact   U.S. Department of Justice, Bureau of Justice Statistics Clearinghouse, Box 6000, Rockville, MD 20850. (800) 732-3277. A World Wide Web server is operated at http://ncjrs.aspensys.com:81/ncjrshome.html. Inquiries can also be sent by e-mail to askncjrs@aspensys.com.

How often are thefts and household crimes reported?

The percentage of theft and household crime victimizations reported to the police, 1973–92.

Year	Theft	Burglary	Larceny	Motor Vehicle Theft
1973	22%	47%	25%	68%
1974	25%	48%	25%	67%
1975	26%	49%	27%	71%
1976	27%	48%	27%	69%
1977	25%	49%	25%	68%
1978	25%	47%	24%	66%
1979	24%	48%	25%	68%
1980	27%	51%	28%	69%
1981	27%	51%	26%	67%
1982	27%	49%	27%	72%
1983	26%	49%	25%	69%
1984	26%	49%	27%	69%
1985	27%	50%	27%	71%
1986	28%	52%	28%	73%
1987	28%	52%	27%	75%
1988	27%	51%	26%	73%
1989	29%	50%	28%	76%
1990	29%	51%	27%	75%
1991	29%	50%	28%	74%
1992	30%	54%	26%	75%

Burglary is the unlawful or forcible entry or attempted entry of a residence, but does not always result in theft. Larceny is theft or attempted theft of property or cash without using force or an illegal entry. Motor vehicle theft involves the stealing of a car, truck, or motorcycle.

Comments During 1973–92, the general tendency of victims to report the incident increased slightly for all types of theft and household crimes, according to the National Crime Victimization Survey (NCVS). The NCVS annually collects information on experiences with crime from over 100,000 people, regardless of whether or not the incident was reported to the police.

Motor vehicle thefts consistently were reported most frequently, between 67% and 76% of the time. Burglaries consistently were reported second most often, from 47% to 54%. Larcenies were reported only 24% to 28% of the time, while the percentage of thefts reported ranged from 22% to 30%. These two types of crime often traded places as the type of crime reported least often.

Source U.S. Department of Justice, Bureau of Justice Statistics, *Criminal Victimization in the United States, 1992* (Washington, D.C.: U.S. Government Printing Office, 1994), p. 7.

Contact U.S. Department of Justice, Bureau of Justice Statistics Clearinghouse, Box 6000, Rockville, MD 20850. (800) 732-3277. A World Wide Web server is operated at http://ncjrs.aspensys.com:81/ncjrshome.html. Inquiries can also be sent by e-mail to askncjrs@aspensys.com.

How often are crimes of violence reported?

The percentage of nonfatal violent crime victimizations reported to the police, 1973–92.

Year	Rape	Robbery	Aggravated Assault	Simple Assault
1973	49%	52%	52%	38%
1974	52%	54%	53%	39%
1975	56%	53%	55%	39%
1976	53%	53%	58%	41%
1977	58%	56%	51%	39%
1978	49%	51%	53%	37%
1979	51%	55%	51%	37%
1980	41%	57%	54%	40%
1981	56%	56%	52%	39%
1982	53%	56%	58%	40%
1983	47%	53%	56%	41%
1984	56%	54%	55%	40%
1985	61%	54%	58%	40%
1986	48%	58%	59%	41%
1987	52%	55%	60%	38%
1988	45%	57%	54%	41%
1989	51%	51%	52%	38%
1990	54%	50%	59%	42%
1991	59%	55%	58%	42%
1992	53%	51%	62%	43%

Comments Victims typically report only about half of all violent crimes to the police, according to these survey statistics gathered since 1973. The NCVS annually collects information on experiences with crime from over 100,000 people, regardless of whether or not the incident was reported to the police. Murder statistics are not included because the victims cannot be surveyed.

Among the specific violent crimes indicated here, reports of aggravated assault are the most frequent. Also, the frequency of reporting assault has grown, especially aggravated assault. The percent of reported victimizations from rape and robbery fluctuated from year to year without providing any clear trends.

If only half the violent crimes are ever reported to police, it can be difficult for them to act effectively. Missing information from unreported incidents could be useful in setting up strategies to reduce violent crime.

Source U.S. Department of Justice, Bureau of Justice Statistics, *Criminal Victimization in the United States, 1992* (Washington, D.C.: U.S. Government Printing Office, 1994), p. 7.

Contact U.S. Department of Justice, Bureau of Justice Statistics Clearinghouse, Box 6000, Rockville, MD 20850. (800) 732-3277. A World Wide Web server is operated at http://ncjrs.aspensys.com:81/ncjrshome.html. Inquiries can also be sent by e-mail to askncjrs@aspensys.com.

At what time of day are most crimes committed?

Percent distribution of nonfatal victimization incidents in the U.S. during 1992, by type of crime and time of occurrence.

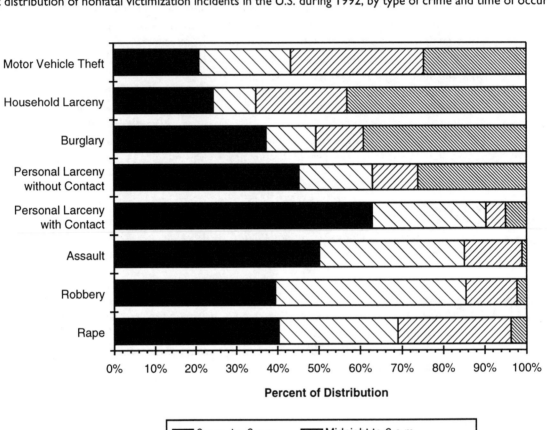

Type of Crime	Number of Incidents	6 a.m. to 6 p.m.	6 p.m. to Midnight	Midnight to 6 a.m.	Not Known or Not Available
Rape	131,530	40.3%	28.6%	27.3%	3.7%
Robbery	1,113,300	39.5%	46.0%	12.2%	2.3%
Assault	4,719,250	50.2%	35.0%	13.8%	1.1%
Personal larceny with contact	478,170	62.9%	27.4%	4.7%	5.0%
Personal larceny without contact	11,719,710	45.3%	17.7%	10.9%	26.1%
Burglary	4,757,420	37.4%	12.1%	11.5%	39.2%
Household larceny	8,101,150	24.4%	10.5%	22.1%	43.1%
Motor vehicle theft	1,958,780	21.0%	22.5%	32.1%	24.7%

Comments Violent crimes such as rape, robbery, and assault occurred almost as frequently during daylight hours (6 a.m. to 6 p.m.) as they did at night in 1992. Crimes of theft like personal larcenies usually took place during the day. Motor vehicle theft, however, was usually a nighttime crime.

The time of day was sometimes unknown or not available. For household larceny, burglary, personal larceny without contact, and motor vehicle theft, the unknown category was a sizeable portion of the total. Therefore, any conclusions as to when these crimes take place are less reliable.

Source U.S. Department of Justice, Bureau of Justice Statistics. *Criminal Victimization in the United States, 1992* (Washington, D.C.: U.S. Government Printing Office, 1994).

Contact U.S. Department of Justice, Bureau of Justice Statistics Clearinghouse, Box 6000, Rockville, MD 20850. (800) 732-3277. A World Wide Web server is operated at http://ncjrs.aspensys.com:81/ncjrshome.html. Inquiries can also be sent by e-mail to askncjrs@aspensys.com.

At what time of year do violent and property crimes occur most frequently?

Percent distribution of reported violent and property crimes in the U.S. by month during 1993.

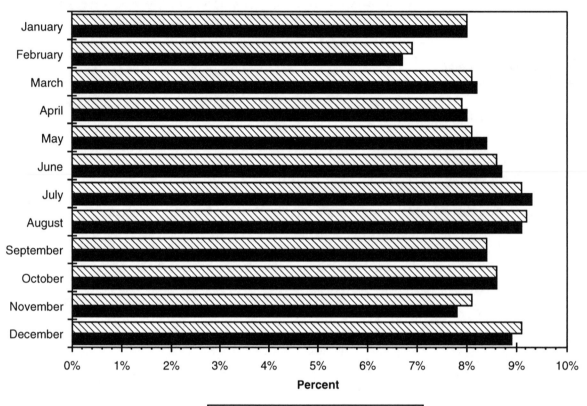

Month	Violent Crime	Property Crime
January	8.0%	8.0%
February	6.7%	6.9%
March	8.2%	8.1%
April	8.0%	7.9%
May	8.4%	8.1%
June	8.7%	8.6%
July	9.3%	9.1%
August	9.1%	9.2%
September	8.4%	8.4%
October	8.6%	8.6%
November	7.8%	8.1%
December	8.9%	9.1%

Comments The FBI indicated that in 1993 violent crimes took place most often in July, and property crimes most often in August. Summer is generally the most common time of year for crimes to happen.

During June, July, and August of 1993, 27.1% of all violent crimes and 26.9% of all property crimes took place. If crime happened equally throughout the year, then 25% should happen within any three-month span, since 100% would occur within twelve months. Since the June–August percentages are greater than 25%, this indicates that these months are popular times to commit criminal offenses.

During some months the percentage of property crimes is greater than the percentage of violent crimes. This does not mean that the number of property crimes exceeds that of violent crimes, only that the tendency for a property crime to occur during that month is greater than the tendency for a violent crime to occur. For example, the percentage of property crimes happening in November and December is greater than that of violent crimes. Property crimes are possibly more common during these months because of the holiday shopping season. As a result, crimes like shoplifting, pocket picking, burglary, thefts of items from cars, and other kinds of larceny increase because thieves have better opportunities to steal at that time of year.

Source U.S. Department of Justice, Federal Bureau of Investigation, *Crime in the United States, 1993* (Washington, D.C.: U.S. Government Printing Office, 1994), pp. 11, 36.

Contact U.S. Department of Justice, Federal Bureau of Investigation, Uniform Crime Reports, Criminal Justice Information Services Division, Washington, D.C. 20535. Information Dissemination: (202) 324-5015.

Does more poverty lead to more crime?

The rate of poverty for families in the U.S. compared with the rate of reported criminal offenses during 1960–92.

Year	Rate of Poverty per 100 Families	Rate of Reported Criminal Offenses per 100 Inhabitants	Rate of Personal Crime Victimizations per 100 Persons Age 12 and Older
1960	18.1	1.9	—
1961	18.1	1.9	—
1962	17.2	2.0	—
1963	15.9	2.2	—
1964	15.0	2.4	—
1965	13.9	2.5	—
1966	11.8	2.7	—
1967	11.4	3.0	—
1968	10.0	3.4	—
1969	9.7	3.7	—
1970	10.1	4.0	—
1971	10.0	4.2	—
1972	9.3	4.0	—
1973	8.8	4.2	12.4
1974	8.8	4.9	12.8
1975	9.7	5.3	12.9
1976	9.4	5.3	12.9
1977	9.3	5.1	13.1
1978	9.1	5.1	13.1
1979	9.2	5.6	12.7
1980	10.3	6.0	11.7
1981	11.2	5.9	12.1
1982	12.2	5.6	11.7
1983	12.3	5.2	10.8
1984	11.6	5.0	10.3
1985	11.4	5.2	9.9
1986	10.9	5.5	9.6
1987	10.7	5.6	9.8
1988	10.4	5.7	10.0
1989	10.3	5.7	9.8
1990	10.7	5.8	9.3
1991	11.5	5.9	9.5
1992	11.7	5.7	9.1

Comments This table shows the proportion of American families who lived below the poverty level from 1960–92, and also the proportion of reported criminal offenses during those years. It also shows the crime victimization rate, beginning with 1973. The victimization rate measures both recorded and unrecorded crimes, but does not include murders or crimes against children under 12.

According to these statistics, crime steadily grew throughout the 1960s and 1970s. At the same time, the percentage of American families living in poverty shrank from about 18% in 1960, to less than 9% by 1974.

This suggests that as poverty decreased from 1960 to 1974, crime tended to increase during those same years. This idea is exactly

the opposite of thinking that more poverty leads to more crime.

From the mid-1970s through the 1980s, the poverty rate fluctuated. The reported crime rate grew, but has stabilized between 5%–6%. The crime victimization rate has steadily fallen since the late 1970s. Thus it is difficult to interpret any correlation between the levels of poverty and crime for these later years.

It is important to remember, however, that none of the measurements cited here measure exactly the same thing. The statistics on poverty measure families, while the reported crime statistics measure individuals, and the crime victimization statistics measure individuals over age 12.

Source U.S. Department of Commerce, Economics and Statistics Administration, *Poverty in the United States: 1992* (Washington, D.C.: U.S. Government Printing Office, 1993), p. xvi.

U.S. Department of Justice, Federal Bureau of Investigation, *Crime in the United*

States, 1993 (Washington, D.C.: U.S. Government Printing Office, 1994), p. 5.

U.S. Department of Justice, Bureau of Justice Statistics. *Criminal Victimization in the United States, 1992* (Washington, D.C.: U.S. Government Printing Office, 1994), p. 6.

Contact U.S. Department of Commerce, Economics and Statistics Administration, Bureau of the Census, Washington, D.C., 20233. (301) 763-4040.

U.S. Department of Justice, Federal Bureau of Investigation, Uniform Crime Reports, Criminal Justice Information Services Division, Washington, D.C. 20535. Information Dissemination: (202) 324-5015.

U.S. Department of Justice, Bureau of Justice Statistics Clearinghouse, Box 6000, Rockville, MD 20850. (800) 732-3277. A World Wide Web server is operated at http://ncjrs.aspensys.com:81/ncjrshome.html. Inquiries can also be sent by e-mail to askncjrs@aspensys.com.

How often are men and women victims of violent crimes?

Victimization rates for persons age 12 and over in the U.S. during 1992, by type of crime and sex of victims.

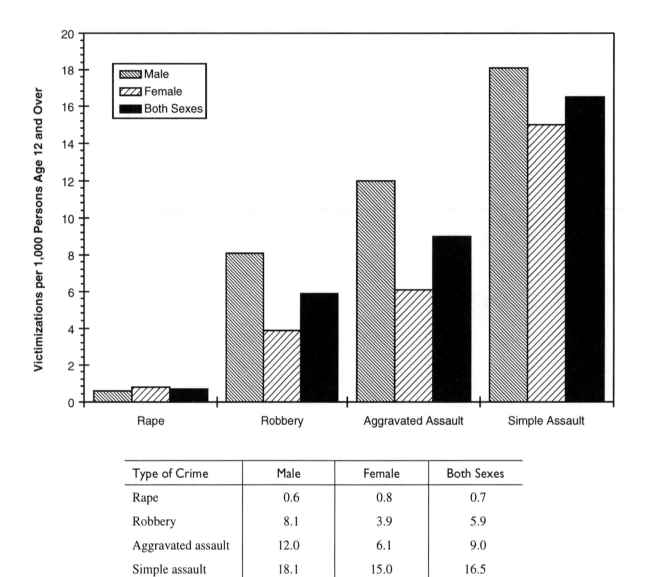

Type of Crime	Male	Female	Both Sexes
Rape	0.6	0.8	0.7
Robbery	8.1	3.9	5.9
Aggravated assault	12.0	6.1	9.0
Simple assault	18.1	15.0	16.5

Comments In 1992, violent crime victims were more likely male than female. This information is based on a survey of over 100,000 citizens age 12 and older that asks questions about experiences with crime. This method is useful because it measures both reported and unreported crimes (although it does not include murder).

Males had higher victimization rates than females for every type of nonfatal violent crime except rape. The greatest disparity between the rate for males and females was for aggravated assault. For that type of victimization, the rate for men was 12.0 per 1,000 males and the rate for women was 6.1 per 1,000 females, a difference of 5.9.

Source U.S. Department of Justice, Bureau of Justice Statistics, *Criminal Victimization in the United States, 1992* (Washington, D.C.: U.S. Government Printing Office, 1994), p. 22.

Contact U.S. Department of Justice, Bureau of Justice Statistics Clearinghouse, Box 6000, Rockville, MD 20850. (800) 732-3277. A World Wide Web server is operated at http://ncjrs.aspensys.com:81/ncjrshome.html. Inquiries can also be sent by e-mail to askncjrs@aspensys.com.

How old are crime victims?

Victimization rates in 1993 for persons age 12 and older, by age group.

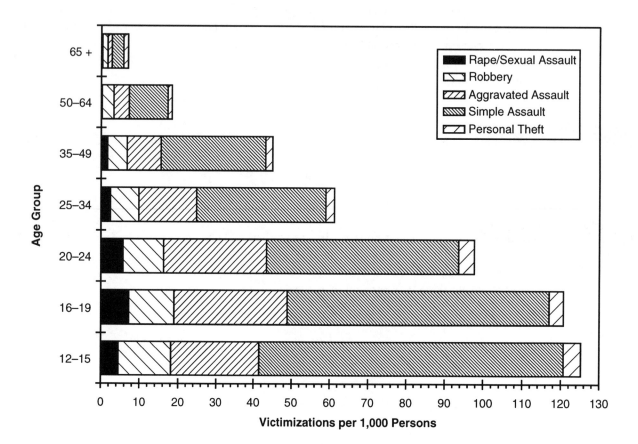

Age Group	Rape/Sexual Assault (per 1,000 persons)	Robbery (per 1,000 persons)	Aggravated Assault (per 1,000 persons)	Simple Assault (per 1,000 persons)	Personal Theft (per 1,000 persons)	Total (per 1,000 persons)
12–15	4.5	13.6	23.3	79.3	4.5	125.3
16–19	7.2	11.7	30.0	68.1	3.7	120.7
20–24	5.7	10.5	27.1	50.3	4.1	97.7
25–34	2.4	7.4	15.0	34.1	2.3	61.2
35–49	1.6	5.1	8.8	27.5	1.9	44.9
50–64	0.2	3.0	4.0	10.0	1.1	18.3
65 +	0.3	1.3	1.1	3.0	1.2	7.9

Comments The chance that an individual will be a victim of crime generally decreases with age, according to these statistics from the U.S. Department of Justice's 1993 National Crime Victimization Survey. Persons under age 25 had higher victimization rates than older persons. Those 65 and older generally had the lowest victimization rates.

Much of the difference in the rates of victimization between the age groups was caused by the frequency of aggravated and simple assaults. The combined rate of aggravated and simple assault, for example, was 98.1 per 1,000 persons age 16 to 19, but just 4.1 per 1,000 persons 65 or older.

Source U.S. Department of Justice, Bureau of Justice Statistics, "Criminal Victim-ization 1993" (Washington, D.C.: U.S. Government Printing Office, May 1995).

Contact U.S. Department of Justice, Bureau of Justice Statistics Clearinghouse, Box 6000, Rockville, MD 20850. (800) 732-3277. A World Wide Web server is operated at http://ncjrs.aspensys.com:81/ncjrshome.html. Inquiries can also be sent by e-mail to askncjrs@aspensys.com.

How old are murder victims?

Age distribution of murder victims in 1993.

Age Group	Male	Female
≤ 4	408	320
5–9	84	89
10–14	258	129
15–19	2,652	432
20–24	3,667	684
25–29	2,729	736
30–34	2,338	745
35–39	1,767	550
40–44	1,226	394
45–49	825	252
50–54	549	166
55–59	352	112
60–64	285	108
65–69	210	109
70–74	171	121
≥ 75	212	255
Unknown	216	76
Total*	17,949	5,278

* Does not add to total murders (23,271) because the gender of 44 murder victims was unknown. The age distribution for unknowns was as follows: 4 and under, 3; 20–24, 4; 25–29, 1; 35–39, 1; 50–54, 2; 55–59, 1; and unknown age, 32.

Comments
In 1993, police agencies across the U.S. recorded 23,271 murders. The victim was male in 17,949 of the murders, female in 5,278 murders, and the gender of 44 victims was unknown.

According to these records, the chances of being a murder victim steadily decreased after age 24, until rising slightly after age 75. There were more murdered children age 4 or younger than there were murdered 5–9 year-olds and 10–14 year-olds combined.

Males accounted for the majority of all murder victims, and outnumbered females in every category except 5–9 years of age.

The 5–9 age category had the fewest number of murder victims, with just 173 (84 males, 89 females). The 20–24 age category had the most murder victims with 4,355 (3,667 males, 684 females, and 4 unknowns). This age category accounted for about 18.7% of the total.

Source
U.S. Department of Justice, Federal Bureau of Investigation, *Crime in the United States, 1993* (Washington, D.C.: U.S. Government Printing Office, 1994), p. 16.

Contact
U.S. Department of Justice, Federal Bureau of Investigation, Uniform Crime Reports, Criminal Justice Information Services Division, Washington, D.C. 20535. Information Dissemination: (202) 324-5015.

What is the racial diversity of murder victims and murderers?

The racial composition of 11,721 murder victims and their murderers in 1993. The information is based on reported murders involving only one victim and one offender.

Race of Victim	Race of Offender				Total Victims, by Race of Victim
	White	Black	Other	Unknown	
Total white victims	4,686	849	58	55	5,648
Total black victims	304	5,393	18	67	5,782
Total other race victims	61	40	137	2	240
Total unknown race	11	17	1	22	51
Total victims, by race of offender	5,062	6,299	214	146	11,721

Comments

According to the FBI, most murder victims were the same race as their murderers in 1993. When the race of the victim and offender were both known, whites killed 4,686 whites, or 92.6% of 5,062 murders committed by whites. Blacks killed 5,393 blacks, or 85.6% of 6,299 murders committed by blacks. Although the category "other" includes more than one race (mostly Asians and Native Americans), it still supports this trend.

This type of table, where each category is compared with every other category, is called a *cross-tabulation*. This one counts murders two different ways: by the race of the victim and by the race of the offender. By analyzing the table, it is possible to see how frequently murder occurred in 1993 for any racial combination of victim and offender.

For example, whites accounted for 5,648 (48%) of the 11,721 victims and for 5,062 (43%) of the 11,721 murderers. Blacks accounted for 5,782 (49.3%) of all victims and for 6,299 (53.7%) of all murderers.

Source

U.S. Department of Justice, Federal Bureau of Investigation, *Crime in the United States, 1993* (Washington, D.C.: U.S. Government Printing Office, 1994), p. 17.

Contact

U.S. Department of Justice, Federal Bureau of Investigation, Uniform Crime Reports, Criminal Justice Information Services Division, Washington, D.C. 20535. Information Dissemination: (202) 324-5015.

Personal crime victimization rates by race

Victimization rates in the U.S. for personal crimes by race and ethnicity, 1993. Victimization rates are given per 1,000 persons age 12 and older.

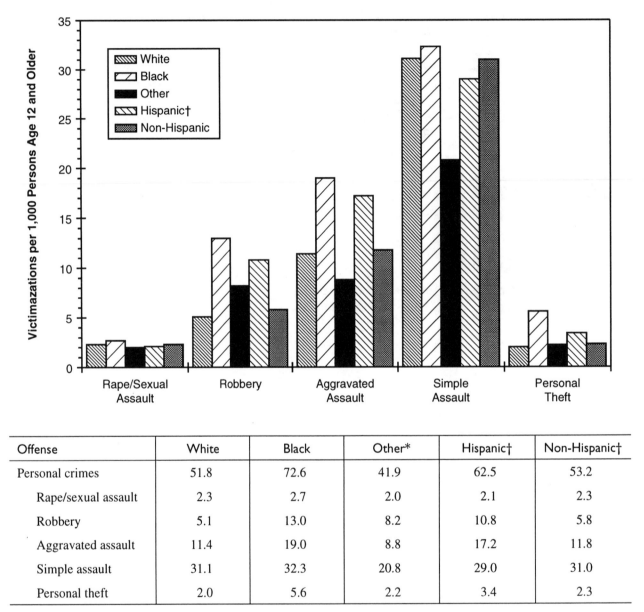

Offense	White	Black	Other*	Hispanic†	Non-Hispanic†
Personal crimes	51.8	72.6	41.9	62.5	53.2
Rape/sexual assault	2.3	2.7	2.0	2.1	2.3
Robbery	5.1	13.0	8.2	10.8	5.8
Aggravated assault	11.4	19.0	8.8	17.2	11.8
Simple assault	31.1	32.3	20.8	29.0	31.0
Personal theft	2.0	5.6	2.2	3.4	2.3

* This category consists primarily of Asians and Pacific Islanders as well as Native Americans.
† Hispanic status is defined as an ethnicity. A person of Hispanic origin may be of any race.

Comments Blacks were more likely than persons of other races to be victims of personal crime (except in the categories of rape/sexual assault and simple assault). This information was obtained through the National Crime Victimization Survey which annually collects information on experiences with crime from over 100,000 people, regardless of whether or not the incident was reported to the police. Murder statistics are not included because the victims cannot be surveyed.

Total personal crimes in 1993 were most frequent among blacks, with about 72.6 crimes per 1,000 black persons. The rate was 51.8 crimes per 1,000 whites, and 41.9 per 1,000 persons of other racial categories. For example, there were 19 aggravated assaults per 1,000 black persons, 11.4 per 1,000 whites, and 8.8 per 1,000 persons in other racial categories. The victimization rates for rape/sexual assault were not significantly different among the three racial groups. In 1993, blacks accounted for about 12.5% of the U.S. population; whites, 83%; and persons of other races, 4.5%.

The rate of personal crime victimization was also higher for Hispanics (62.5 per 1,000) than for non-Hispanics (53.2 per 1,000). Hispanics and non-Hispanics had similar victimization rates for the crimes of rape/sexual assault, simple assault, and personal theft. However, Hispanics had significantly higher rates for aggravated assault and especially robbery, with a robbery rate nearly twice that of non-Hispanics (10.8 as opposed to 5.8). As of 1993, about 10% of the U.S. population was Hispanic.

Source U.S. Department of Justice, Bureau of Justice Statistics, "Criminal Victimization 1993" (Washington, D.C.: U.S. Government Printing Office, May 1995).

Contact U.S. Department of Justice, Bureau of Justice Statistics Clearinghouse, Box 6000, Rockville, MD 20850. (800) 732-3277. A World Wide Web server is operated at http://ncjrs.aspensys.com:81/ncjrshome.html. Inquiries can also be sent by e-mail to askncjrs@aspensys.com.

What is the annual family income of crime victims?

Victimization rates per 1,000 persons age 12 and over, by type of crime and annual family income of victims in 1992.

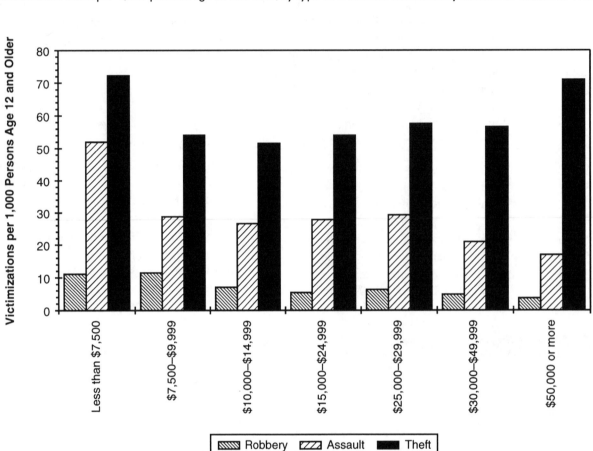

Annual Family Income of Victim	Robbery	Assault	Theft
Less than $7,500	11.1	52.0	72.3
$7,500–$9,999	11.5	28.8	54.1
$10,000–$14,999	7.1	26.6	51.6
$15,000–$24,999	5.4	27.8	54.0
$25,000–$29,999	6.3	29.3	57.6
$30,000–$49,999	4.8	20.9	56.6
$50,000 or more	3.7	16.9	71.0

Comments In 1992, persons from families that earned less than $7,500 per year were most often the victims of assaults and thefts, while victims of robbery most often belonged to families that earned between $5,000 and $10,000 per year. The victimization rates for robbery and assault generally declined as family income went up. The rate of theft, however, was less common for persons in middle income families and most common among persons from the lowest and highest income groups.

It may seem odd that these crimes often occur more frequently to persons from lower income families, because it might seem that someone with a higher income would have more wealth to steal. However, there are several possible explanations for these trends. In cities, people with lower incomes often live in areas with low property values and low employment, which affects the community's ability to pay for police and other services. In any densely populated area, there are more potential victims for a criminal to prey upon. A criminal may decide that a densely populated area with limited police services provides the best chance of getting away with a crime.

Persons with higher incomes often spend more on security devices, and also pay higher taxes for better police protection. Also, persons from higher income families may use checks or credit cards instead of cash. If a robber or thief thinks that there will not be very much cash on hand, he may be less inclined to commit the crime.

However, families with incomes over $50,000 are the targets of thieves more often than all but the lowest income group. In this case, a thief may decide that the possibility of a very profitable haul is worth any added risk.

Source U.S. Department of Justice, Bureau of Justice Statistics, *Criminal Victimization in the United States, 1992* (Washington, D.C.: U.S. Government Printing Office, 1994), p. 33.

Contact U.S. Department of Justice, Bureau of Justice Statistics Clearinghouse, Box 6000, Rockville, MD 20850. (800) 732-3277. A World Wide Web server is operated at http://ncjrs.aspensys.com:81/ncjrshome.html. Inquiries can also be sent by e-mail to askncjrs@aspensys.com.

What is the annual family income of household property crime victims?

Victimization rates per 1,000 households, by type of crime and annual family income of victims in 1993.

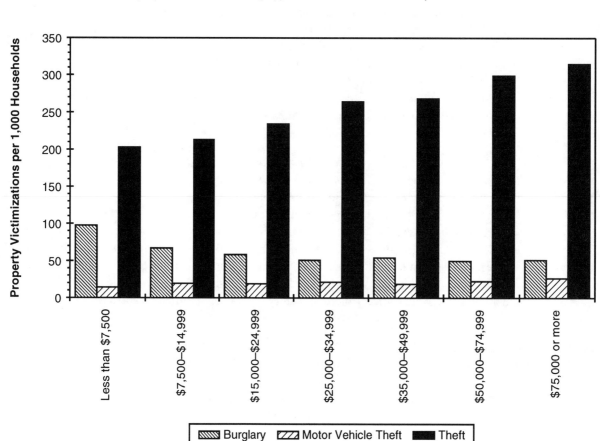

Annual Family Income of Victim	Burglary	Motor Vehicle Theft	Theft	Total
Less than $7,500	97.5	14.1	202.8	314.4
$7,500–$14,999	67.1	19.2	213.0	299.3
$15,000–$24,999	58.2	18.8	234.2	311.2
$25,000–$34,999	50.8	21.2	263.9	335.9
$35,000–$49,999	54.1	18.6	268.1	358.8
$50,000–$74,999	49.7	22.4	298.8	370.9
$75,000 or more	51.2	26.4	314.6	392.2

Comments Households with higher annual family incomes generally were victimized by household property crimes more frequently than households with lower incomes, according to the 1993 National Crime Victimization Survey (NCVS). The NCVS annually collects information on experiences with crime from over 100,000 people, regardless of whether or not the incident was reported to the police.

The income level experiencing household property crime least often was the $7,500–$14,999 group, at 299.3 victimizations per 1,000 households. Experiencing it most often was the over $75,000 group, at 392.2 victimizations per 1,000 households.

However, households earning under $7,500 sustained burglaries at almost twice the rate of households with the highest annual earnings. Burglary accounted for only 13% of the total household property crimes among households in the highest income group, but for 31% among the lowest income group.

Source U.S. Department of Justice, Bureau of Justice Statistics, "Criminal Victimization 1993" (Washington, D.C.: U.S. Government Printing Office, May 1995).

Contact U.S. Department of Justice, Bureau of Justice Statistics Clearinghouse, Box 6000, Rockville, MD 20850. (800) 732-3277. A World Wide Web server is operated at http://ncjrs.aspensys.com:81/ncjrshome.html. Inquiries can also be sent by e-mail to askncjrs@aspensys.com.

How often does the victim of a violent crime know the offender?

Number of nonfatal violent victimizations and the victimization rates (per 1,000 persons age 12 and older), by type of crime and victim-offender relationship in 1992.

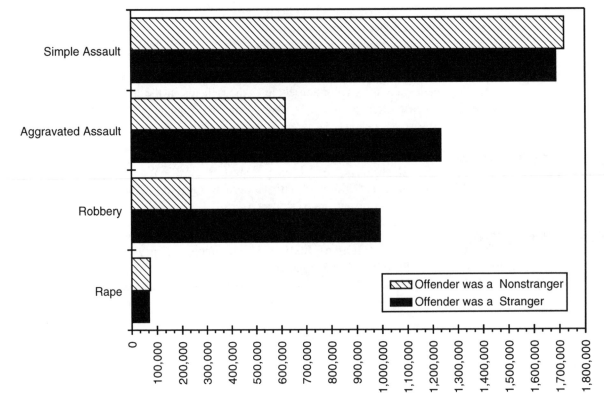

Victimizations

Type of Violent Crime	Offender was a Stranger	Offender was a Nonstranger*	Rate for Cases Involving Strangers (per 1,000 persons)	Rate for Cases Involving Nonstrangers* (per 1,000 persons)
Rape	68,140	72,790	0.3	0.4
Robbery	991,120	234,380	4.8	1.1
Aggravated assault	1,232,340	616,180	6.0	3.0
Simple assault	1,687,270	1,718,890	8.2	8.3
Any violent crime	3,978,890	2,642,250	19.3	12.8

* A "nonstranger" offender is someone who is either related to, well known to, or casually acquainted with the victim.

Comments Violent crimes in general were more likely to have been committed by strangers than nonstrangers in 1992, according to these statistics from the National Crime Victimization Survey (NCVS). The NCVS is a nationwide survey of over 100,000 residents which measures both reported and unreported crimes. Murder statistics are not included because the victims cannot be surveyed. The NCVS estimated that in 1992, 60% of all non-fatal violent victimizations were committed by strangers and 40% by nonstrangers.

Robberies and aggravated assaults were especially likely to have been committed by strangers. Of the estimated 1,225,500 robberies, nearly 81% (991,120) were committed by someone who was a stranger to the victim. Strangers also committed about 67% (1,232,340) of the aggravated assaults.

Simple assaults and rapes were slightly more likely to have been committed by someone the victim knew than by a stranger. Simple assaults committed by nonstrangers (1,718,890) accounted for 50.4% of all simple assaults. Rapes committed by nonstrangers (72,790) comprised 51.6% of all rapes.

Source U.S. Department of Justice, Bureau of Justice Statistics, *Criminal Victimization in the United States, 1992* (Washington, D.C.: U.S. Government Printing Office, 1994), p. 55.

Contact U.S. Department of Justice, Bureau of Justice Statistics Clearinghouse, Box 6000, Rockville, MD 20850. (800) 732-3277. A World Wide Web server is operated at http://ncjrs.aspensys.com:81/ncjrshome.html. Inquiries can also be sent by e-mail to askncjrs@aspensys.com.

Crime rates for cities, suburban, and rural areas

The frequency of reported property and violent crime in the U.S. during 1993, by population group.
Rates shown are per 100,000 inhabitants.

Population Group	Property Crime Rate	Violent Crime Rate	Total Crime Rate
Cities	5,806.3	951.2	6,757.5
250,000 +	7,492.5	1,708.0	9,200.5
100,000–250,000	6,844.8	1,073.8	7,918.6
50,000–100,000	5,528.3	754.1	6,282.4
25,000–50,000	4,939.6	574.2	5,513.8
10,000–25,000	4,231.6	435.0	4,666.6
Under 10,000	4,160.2	405.2	4,565.4
Suburban counties	3,411.3	454.4	3,865.7
Rural counties	1,859.8	227.7	2,087.5

Comments In 1993, crime occurred more frequently in cities than in suburban or rural counties, and crime within cities was more frequent as city size increased.

Not only did large cities have the greatest frequency of crime, but they also had the highest frequency of violent crime. For example, cities with more than 250,000 inhabitants had the highest crime rate, at 9,200.5 reported crimes per 100,000 inhabitants. This means that about 9.2% of those inhabitants were crime victims. The violent crime rate for cities of this size was 1,708.0 per 100,000 persons, making up 18.6% of the total crime rate.

At the other end of the scale were rural counties, which had the lowest crime rate, at 2,087.5 offenses per 100,000 inhabitants (about 2.1% of inhabitants). The violent crime rate among rural counties was 227.7 per 100,000, also the lowest. Violent crimes contributed 10.9% to the total crime rate.

Although the total crime rate is low, the percentage of violent crime in rural counties is higher than in the smallest cities. Violent crimes contribute just 8.9% of the total crime rate for cities with fewer than 10,000 residents, and 10.4% for cities with 25,000–50,000 inhabitants.

Source U.S. Department of Justice, Federal Bureau of Investigation, *Crime in the United States, 1993* (Washington, D.C.: U.S. Government Printing Office, 1994), pp. 190–1.

Contact U.S. Department of Justice, Federal Bureau of Investigation, Uniform Crime Reports, Criminal Justice Information Services Division, Washington, D.C. 20535. Information Dissemination: (202) 324-5015.

Urban, suburban, and rural crime victims

Victimizations in the U.S. per 1,000 persons age 12 and older in 1993, by locality of residence of victims.

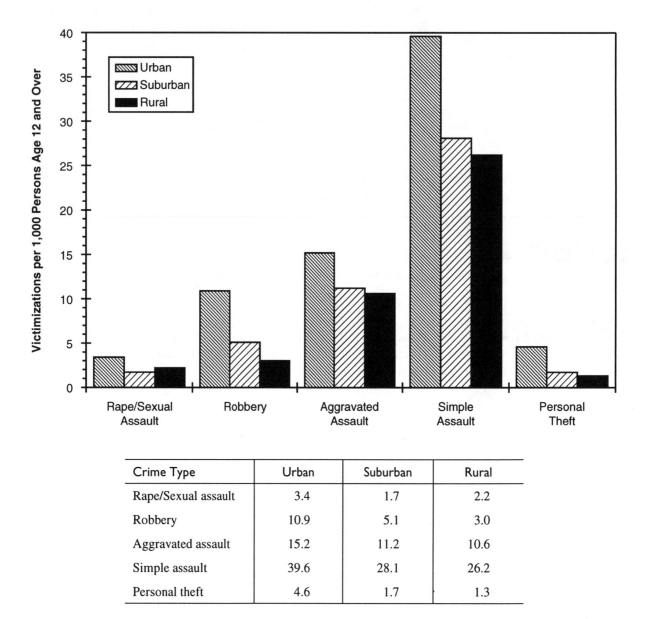

Crime Type	Urban	Suburban	Rural
Rape/Sexual assault	3.4	1.7	2.2
Robbery	10.9	5.1	3.0
Aggravated assault	15.2	11.2	10.6
Simple assault	39.6	28.1	26.2
Personal theft	4.6	1.7	1.3

Comments People who live in urban areas generally have a greater chance of being a crime victim than someone living in a suburban area. Similarly, suburban residents have a greater chance than people living in rural areas. This information was gathered by the National Crime Victimization Survey, which annually polls over 100,000 residents to measure both reported and unreported crimes. Murder statistics are not included because the victims cannot be surveyed.

Residents of urban areas had higher victimization rates for all personal crimes. In fact, the robbery rate of 10.9 per 1,000 persons for urban residents was more than three times the rate for rural residents (3.0) and more than twice the rate for suburban residents (5.1). Urban residents were also raped or sexually assaulted at twice the rate of suburban residents.

The difference between the suburban and rural rates is not nearly as wide as the difference between the urban and suburban rates. Victimizations among rural residents occurred less frequently than for suburbanites for all the crimes listed here except for rape/sexual assault.

Source U.S. Department of Justice, Bureau of Justice Statistics, "Criminal Victimization 1993" (Washington, D.C.: U.S. Government Printing Office, May 1995).

Contact U.S. Department of Justice, Bureau of Justice Statistics Clearinghouse, Box 6000, Rockville, MD 20850. (800) 732-3277. A World Wide Web server is operated at http://ncjrs.aspensys.com:81/ncjrshome.html. Inquiries can also be sent by e-mail to askncjrs@aspensys.com.

Crime in metropolitan areas

Index of crime (reported offenses per 100,000 inhabitants) in 44 of the nation's 50 largest metropolitan areas in 1994.*

Metropolitan Statistical Area	Crime Index	Crime Index Rank	Violent Crime Index	Violent Crime Index Rank	Property Crime Index	Property Crime Index Rank
Albany-Schenectady-Troy, NY	3,958.6	43	413.5	40	3,545.0	43
Atlanta, GA	7,333.0	12	846.6	19	6,486.4	11
Baltimore, MD	7,285.1	13	1,296.3	4	5,988.8	13
Birmingham, AL	6,415.3	20	1,085.0	12	5,330.3	22
Boston, MA-NH	4,459.4	39	686.6	28	3,772.8	40
Charlotte-Gastonia-Rock Hill, NC-SC	6,886.5	15	1,081.5	13	5,805.0	17
Cincinnati, OH-KY-IN	4,773.5	38	551.5	34	4,222.1	37
Columbus, OH	5,975.7	26	649.2	30	5,326.4	23
Dallas, TX	6,738.0	16	867.8	18	5,870.2	14
Dayton-Springfield, OH	5,155.1	35	521.9	37	4,633.2	35
Denver, CO	5,600.7	31	650.5	29	4,950.1	28
Detroit, MI	6,373.8	22	987.5	14	5,386.3	21
Greensboro-Winston Salem-High Point, NC	6,288.1	23	721.9	23	5,566.2	20
Hartford, CT	4,850.1	37	546.5	35	4,303.7	36
Houston, TX	5,644.0	28	877.7	17	4,766.3	32
Jacksonville, FL	8,119.4	5	1,255.6	5	6863.8	6
Los Angeles-Long Beach, CA	6,425.1	19	1,498.2	3	4,926.8	29
Louisville, KY-IN	4,885.2	36	707.1	26	4,178.0	38
Memphis, TN-AR-MS	7,508.8	9	1,115.2	10	6,393.6	12
Miami, FL	12,839.3	1	1,914.2	1	10,925.1	1
Milwaukee-Waukesha, WI	5,356.6	33	518.9	38	4,837.7	31
Minneapolis-St. Paul, MN-WI	5,215.8	34	496.5	39	4,719.3	33
Nashville, TN	6,913.6	14	1,132.5	8	5,781.1	19
New Orleans, LA	8,041.6	6	1,227.2	7	6,814.3	7
New York, NY	6,648.7	17	1,640.6	2	5,008.2	27
Norfolk-Virginia Beach-Newport News, VA-NC	5,638.5	29	580.7	32	5,057.9	25
Oklahoma City, OK	8,172.2	4	846.2	20	7,326.0	4
Orlando, FL	7,628.2	8	1,126.9	9	6,501.3	10
Philadelphia, PA-NJ	4,422.3	40	693.6	27	3,728.7	42
Phoenix-Mesa, AZ	8,290.3	3	768.0	22	7,522.3	3
Pittsburgh, PA	3,000.6	44	382.1	42	2,618.4	44

[Continued]

Crime in metropolitan areas

[Continued]

Metropolitan Statistical Area	Crime Index	Crime Index Rank	Violent Crime Index	Violent Crime Index Rank	Property Crime Index	Property Crime Index Rank
Portland-Vancouver, OR-WA	6,539.9	18	721.6	24	5,818.3	16
Providence-Fall River-Warwick, RI-MA	4,153.3	42	386.8	41	3,766.4	41
Richmond-Petersburg, VA	5,624.5	30	597.1	31	5,027.3	26
Rochester, NY	4,367.1	41	353.4	44	4,013.7	39
Sacramento, CA	7,342.8	11	836.8	21	6,505.9	9
Salt Lake City-Ogden, UT	6,174.6	24	375.7	43	5,798.9	18
San Antonio, TX	7,476.8	10	573.6	33	6,903.1	5
San Diego, CA	5,773.6	27	882.8	16	4,890.8	30
San Francisco, CA	5,998.8	25	915.6	15	5,083.2	24
Seattle-Bellevue-Everett, WA	6,397.8	21	542.3	36	5,855.5	15
Tampa-St. Petersburg-Clearwater, FL	7,953.9	7	1,238.2	6	6,715.6	8
Washington, DC-MD-VA-WV	5,382.9	32	714.5	25	4,668.5	34
West Palm Beach-Boca Raton, FL	8,892.6	2	1,107.3	11	7,785.3	2

*Information for six of the 50 largest metropolitan areas is missing, due to statistical differences. Only the 44 metropolitan areas shown are ranked. The missing metropolitan areas include: Chicago, IL; Cleveland, OH; Kansas City, MO; Indianapolis, IN; St. Louis, MO; and Buffalo-Niagara Falls, NY.

Comments

These statistics measure the frequency of crime in 44 of the nation's 50 largest metropolitan areas in 1994. Miami, Florida, had the worst overall crime rate, worst violent crime rate, and worst property crime rate.

However, keep in mind that these statistics are based on reported crimes. Sometimes people in one city may be more willing to report a crime than those in another city.

Source

U.S. Department of Justice, Federal Bureau of Investigation, *Crime in the United States, 1994* (Washington, D.C.: U.S. Government Printing Office, 1995), pp. 79–105.

Contact

U.S. Department of Justice, Federal Bureau of Investigation, Uniform Crime Reports, Criminal Justice Information Services Division, Washington, D.C. 20535. Information Dissemination: (202) 324-5015.

How frequent is violent crime among the states?

Violent crime rates (per 100,000 inhabitants) by state, 1994.

State	Violent Crime*	Murder	Forcible Rape	Robbery	Aggravated Assault
Alabama	683.7	11.9	35.2	171.2	465.3
Alaska	766.3	6.3	69.0	146.2	544.9
Arizona	703.1	10.5	36.0	162.0	494.7
Arkansas	595.1	12.0	41.9	128.7	412.5
California	1,013.0	11.8	34.9	356.8	609.4
Colorado	509.6	5.4	43.2	106.9	354.0
Connecticut	455.5	6.6	24.6	187.8	236.5
Delaware	561.0	4.7	75.6	125.9	354.8
District of Columbia	2,662.6	70.0	43.7	1,107.2	1,441.8
Florida	1,146.8	8.3	52.3	328.8	757.4
Georgia	667.7	10.0	34.7	222.6	400.4
Hawaii	262.2	4.2	30.4	103.6	123.9
Idaho	285.8	3.5	27.9	18.4	235.9
Illinois	960.9	11.7	33.3	372.6	543.3
Indiana	525.1	7.9	35.6	130.2	351.5
Iowa	315.1	1.7	23.5	46.9	243.0
Kansas	478.7	5.8	37.1	119.8	316.0
Kentucky	605.3	6.4	35.3	93.9	469.7
Louisiana	981.9	19.8	44.6	267.2	650.3
Maine	129.9	2.3	25.6	22.4	79.6
Maryland	948.0	11.6	40.7	402.5	493.3
Massachusetts	707.6	3.5	30.2	168.2	505.7
Michigan	766.1	9.8	70.8	228.9	456.7
Minnesota	359.0	3.2	59.7	117.6	178.6
Mississippi	493.7	15.3	45.4	162.5	270.5
Missouri	743.5	10.5	37.0	230.7	465.2
Montana	177.1	3.3	27.2	32.7	113.9
Nebraska	389.5	3.1	30.8	75.4	280.2
Nevada	1,001.9	11.7	68.7	352.4	569.1
New Hampshire	116.8	1.4	35.8	27.1	52.5
New Jersey	614.2	5.0	24.9	288.0	296.2
New Mexico	889.2	10.7	52.4	140.8	685.4
New York	965.6	11.1	25.9	476.7	451.9
North Carolina	655.0	10.9	33.0	181.2	429.9
North Dakota	81.8	0.2	23.4	11.1	47.2
Ohio	485.8	6.0	47.1	187.5	245.1
Oklahoma	651.5	6.9	49.6	128.1	466.8
Oregon	520.6	4.9	43.2	138.2	334.4
Pennsylvania	426.7	5.9	26.1	186.7	208.0
Rhode Island	375.5	4.1	27.4	87.3	256.8

[Continued]

How frequent is violent crime among the states?

[Continued]

State	Violent Crime*	Murder	Forcible Rape	Robbery	Aggravated Assault
South Carolina	1,030.5	9.6	54.3	186.1	780.4
South Dakota	277.6	1.4	42.0	18.7	165.5
Tennessee	747.9	9.3	49.2	207.4	482.0
Texas	706.5	11.0	49.5	204.8	441.1
Utah	304.5	2.9	42.2	63.6	195.8
Vermont	96.9	1.0	27.6	12.2	56.0
Virginia	357.7	8.7	28.5	132.8	187.6
Washington	511.3	5.5	60.5	139.7	305.6
West Virginia	215.8	5.4	20.3	42.4	147.6
Wisconsin	270.5	4.5	23.5	112.9	129.7
Wyoming	272.5	3.4	33.6	16.6	218.9
U.S. Total	716.0	9.0	39.2	237.7	430.2

*Violent crimes are offenses of murder (and nonnegligent manslaughter), forcible rape, robbery, and aggravated assault.

Comments The number of violent crimes varies widely from one state to another. The accompanying table lists 1994 violent crime rates among the 50 states and the District of Columbia. This is based on the frequency of crime per 100,000 inhabitants, not just on the number of crimes, which varies significantly between large and small states.

The District of Columbia, Florida, South Carolina, California, and Nevada had the highest rates of violent crime in 1994, with each state having over 1,000 offenses per 100,000 inhabitants. On the other extreme, North Dakota, Vermont, New Hampshire, Maine, and Montana had the lowest violent crime rates, all below 200 offenses per 100,000 inhabitants.

The District of Columbia had the worst violent crime in general, and also the worst murder, robbery, and aggravated assault rates. After D.C., murder rates were highest in Louisiana, Mississippi, and California; robbery rates highest after D.C. in New York, Maryland, and Illinois; and aggravated assault rates highest after D.C. in South Carolina, Florida, and New Mexico. Forcible rape rates were the worst in Delaware, followed by Michigan, Alaska, and Nevada.

Source U.S. Department of Justice, Federal Bureau of Investigation, *Crime in the United States, 1994* (Washington, D.C.: U.S. Government Printing Office, 1995), pp. 68–78, 189.

Contact U.S. Department of Justice, Federal Bureau of Investigation, Uniform Crime Reports, Criminal Justice Information Services Division, Washington, D.C. 20535. Information Dissemination: (202) 324-5015.

How frequent is property crime among the states?

Property crime rates (per 100,000 inhabitants) by state, 1994.

State	Property Crime	Burglary	Larceny-Theft	Motor Vehicle Theft
Alabama	4,219.4	1,044.4	2,843.1	331.8
Alaska	4,941.7	800.0	3,601.3	540.4
Arizona	7,221.4	1,476.2	4,678.5	1,066.7
Arkansas	4,203.6	1,097.1	2,791.6	315.0
California	5,160.8	1,222.5	2,957.7	980.6
Colorado	4,808.8	925.7	3,490.2	392.9
Connecticut	4,092.5	889.8	2,586.9	615.8
Delaware	3,586.5	790.4	2,446.2	350.0
District of Columbia	8,422.6	1,760.9	5,212.5	1,449.3
Florida	7,103.2	1,701.0	4,490.6	911.5
Georgia	5,342.7	1,153.9	3,631.6	557.2
Hawaii	6,418.3	1,189.9	4,687.0	541.4
Idaho	3,791.2	719.1	2,877.1	195.1
Illinois	4,664.9	1,005.1	3,096.4	563.5
Indiana	4,067.7	850.5	2,782.4	434.8
Iowa	3,339.5	667.1	2,492.3	180.1
Kansas	4,415.1	1,121.2	2954.5	339.4
Kentucky	2,893.3	750.4	1,919.2	223.6
Louisiana	5,689.2	1,279.0	3,802.6	607.6
Maine	3,142.8	720.8	2,278.8	143.2
Maryland	5,174.6	1,043.4	3,368.1	763.0
Massachusetts	3,733.4	881.0	2,151.3	701.0
Michigan	4,679.1	967.2	3,055.7	656.1
Minnesota	3,982.0	791.7	2,875.9	314.3
Mississippi	4,343.3	1,292.4	2,646.0	405.0
Missouri	4,564.2	1,053.0	2,998.9	512.3
Montana	4,841.7	721.7	3,833.8	286.2
Nebraska	4,050.9	675.5	2,991.2	384.2
Nevada	5,675.6	1,354.5	3,561.6	759.4
New Hampshire	2,624.2	463.9	1,957.8	202.5
New Jersey	4,046.8	911.9	2,474.9	660.0
New Mexico	5,298.5	1,326.8	3,466.9	504.8
New York	4,105.0	906.2	2,489.5	709.3
North Carolina	4,970.3	1,472.7	3,195.7	301.9
North Dakota	2,654.1	324.5	2,178.5	151.1
Ohio	3,975.7	866.3	2,682.3	427.1
Oklahoma	4,918.7	1,251.2	3,192.9	474.6

[Continued]

How frequent is property crime among the states?

[Continued]

State	Property Crime	Burglary	Larceny-Theft	Motor Vehicle Theft
Oregon	5,775.8	1,100.8	3,969.7	705.2
Pennsylvania	2,845.2	551.5	1,844.3	449.3
Rhode Island	3,743.5	912.8	2,310.8	519.9
South Carolina	4,970.4	1,274.0	3,336.6	359.8
South Dakota	2,874.6	546.2	2,207.5	120.9
Tennessee	4,371.9	1,141.6	2,670.0	560.3
Texas	5,165.9	1,168.2	3,395.1	602.6
Utah	4,996.4	790.8	3,907.4	298.2
Vermont	3,153.4	736.9	2,267.9	148.6
Virginia	3,689.9	638.8	2,272.0	279.1
Washington	5,516.3	1,044.2	3,971.5	500.5
West Virginia	2,312.6	585.8	1,547.1	179.7
Wisconsin	3,673.8	645.9	2,667.4	360.5
Wyoming	4,017.2	650.6	3,204.6	162.0
U.S. Total	4,658.3	1,041.8	3,025.4	591.2

*Property crimes are offenses of burglary, larceny-theft, and motor vehicle theft. Data is not included for the property crime of arson.

Comments The number of property crimes varies widely from one state to another. The accompanying table lists 1994 property crime rates among the 50 states and the District of Columbia. This is based on the frequency of crime per 100,000 inhabitants, not just on the number of crimes, which varies significantly between large and small states.

The District of Columbia, Arizona, Florida, Hawaii, and Oregon had the highest rates of property crime in 1994, with each state having over 5,700 offenses per 100,000 inhabitants. On the other extreme, West Virginia, New Hampshire, North Dakota, Pennsylvania, and South Dakota had the lowest property crime rates.

The District of Columbia had the worst property crime in general, and also the worst burglary, larceny-theft, and motor vehicle theft rates. After D.C., burglary rates were highest in Florida, Arizona, and North Carolina; larceny-theft rates highest after D.C. in Hawaii, Arizona, and Florida; and motor vehicle theft rates highest after D.C. in Arizona, California, and Florida.

Source U.S. Department of Justice, Federal Bureau of Investigation, *Crime in the United States, 1994* (Washington, D.C.: U.S. Government Printing Office, 1995), pp. 59, 68–78.

Contact U.S. Department of Justice, Federal Bureau of Investigation, Uniform Crime Reports, Criminal Justice Information Services Division, Washington, D.C. 20535. Information Dissemination: (202) 324-5015.

Residential and nonresidential burglaries, 1988–94

Reported burglaries in the U.S. during 1988–94, by type of premises.

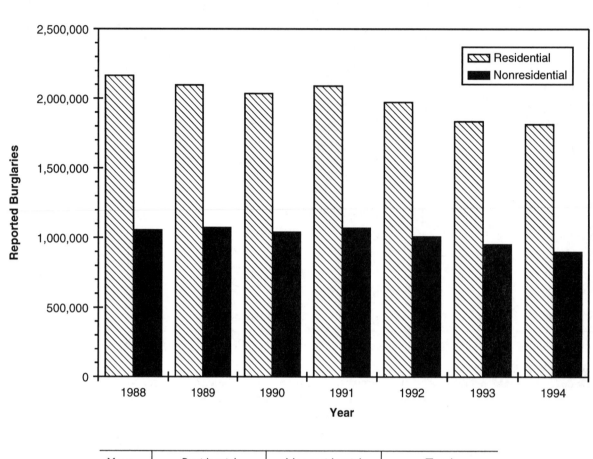

Year	Residential	Nonresidential	Total
1988	2,164,309	1,053,791	3,218,100
1989	2,096,233	1,071,967	3,168,200
1990	2,034,865	1,039,035	3,073,900
1991	2,088,343	1,068,807	3,157,200
1992	1,972,919	1,006,981	2,979,900
1993	1,833,907	950,893	2,834,800
1994	1,813,771	898,429	2,712,200

Comments

During 1988–94 in the U.S., there were about twice as many residential burglaries each year as there were nonresidential burglaries. A residential burglary occurs on property where people live, such as in a house, apartment, or condominium. A nonresidential burglary occurs on commercial property, such as in a store, office, factory, or warehouse.

From 1988 to 1994, the number of reported nonresidential burglaries held steady at about 1 million per year. Burglaries of residences, however, fell from about 2.2 million in 1988 to around 1.8 million in 1994, a drop of 16%.

This decline in residential burglaries could have several possible explanations. First, willingness to report a burglary may have dropped during those years. If so, the actual number of residential burglaries may not have changed much.

If the actual number of residential burglaries did fall, however, it could be from increased security methods, such as more police presence, electronic alarms systems, fences and barred windows, or guard dogs.

Source

U.S. Department of Justice, Federal Bureau of Investigation, *Crime in the United States, 1994* (Washington, D.C.: U.S. Government Printing Office, 1995), p. 107.

U.S. Department of Justice, Federal Bureau of Investigation, *Crime in the United States, 1993* (Washington, D.C.: U.S. Government Printing Office, 1994), p. 108.

U.S. Department of Justice, Federal Bureau of Investigation, *Crime in the United States, 1991* (Washington, D.C.: U.S. Government Printing Office, 1992), p. 107.

Contact

U.S. Department of Justice, Federal Bureau of Investigation, Uniform Crime Reports, Criminal Justice Information Services Division, Washington, D.C. 20535. Information Dissemination: (202) 324-5015.

Where do robberies happen most often?

Robberies by site of offense, 1988–94.

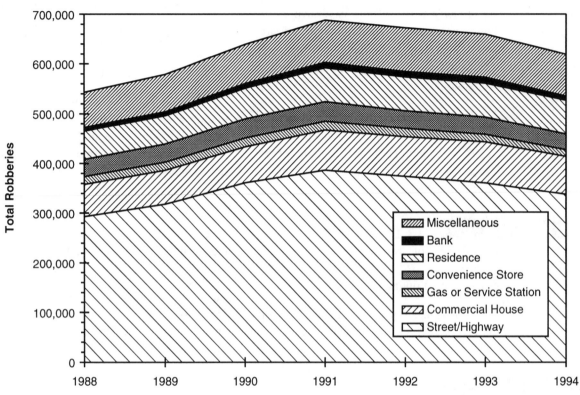

Site of Offense	1988	1989	1990	1991	1992	1993	1994
Street/highway	293,229	318,017	360,861	386,552	374,157	360,739	337,687
Commercial house	64,769	68,173	72,589	80,448	79,717	82,371	76,114
Gas or service station	15,745	16,355	17,394	17,829	16,752	15,389	13,433
Convenience store	34,516	36,381	38,643	39,429	35,312	34,811	31,824
Residence	56,853	56,928	61,733	67,592	67,619	67,902	67,375
Bank	7,739	7,932	9,345	11,019	11,121	11,854	8,959
Miscellaneous	70,119	74,544	78,705	84,863	87,802	86,693	83,429
Total	542,970	578,330	639,270	687,730	672,480	659,760	618,820

Comments

About 56% of all reported robberies occurred on the street or highway during 1988–94, and not in a place of business or residence according to the FBI's Uniform Crime Reports system.

Robberies on the street or highway often involve just one victim and one offender. If a robber picks a victim randomly, then the chance to steal a lot of money is hit-or-miss. Also, residential robberies (which include the use of force or the threat of force) may result in a violent confrontation with a member of the household.

Robberies at places of business often involve multiple victims because several employees as well as customers may be present. Robbers of commercial establishments often will work in teams of two or more, where different individuals have different functions within the robbery. Such roles can include grabbing cash or valuables, maintaining control over employees and customers, searching for any approaching police, and finding a quick escape.

Robberies of different types of establishments have different levels of risk and reward. For example, robbers of convenience stores and gas and service stations are often successful. The cash taken by such robberies, however, is often very little compared to the risk of apprehension and punishment. On the other hand, the risks in bank robbery are often greater, but the potential of gaining a lot of cash from a single robbery is also increased.

Source

U.S. Department of Justice, Federal Bureau of Investigation, *Crime in the United States, 1994* (Washington, D.C.: U.S. Government Printing Office, 1995), p. 107.

U.S. Department of Justice, Federal Bureau of Investigation, *Crime in the United States, 1993* (Washington, D.C.: U.S. Government Printing Office, 1994), p. 108.

U.S. Department of Justice, Federal Bureau of Investigation, *Crime in the United States, 1992* (Washington, D.C.: U.S. Government Printing Office, 1993), p. 107.

U.S. Department of Justice, Federal Bureau of Investigation, *Crime in the United States, 1991* (Washington, D.C.: U.S. Government Printing Office, 1992), p. 107.

Contact

U.S. Department of Justice, Federal Bureau of Investigation, Uniform Crime Reports, Criminal Justice Information Services Division, Washington, D.C. 20535. Information Dissemination: (202) 324-5015.

How many murders are committed in the U.S. each year?

The number of murders in the U.S. during 1960–94 and the murder rate per 100,000 inhabitants.

Year	Number of Murders	Rate per 100,000 Inhabitants
1960	9,110	5.1
1961	8,740	4.8
1962	8,530	4.6
1963	8,640	4.6
1964	9,360	4.9
1965	9,960	5.1
1966	11,040	5.6
1967	12,240	6.2
1968	13,800	6.9
1969	14,760	7.3
1970	16,000	7.9
1971	17,780	8.6
1972	18,670	9.0
1973	19,640	9.4
1974	20,710	9.8
1975	20,510	9.6
1976	18,780	8.8
1977	19,120	8.8
1978	19,560	9.0
1979	21,460	9.7
1980	23,040	10.2
1981	22,520	9.8
1982	21,010	9.1
1983	19,310	8.3
1984	18,690	7.9
1985	18,980	7.9
1986	20,610	8.6
1987	20,100	8.3
1988	20,680	8.4
1989	21,500	8.7
1990	23,440	9.4
1991	24,700	9.8
1992	23,760	9.3
1993	24,530	9.5
1994	23,300	9.0

Comments The total number of murders committed in the U.S. steadily climbed from 9,110 in 1960 to 23,300 in 1994, an increase of 156%. The murder rate increased from 5.1 murders per 100,000 inhabitants to 9.0, a rise of about 86%.

Although the annual number of murders has more than doubled since the mid-1960s, the murder rate has not increased as rapidly.

That is because the murder rate accounts for changes in population size.

The number of murders peaked in 1991, at 24,700, but the murder rate was at its highest in 1980 when there were 10.2 murders per 100,000 inhabitants. This means that since 1980, the frequency of murder in the U.S. has slightly declined even though the total number of murders has risen.

Source U.S. Department of Justice, Federal Bureau of Investigation, *Crime in the United States,* 1960–93 (Washington, D.C.: U.S. Government Printing Office).

U.S. Department of Justice, Federal Bureau of Investigation, *Crime in the United States, 1994* (Washington, D.C.: U.S. Government Printing Office, 1995), p. 13.

Contact U.S. Department of Justice, Federal Bureau of Investigation, Uniform Crime Reports, Criminal Justice Information

Services Division, Washington, D.C. 20535. Information Dissemination: (202) 324-5015.

Why do murders happen?

Circumstances of murders occurring in the U.S. during 1994.

Circumstance	1994 Murders	Percent of Total*
Felony type total	4,071	18.4
Rape	78	0.4
Robbery	2,072	9.4
Burglary	158	0.7
Larceny-theft	30	0.1
Motor vehicle theft	53	0.2
Arson	132	0.6
Prostitution and commercialized vice	14	0.1
Other sex offenses	41	0.2
Narcotic drug laws	1,239	5.6
Gambling	12	0.1
Other–not specified	242	1.1
Suspected felony type	136	0.6
Other than felony type	11,675	52.9
Romantic triangle	371	1.7
Child killed by babysitter	22	0.1
Brawl due to influence of alcohol	316	1.4
Brawl due to influence of narcotics	211	1.0
Argument over money or property	387	1.8
Other argument	5,812	26.3
Gangland killings	111	0.5
Juvenile gang killings	1,157	5.2
Institutional killings	14	0.1
Sniper attack	2	†
Others–not specified	3,272	14.8
Unknown	6,194	28.1
Total	22,076	100.0

* May not add to total because of rounding.
† Less than 0.01%.

Comments   In 1994, the FBI gathered information about the circumstances behind 22,076 of the 23,305 murders (about 95%) recorded across the U.S. that year. The FBI annually tabulates the reasons why murders take place when such details are available.

Most of the murders recorded in 1994 were not the result of any kind of felony. Murders that were related to felonies only accounted for 18.4% of all murders, and murders that were suspected to be related to felonies made up 0.6%.

Most of the murders related to felonies were committed in the course of a robbery or a violation of narcotics drug laws. These two circumstances accounted for 81% of all felony-related murders, and accounted for 15% of all murders where the circumstance was known.

Murders that resulted from a non-felony motive accounted for 52.9% of the total. Many of these murders were the result of personal disputes. These situations often involved intense, typically spur-of-the-moment emotional outbursts that culminated in violence. Murders resulting from an argument over money or property or some other type of an argument accounted for about 28% of all murders in 1994. About 2.4% of all murders were due to alcohol- or drug-influenced brawls.

Of recent concern also are the numbers of gangland and juvenile gang killings, which made up 5.7% of all murder circumstances. Murders resulting from a romantic triangle, although highly publicized, accounted for only 1.7%.

Source   U.S. Department of Justice, Federal Bureau of Investigation, *Crime in the United States, 1994* (Washington, D.C.: U.S. Government Printing Office, 1995).

Contact   U.S. Department of Justice, Federal Bureau of Investigation, Uniform Crime Reports, Criminal Justice Information Services Division, Washington, D.C. 20535. Information Dissemination: (202) 324-5015.

How many victims of rape and sexual assault are there, and how many of them report the crime to the police?

Rape/sexual assault* victimizations and victimizations reported to the police in the U.S. during 1993.

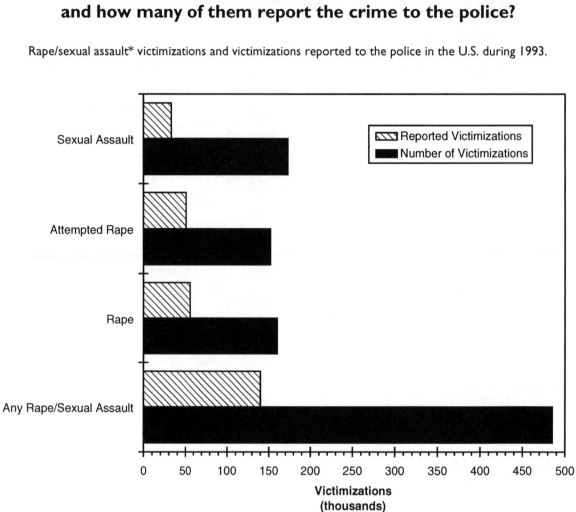

Type of Rape	Number of Victimizations	Number of Reported Victimizations
Sexual assault	173,000	· 33,000
Attempted rape	152,000	51,000
Rape	160,000	56,000
Total Rape/Sexual assault	485,000	140,000

*Distinct from rape or attempted rape, sexual assault includes attacks or attempted attacks generally involving unwanted sexual contact between the victim and the offender; this may or may not involve force.

Comments In 1993 there were about 485,000 victims of rape and sexual assault, according to the National Crime Victimization Survey (NCVS). The NCVS is a nationwide survey of over 100,000 residents which measures both reported and unreported crimes.

About 36% of those victimizations were sexual assaults while the remaining 64% were rapes. Of the total number of rapes, 51% were completed rapes and 49% were attempted rapes.

About 29% (140,000 of 485,000) of all rape/sexual assault victimizations were reported to the police, with the rate of reporting differing according to the type of crime. Sexual assault was reported about 19% of the time; attempted rape was reported about 34% of the time; and completed rape was reported about 35% of the time.

Source U.S. Department of Justice, Bureau of Justice Statistics, "Criminal Victimization 1993" (Washington, D.C.: U.S. Government Printing Office, May 1995).

Contact U.S. Department of Justice, Federal Bureau of Investigation, Uniform Crime Reports, Criminal Justice Information Services Division, Washington, D.C. 20535. Information Dissemination: (202) 324-5015.

How many rapes are committed in the U.S. each year?

The number of reported forcible rapes in the U.S. during 1960–94 and the rate of rape per 100,000 inhabitants.

Year	Number of Rapes	Rate per 100,000 Inhabitants
1960	17,190	9.6
1961	17,220	9.4
1962	17,550	9.4
1963	17,650	9.4
1964	21,420	11.2
1965	23,410	12.1
1966	25,820	13.2
1967	27,620	14.0
1968	31,670	15.9
1969	37,170	18.5
1970	37,990	18.7
1971	42,260	20.5
1972	46,850	22.5
1973	51,400	24.5
1974	55,400	26.2
1975	56,090	26.3
1976	57,080	26.6
1977	63,500	29.4
1978	67,610	31.0
1979	76,390	34.7
1980	82,990	36.8
1981	82,500	36.0
1982	78,770	34.0
1983	78,920	33.7
1984	84,230	35.7
1985	88,670	37.1
1986	91,460	37.9
1987	91,110	37.4
1988	92,490	37.6
1989	94,500	38.1
1990	102,560	41.2
1991	106,590	42.3
1992	109,060	42.8
1993	106,000	41.1
1994	102,100	39.2

Comments The total number of rapes reported in the U.S. in 1994 was 102,096, almost six times greater than the 17,190 rapes reported in 1960. During this period the rate of rape per 100,000 inhabitants increased by a factor of over four times, from 9.6 in 1960 to 39.2 in 1994.

The rate of rape has not increased as rapidly as the annual number of reported rapes because the rate accounts for increases in population.

The number of reported rapes peaked in 1992, at 109,060. The rape rate also was at its highest in 1992, at 42.8 rapes per 100,000 inhabitants. The rate of rape steadily increased during the 1960s and 1970s, but stabilized during much of the 1980s.

It is important to remember that these statistics include only reported offenses against females. Unreported offenses and all offenses against males are not included. Many criminologists believe that rape may have been greatly underreported in the past and that the increases in reported rapes in the recent years may be a reflection of a new open attitude toward reporting victimization, rather than a sharp increase in the actual frequency of rape.

Source U.S. Department of Justice, Federal Bureau of Investigation, *Crime in the United States,* 1960–93 (Washington, D.C.: U.S. Government Printing Office).

U.S. Department of Justice, Federal Bureau of Investigation, *Crime in the United States, 1994* (Washington, D.C.: U.S. Government Printing Office, 1995), p. 23.

Contact U.S. Department of Justice, Federal Bureau of Investigation, Uniform Crime Reports, Criminal Justice Information Services Division, Washington, D.C. 20535. Information Dissemination: (202) 324-5015.

How many victims of robbery are there, and how many of them report the crime to the police?

Robbery victimizations and victimizations reported to the police in the U.S. during 1993.

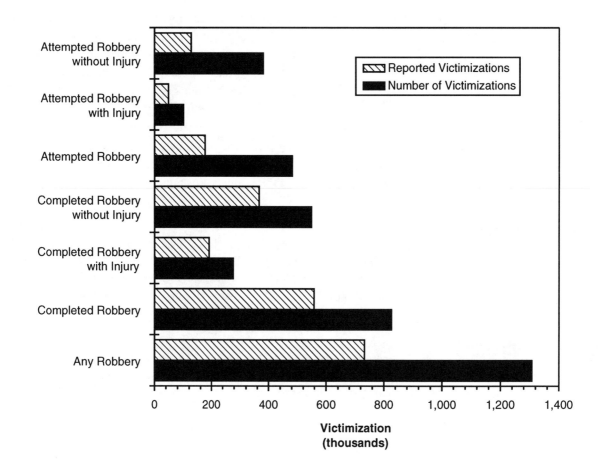

Type of Robbery	Number of Victimizations	Number of Reported Victimizations
Completed robbery	826,000	558,000
With injury	276,000	191,000
Without injury	549,000	366,000
Attempted robbery	481,000	176,000
With injury	100,000	49,000
Without injury	381,000	127,000
Any robbery	1,307,000	733,000

Comments In 1993 there were over 1.3 million robbery victims, according to estimates from the National Crime Victimization Survey (NCVS). The NCVS is a nationwide survey of over 100,000 residents which measures both reported and unreported crimes.

About 826,000 victimizations were completed robberies while the remaining 481,000 were attempted robberies, indicating that 63.2% of all robbery attempts were successful.

However, only 56% (733,000) of all robbery victimizations were reported to the police. Of those reported, 76% were for completed robberies, and 24% for attempted robberies.

Individuals are more likely to report a completed robbery than an attempted one. In fact, 67.6% of the completed robberies were reported, while only 36.6% of the attempted robberies were reported.

Source U.S. Department of Justice, Bureau of Justice Statistics, "Criminal Victimization 1993" (Washington, D.C.: U.S. Government Printing Office, May 1995).

Contact U.S. Department of Justice, Federal Bureau of Investigation, Uniform Crime Reports, Criminal Justice Information Services Division, Washington, D.C. 20535. Information Dissemination: (202) 324-5015

How many robberies are committed in the U.S. each year?

The number of reported robberies in the U.S. during 1960–94 and the robbery rate per 100,000 inhabitants.

Year	Number of Robberies	Rate per 100,000 Inhabitants
1960	107,840	60.1
1961	106,670	58.3
1962	110,860	59.7
1963	116,470	61.8
1964	130,390	68.2
1965	138,690	71.7
1966	157,990	80.8
1967	202,910	102.8
1968	262,840	131.8
1969	298,850	148.4
1970	349,860	172.1
1971	387,700	188.0
1972	376,290	180.7
1973	384,220	183.1
1974	442,400	209.3
1975	470,500	220.8
1976	427,810	199.3
1977	412,610	190.7
1978	426,930	195.8
1979	480,700	218.4
1980	565,840	251.1
1981	592,910	258.7
1982	553,130	238.9
1983	506,570	216.5
1984	485,010	205.4
1985	497,870	208.5
1986	542,780	225.1
1987	517,700	212.7
1988	542,970	220.9
1989	578,330	233.0
1990	639,270	257.0
1991	687,730	272.7
1992	672,480	263.6
1993	659,870	255.9
1994	618,817	237.7

Comments The total number of robberies reported in the U.S in 1993 was 659,870, over six times greater than the 107,840 robberies reported in 1960. During this period, the rate of robbery per 100,000 inhabitants increased by a factor of over four times, from 60.1 in 1960 to 255.9 in 1993.

The rate of robbery has not increased as rapidly as the annual number of reported robberies because the rate accounts for increases in population.

The number of reported robberies peaked in 1991, at 687,730. The robbery rate also was at its highest in 1991, at 272.7 robberies per 100,000 inhabitants. The robbery rate steadily increased during the 1960s, but fluctuated throughout the 1970s and 1980s.

Source U.S. Department of Justice, Federal Bureau of Investigation, *Crime in the United States,* 1960–93 (Washington, D.C.: U.S. Government Printing Office).

U.S. Department of Justice, Federal Bureau of Investigation, *Crime in the United States, 1994* (Washington, D.C.: U.S. Government Printing Office, 1995), p. 26.

Contact U.S. Department of Justice, Federal Bureau of Investigation, Uniform Crime Reports, Criminal Justice Information Services Division, Washington, D.C. 20535. Information Dissemination: (202) 324-5015.

How often does aggravated assault occur in the U.S. each year?

The rate of reported aggravated assault offenses and the rate of aggravated assault victimizations, 1973–93. Although both measure the frequency of aggravated assault, the rates are not entirely compatible.

Year	Reported Aggravated Assaults per 100,000 Inhabitants	Aggravated Assault Victimizations per 1,000 Persons Age 12 and Older
1973	200.5	10.1
1974	215.8	10.4
1975	231.1	9.6
1976	233.2	9.9
1977	247.0	10.0
1978	262.1	9.7
1979	286.0	9.9
1980	298.5	9.3
1981	289.7	9.6
1982	289.2	9.3
1983	279.2	8.0
1984	290.2	9.0
1985	302.9	8.3
1986	346.1	7.9
1987	351.3	8.0
1988	370.2	8.7
1989	383.4	8.3
1990	424.1	7.9
1991	433.3	8.0
1992	441.8	9.0
1993	440.1	12.2*

* Beginning in 1993, the procedures used in conducting the survey changed, making it unwise to compare the data from the old survey and the new redesigned survey.

Comments

Aggravated assault is the unlawful intention of inflicting serious bodily injury on someone. It also includes unlawful threats or attempts to inflict bodily injury or death by means of a dangerous weapon with or without actually resulting in injury.

Although the rate of aggravated assault victimizations generally declined in the 1970s and 1980s, the rate of reported aggravated assaults steadily increased during the same period. The rate of aggravated assault victimizations fell from 10.1 incidents per 1,000 persons in 1973 to 9.0 in 1992, a decline of about 10%. Meanwhile, the rate of reported aggravated assault increased from 200.5 to 441.8 incidents per 100,000 inhabitants, a rise of about 120%.

At first it may seem that these two figures conflict, but it is important to remember that although both measure the frequency of aggravated assault, the two sources measure it using different techniques. The FBI's Uniform Crime Report (UCR) system measures aggravated assault according to police reports, while the Bureau of Justice Statistics' National Crime Victimization Survey (NCVS) estimates the frequency of reported and unreported aggravated assaults, based on a survey of over 100,000 Americans.

Based on the findings of these two sources, it is possible to make speculations that are not possible when only one source is used. So although the UCR information indicates a rapid rise in the frequency of aggravated assault, one possible explanation could be that an increase occurred, but was combined with an increase in the willingness of victims to report the crime. If this was true, it would mean that aggravated assaults were underreported to police in the past.

Source

U.S. Department of Justice, Federal Bureau of Investigation, *Crime in the United States,* 1960–93 (Washington, D.C.: U.S. Government Printing Office).

U.S. Department of Justice, Bureau of Justice Statistics. *Criminal Victimization in the United States, 1992* (Washington, D.C.: U.S. Government Printing Office, 1994), p. 4.

U.S. Department of Justice, Bureau of Justice Statistics, "Criminal Victimization 1993" (Washington, D.C.: U.S. Government Printing Office, May 1995).

Contact

U.S. Department of Justice, Federal Bureau of Investigation, Uniform Crime Reports, Criminal Justice Information Services Division, Washington, D.C. 20535. Information Dissemination: (202) 324-5015.

U.S. Department of Justice, Bureau of Justice Statistics Clearinghouse, Box 6000, Rockville, MD 20850. (800) 732-3277. A World Wide Web server is operated at http://ncjrs.aspensys.com:81/ncjrshome.html. Inquiries can also be sent by e-mail to askncjrs@aspensys.com.

How often do assaults occur in each state?

Reported aggravated assaults per 100,000 population for the 50 states and the District of Columbia, 1991–94.

State	1991	1992	1993	1994
Alabama	644.4	654.6	574.3	465.3
Alaska	401.6	445.3	545.6	544.9
Arizona	454.8	466.6	505.7	494.7
Arkansas	401.9	399.0	415.8	412.5
California	623.5	641.6	621.8	609.4
Colorado	398.9	404.9	399.0	354.0
Connecticut	280.5	252.5	228.7	236.5
Delaware	407.6	379.5	417.1	354.8
District of Columbia	1,121.4	1,454.7	1,557.6	1,441.8
Florida	723.4	777.2	785.7	757.4
Georgia	415.0	427.1	428.3	400.4
Hawaii	117.9	117.7	120.1	123.9
Idaho	238.9	224.7	226.7	235.9
Illinois	531.8	516.4	532.6	543.3
Indiana	340.5	335.7	322.6	351.5
Iowa	235.4	218.0	244.8	243.0
Kansas	310.3	333.7	326.3	316.0
Kentucky	312.7	410.4	331.4	469.7
Louisiana	614.3	653.4	715.4	650.3
Maine	86.3	82.0	76.3	79.6
Maryland	491.5	512.6	506.4	493.3
Massachusetts	505.2	555.0	592.0	505.7
Michigan	470.3	458.6	472.1	456.7
Minnesota	175.3	184.1	175.8	178.6
Mississippi	213.7	230.4	238.4	270.5
Missouri	467.4	466.5	455.2	465.2
Montana	98.9	114.6	114.2	113.9
Nebraska	249.2	256.2	252.0	280.2
Nevada	268.7	291.8	463.9	569.1
New Hampshire	52.8	52.9	64.1	52.5
New Jersey	307.3	304.8	297.5	296.2
New Mexico	651.6	724.1	731.1	685.4
New York	499.4	483.5	471.5	451.9
North Carolina	434.4	447.7	441.3	429.9
North Dakota	38.0	50.3	48.7	47.2
Ohio	287.0	268.2	256.3	245.1
Oklahoma	396.7	431.6	455.3	466.8
Oregon	298.2	301.1	317.6	334.4

[Continued]

How often do assaults occur in each state?

[Continued]

State	1991	1992	1993	1994
Pennsylvania	221.1	212.4	205.1	208.0
Rhode Island	304.5	265.5	268.1	256.8
South Carolina	731.2	706.0	773.4	780.4
South Dakota	122.0	125.3	145.6	165.5
Tennessee	455.6	470.3	485.5	482.0
Texas	484.9	487.7	470.8	441.1
Utah	183.1	186.2	194.7	195.8
Vermont	72.3	73.5	61.8	56.0
Virginia	196.4	196.8	189.8	187.6
Washington	302.5	317.8	307.9	305.6
West Virginia	118.5	140.0	138.5	147.6
Wisconsin	127.7	125.3	121.4	129.7
Wyoming	263.9	262.9	231.3	218.9
U.S. Total	433.3	441.8	440.1	430.2

Comments

Aggravated assault is the unlawful intention of inflicting of serious bodily injury on someone. It also includes unlawful threats or attempts to inflict bodily injury or death by means of a dangerous weapon with or without actual infliction of injury. Across the United States, there were 430.2 reported aggravated assaults per 100,000 persons in 1994, the lowest rate in four years.

The District of Columbia, Florida, South Carolina, and New Mexico were among the top five states with the highest rates of aggravated assault during 1991–94. Alabama was in the top five in 1991 and 1992, but was replaced by Louisiana in 1993 and 1994. North Dakota, New Hampshire, Vermont, Maine, and Montana consistently ranked the lowest in the rate of aggravated assault.

Source

U.S. Department of Justice, Federal Bureau of Investigation, *Crime in the United States, 1994* (Washington, D.C.: U.S. Government Printing Office, 1995), pp. 59, 68–78.

U.S. Department of Justice, Federal Bureau of Investigation, *Crime in the United States, 1993* (Washington, D.C.: U.S. Government Printing Office, 1994), pp. 59, 68–78.

U.S. Department of Justice, Federal Bureau of Investigation, *Crime in the United States, 1992* (Washington, D.C.: U.S. Government Printing Office, 1993), pp. 59, 68–78.

U.S. Department of Justice, Federal Bureau of Investigation, *Crime in the United States, 1991* (Washington, D.C.: U.S. Government Printing Office, 1992), pp. 59, 68–78.

Contact

U.S. Department of Justice, Federal Bureau of Investigation, Uniform Crime Reports, Criminal Justice Information Services Division, Washington, D.C. 20535. Information Dissemination: (202) 324-5015.

How many U.S. households are affected by a crime?

Households experiencing crime, 1975–92.

Year	Total U.S. Households (millions)	Households Experiencing a Crime (millions)	Crime Rate
1975	73.123	23.377	32.1%
1976	74.528	23.540	31.5%
1977	75.904	23.741	31.3%
1978	77.578	24.277	31.3%
1979	78.964	24.730	31.3%
1980	80.622	24.222	30.0%
1981	82.797	24.863	30.0%
1982	85.178	24.989	29.3%
1983	86.146	23.621	27.4%
1984	87.791	22.806	26.0%
1985	88.852	22.191	25.0%
1986	90.014	22.201	24.7%
1987	91.391	22.404	24.5%
1988	92.892	22.844	24.6%
1989	94.553	23.221	24.6%
1990	95.461	22.652	23.7%
1991	96.561	22.855	23.7%
1992	97.614	22.093	22.6%

Comments The annual number of U.S. households experiencing a crime has not significantly increased or decreased since 1975, according to these statistics gathered by the U.S. Department of Justice through the National Criminal Victimization Survey (NCVS). The NCVS is a nationwide survey of over 100,000 residents which measures both reported and unreported crimes. Murder statistics are not included because the victims cannot be surveyed.

However, the percent of all households experiencing a crime fell from 32.1% in 1975 to 25% in 1985 (a decline of 22%). After a period of stability between 1985 and 1989, the percent further decreased to 23.7% in 1991 and to 22.6% in 1992.

The reason why the household crime rate declined during 1975–92 was not because fewer households were affected by crime. There was, however, significant growth in the number of households during those years. The number of U.S. households increased from 73.1 million in 1975 to 97.6 million in 1992, a rise of over 33%. So even though the number of households experiencing a crime remained fairly steady, the percentage fell due to the increase in total households.

Source U.S. Department of Justice, Bureau of Justice Statistics, "Crime and the Nation's Households, 1992" (Washington, D.C.: U.S. Government Printing Office, August 1993).

Contact U.S. Department of Justice, Bureau of Justice Statistics Clearinghouse, Box 6000, Rockville, MD 20850. (800) 732-3277. A World Wide Web server is operated at http://ncjrs.aspensys.com:81/ncjrshome.html. Inquiries can also be sent by e-mail to askncjrs@aspensys.com.

How often are households victimized by thieves each year?

The victimization rates for household crimes (household larceny, burglary, and motor vehicle theft) during 1973–92. The rates shown are per 1,000 U.S. households.

Year	Burglary	Larceny	Motor Vehicle Theft	Total
1973	91.7	107.0	19.1	217.8
1974	93.1	123.8	18.8	235.7
1975	91.7	125.4	19.5	236.5
1976	88.9	124.1	16.5	229.5
1977	88.5	123.3	17.0	228.8
1978	86.0	119.9	17.5	223.4
1979	84.1	133.7	17.5	235.3
1980	84.3	126.5	16.7	227.4
1981	87.9	121.0	17.1	226.0
1982	78.2	113.9	16.2	208.2
1983	70.0	105.2	14.6	189.8
1984	64.1	99.4	15.2	178.7
1985	62.7	97.5	14.2	174.4
1986	61.5	93.5	15.0	170.0
1987	62.1	95.7	16.0	173.9
1988	61.9	90.2	17.5	169.6
1989	56.4	94.4	19.2	169.9
1990	53.8	86.7	20.5	161.0
1991	53.9	90.4	22.2	166.4
1992	48.9	83.2	20.1	152.2

Comments

The chances of a household in the U.S. being victimized by thieves has generally fallen since the mid-1970s. Household crimes include burglary, larceny, and motor vehicle theft. Burglary is the unlawful or forcible entry or attempted entry of a residence, but does not always result in theft. Larceny is theft or attempted theft of property or cash without using force or an illegal entry. Motor vehicle theft involves the stealing of a car, truck, or motorcycle.

Although the household victimization rates for larceny and burglary have fallen since the 1970s, the rate of motor vehicle theft has slowly increased. The frequency of burglary was highest in 1974 at 93.1 incidents per 1,000 households. Larceny was at its peak in 1979, at 133.7 incidents per 1,000 households. Motor vehicle theft, however, was highest in 1991, at 22.2 incidents per 1,000 households.

Source

U.S. Department of Justice, Bureau of Justice Statistics. *Criminal Victimization in the United States, 1992* (Washington, D.C.: U.S. Government Printing Office, 1994), p. 6.

Contact

U.S. Department of Justice, Bureau of Justice Statistics Clearinghouse, Box 6000, Rockville, MD 20850. (800) 732-3277. A World Wide Web server is operated at http://ncjrs.aspensys.com:81/ncjrshome.html. Inquiries can also be sent by e-mail to askncjrs@aspensys.com.

How much do criminals in the U.S. steal, and how much of that stolen property is recovered?

The dollar value of property stolen and recovered in 1993 by type of property.

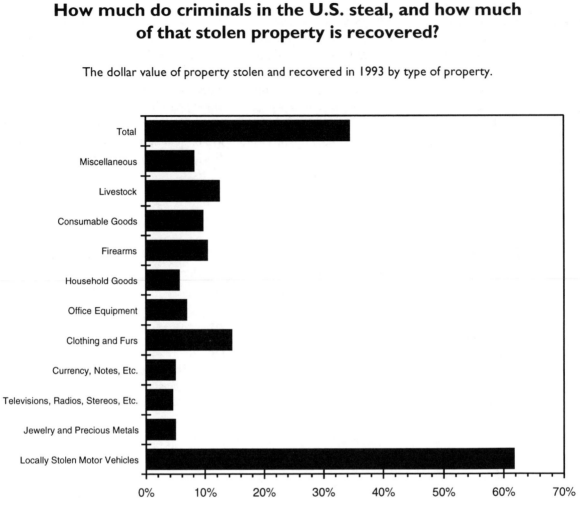

Type of Property	Value of Property Stolen	Value of Property Recovered	Percent Recovered
Locally stolen motor vehicles	$6,682,729,000	$4,125,665,000	61.7%
Jewelry and precious metals	1,145,813,000	55,386,000	4.8%
Televisions, radios, stereos, etc.	1,017,950,000	45,095,000	4.4%
Currency, notes, etc.	886,252,000	42,394,000	4.8%
Clothing and furs	328,787,000	47,445,000	14.4%
Office equipment	327,563,000	22,414,000	6.8%
Household goods	223,149,000	12,327,000	5.5%
Firearms	113,969,000	11,849,000	10.4%
Consumable goods	103,112,000	10,026,000	9.7%
Livestock	36,549,000	4,534,000	12.4%
Miscellaneous	2,438,705,000	201,006,000	8.2%
Total	$13,304,578,000	$4,578,141,000	34.4%

Comments   In 1993 the FBI reported that the value of all property stolen in the U.S. that year exceeded $13.3 billion. Only about $4.6 billion, or 34.4%, of stolen property was recovered in 1993.

Of all the types of stolen property that were recovered, motor vehicles had by far the highest recovery rate, at 61.7%. Recovered motor vehicles alone accounted for just over 90% of all recovered property in 1993.

Clothing and furs (14.4%), livestock (12.4%), and firearms (10.4%) were the types of stolen property next most likely to be recovered. These three categories accounted for about 1.4% of all recovered property.

Stolen jewelry and precious metals were recovered only 4.8% of time; televisions, radios, stereos, etc. 4.4% of the time. Only 4.8% of all stolen currency was recovered. These three categories together made up 3.1% of all recovered property.

There are several reasons why different types of property are recovered more frequently than other types. Motor vehicles may have a high recovery rate because they are difficult to conceal (compared with jewelry or cash). They also require a registration to legally operate on public roads, where they can be spotted by police. Items with low recovery rates, like cash, jewelry, and appliances can be more quickly spent or traded by criminals. Since these types of items can be exchanged so quickly, unless the thief is immediately caught the chance of recovery is often very low.

Source   U.S. Department of Justice, Federal Bureau of Investigation, *Crime in the United States, 1993* (Washington, D.C.: U.S. Government Printing Office, 1994), p. 205.

Contact   U.S. Department of Justice, Federal Bureau of Investigation, Uniform Crime Reports, Criminal Justice Information Services Division, Washington, D.C. 20535. Information Dissemination: (202) 324-5015.

How often are burglaries taking place?

The annual number of reported burglaries in the U.S. and the rate per 100,000 population, 1960–94.

Year	Number of Burglaries	Rate per 100,000 Population
1960	912,100	508.6
1961	949,600	518.9
1962	994,300	535.2
1963	1,086,400	576.4
1964	1,213,200	634.7
1965	1,282,500	662.7
1966	1,410,100	721.0
1967	1,632,100	826.6
1968	1,858,900	932.3
1969	1,981,900	984.1
1970	2,205,000	1,084.9
1971	2,399,300	1,163.5
1972	2,375,500	1,140.8
1973	2,565,000	1,222.5
1974	3,039,200	1,437.7
1975	3,265,300	1,532.1
1976	3,108,700	1,448.2
1977	3,108,700	1,419.8
1978	3,128,300	1,434.6
1979	3,327,700	1,511.9
1980	3,795,200	1,684.1
1981	3,779,700	1,649.5
1982	3,447,100	1,488.8
1983	3,129,900	1,337.7
1984	2,984,400	1,263.7
1985	3,073,300	1,287.3
1986	3,241,400	1,344.6
1987	3,236,200	1,329.6
1988	3,218,100	1,309.2
1989	3,168,200	1,276.3
1990	3,073,900	1,235.9
1991	3,157,200	1,252.0
1992	2,979,900	1,168.2
1993	2,834,800	1,099.2
1994	2,712,200	1,041.8

Comments Burglary is the unlawful or forcible entry or attempted entry of a residence, but it does not always result in theft. The annual number of reported burglaries peaked in 1980, after steadily rising since 1960. In 1980, there were 3,795,200 reported burglaries, over four times greater than the 912,100 burglaries of 1960. Since 1980, however, the number of burglaries reported has fallen to levels similar to those of the mid-1970s. In 1994, there were 2,712,200 reported burglaries, down nearly 27% from the 1980 peak.

Some of the increase in the annual number of burglaries since 1960 should be expected because of population increases. However, the burglary rate per 100,000 inhabitants has also decreased since 1980. The buglary rate generally followed the trend of the number of burglaries, but declined more rapidly during the 1980s.

Source U.S. Department of Justice, Federal Bureau of Investigation, Programs Support Section, Criminal Justice Information Services Division.

U.S. Department of Justice, Federal Bureau of Investigation, *Crime in the United States, 1994* (Washington, D.C.: U.S. Government Printing Office, 1995), p. 38.

Contact U.S. Department of Justice, Federal Bureau of Investigation, Uniform Crime Reports, Criminal Justice Information Services Division, Washington, D.C. 20535. Information Dissemination: (202) 324-5015.

How often are thefts taking place?

The annual number of reported larceny-thefts in the U.S. and the rate per 100,000 population, 1960–94.

Year	Number of Larceny-Thefts	Rate per 100,000 Population
1960	1,855,400	1,034.7
1961	1,913,000	1,045.4
1962	2,089,600	1,124.8
1963	2,297,800	1,219.1
1964	2,514,400	1,315.5
1965	2,572,600	1,329.3
1966	2,822,000	1,442.9
1967	3,111,000	1,575.8
1968	3,482,700	1,746.6
1969	3,888,600	1,930.9
1970	4,225,800	2,079.3
1971	4,424,200	2,145.5
1972	4,151,200	1,993.6
1973	4,347,900	2,071.9
1974	5,262,500	2,489.5
1975	5,977,700	2,804.8
1976	6,270,800	2,921.3
1977	5,905,700	2,729.9
1978	5,991,000	2,747.4
1979	6,601,000	2,999.1
1980	7,136,900	3,167.0
1981	7,194,400	3,139.7
1982	7,142,500	3,084.8
1983	6,712,800	2,868.9
1984	6,591,900	2,791.3
1985	6,926,400	2,901.2
1986	7,257,200	3,010.3
1987	7,499,900	3,081.3
1988	7,705,900	3,134.9
1989	7,872,400	3,171.3
1990	7,945,700	3,194.8
1991	8,142,200	3,228.8
1992	7,915,200	3,103.0
1993	7,820,900	3,032.4
1994	7,876,300	3,025.4

Comments   Larceny is theft or attempted theft of property or cash without using force or illegal entry. This definition includes shoplifting, pocket-picking, purse-snatching, thefts from motor vehicles, thefts of motor vehicle parts and accessories, bicycle thefts, etc., in which no use of force, violence, or fraud occurs.

The annual number of reported larceny-thefts peaked in 1991, at over 8.1 million offenses. This is 339% higher than in 1960. During parts of the early 1970s, the mid-1970s, and the mid-1980s, the annual number of larceny-thefts dropped. In 1994, there were 7.9 million offenses, down nearly 3% from the 1991 peak.

However, the rate of larceny-theft per 100,000 inhabitants has remained fairly stable in recent years because the rate accounts for increases in population. The rate generally followed the trend of the number of larceny-thefts, rising steadily through the late 1970s with only two downward dips in 1972–3 and 1977–8. During the 1980s, however, the difference between the growth in the number of incidents and the growth in the rate per 100,000 inhabitants widened. This means that more offenses were happenning, but the frequency was about the same.

Source   U.S. Department of Justice, Federal Bureau of Investigation, Programs Support Section, Criminal Justice Information Services Division.

U.S. Department of Justice, Federal Bureau of Investigation, *Crime in the United States, 1994* (Washington, D.C.: U.S. Government Printing Office, 1995), p. 43.

Contact   U.S. Department of Justice, Federal Bureau of Investigation, Uniform Crime Reports, Criminal Justice Information

Services Division, Washington, D.C. 20535. Information Dissemination: (202) 324-5015.

What type of larceny-thefts are reported most often?

Reported larceny-thefts in the U.S. in 1993, by type of crime.

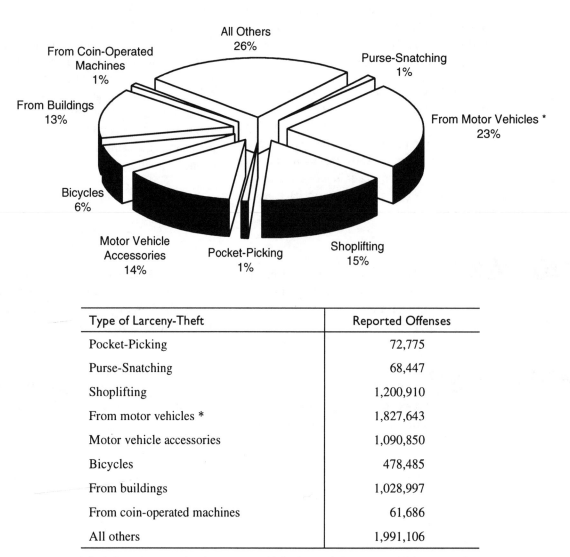

Type of Larceny-Theft	Reported Offenses
Pocket-Picking	72,775
Purse-Snatching	68,447
Shoplifting	1,200,910
From motor vehicles *	1,827,643
Motor vehicle accessories	1,090,850
Bicycles	478,485
From buildings	1,028,997
From coin-operated machines	61,686
All others	1,991,106

* Includes property stolen from motor vehicles but excludes motor vehicle accessories.

Comments In 1993, theft from motor vehicles, shoplifting, and theft of motor vehicle accessories were the most frequent types of larceny-theft. These three types combined accounted for 52% of all reported larceny-thefts. Thefts from buildings (13%) and stolen bicycles (6%) were the next most frequently reported thefts.

Cash and property stored in motor vehicles, as well as motor vehicle accessories (such as stereo equipment and custom vehicle parts) are popular targets for thieves. Since cars and other motor vehicles are often kept outdoors and in public areas, where they are usually unsupervised, a would-be thief has greater opportunities. The thief often completes the crime without being detected, making apprehension and recovery of property very difficult.

Pocket-picking, purse-snatching, and thefts from vending machines each accounted for only 1% of all reported larceny-thefts. With these types, the thief often accomplishes the crime without being noticed, so apprehension can be difficult. Victims who do not see the thief may decide that reporting the incident is futile, thus causing these types of theft to be underreported.

Source U.S. Department of Justice, Federal Bureau of Investigation, *Crime in the United States, 1993* (Washington, D.C.: U.S. Government Printing Office, 1994), p. 108.

Contact U.S. Department of Justice, Federal Bureau of Investigation, Uniform Crime Reports, Criminal Justice Information Services Division, Washington, D.C. 20535. Information Dissemination: (202) 324-5015.

In which states is the problem of motor vehicle theft most severe?

Number of registered vehicles and reported motor vehicle thefts in 1992. Rates of motor vehicle theft are given per 100,000 population and per 100,000 registered vehicles.

State	Population	Number of Registered Vehicles	Number of Thefts	Thefts per 100,000 Population	Thefts per 100,000 Registered Vehicles
Alabama	4,136,000	3,304,064	14,983	362.3	453.5
Alaska	587,000	486,095	2,918	497.1	600.3
Arizona	3,832,000	2,800,901	31,481	821.5	1,124.0
Arkansas	2,399,000	1,501,480	7,900	329.3	526.1
California	30,867,000	22,202,300	320,112	1,037.1	1,441.8
Colorado	3,470,000	2,915,285	17,662	509.0	605.9
Connecticut	3,281,000	2,569,164	23,700	722.3	922.5
Delaware	689,000	544,982	2,109	306.1	387.0
District of Columbia	589,000	256,406	9,118	1,548.0	3,556.1
Florida	13,488,000	10,232,336	111,685	828.0	1,091.5
Georgia	6,751,000	5,899,437	38,913	576.4	659.6
Hawaii	1,160,000	774,094	4,351	375.1	562.1
Idaho	1,067,000	1,034,290	1,679	157.4	162.3
Illinois	11,631,000	7,981,725	71,976	618.8	901.8
Indiana	5,662,000	4,515,850	25,496	450.3	564.6
Iowa	2,812,000	2,705,754	4,474	159.1	165.4
Kansas	2,523,000	1,920,568	8,169	323.8	425.3
Kentucky	3,755,000	2,983,220	8,128	216.5	272.5
Louisiana	4,287,000	3,093,511	26,926	628.1	870.4
Maine	1,235,000	978,134	1,778	144.0	181.8
Maryland	4,908,000	3,688,899	35,654	726.4	966.5
Massachusetts	5,998,000	3,663,400	47,416	790.5	1,294.3
Michigan	9,437,000	7,310,552	59,057	625.8	807.8
Minnesota	4,480,000	3,483,830	15,911	355.2	456.7
Mississippi	2,614,000	1,953,973	8,797	336.5	450.2
Missouri	5,193,000	4,004,062	25,831	497.4	645.1
Montana	824,000	906,789	1,923	233.4	212.1
Nebraska	1,606,000	1,355,050	3,225	200.8	238.0
Nevada	1,327,000	920,936	9,255	697.4	1,005.0
New Hampshire	1,111,000	893,647	2,165	194.9	242.3
New Jersey	7,789,000	5,591,354	63,524	815.6	1,131.3
New Mexico	1,581,000	1,351,695	5,974	377.9	442.0
New York	18,119,000	9,779,554	168,922	932.3	1,727.3
North Carolina	6,843,000	5,306,911	19,613	286.6	369.6
North Dakota	636,000	655,335	950	149.4	145.0
Ohio	11,016,000	9,029,829	51,886	471.0	574.6

[Continued]

In which states is the problem of motor vehicle theft most severe?

[Continued]

State	Population	Number of Registered Vehicles	Number of Thefts	Thefts per 100,000 Population	Thefts per 100,000 Registered Vehicles
Oklahoma	3,212,000	2,736,955	16,601	516.8	606.5
Oregon	2,977,000	2,583,405	15,881	533.5	614.7
Pennsylvania	12,009,000	8,179,231	56,171	467.7	686.8
Rhode Island	1,005,000	622,025	7,463	742.6	1,199.8
South Carolina	3,603,000	2,600,929	12,443	345.4	478.4
South Dakota	711,000	719,690	719	101.1	99.9
Tennessee	5,024,000	4,645,083	28,935	575.9	622.9
Texas	17,656,000	12,767,438	145,071	821.7	1,136.3
Utah	1,813,000	1,252,268	4,313	237.9	344.4
Vermont	570,000	464,810	600	105.3	129.1
Virginia	6,377,000	5,238,706	19,488	305.6	372.0
Washington	5,136,000	4,465,843	24,214	471.5	542.2
West Virginia	1,812,000	1,272,907	2,968	163.8	233.2
Wisconsin	5,007,000	3,734,711	21,605	431.5	578.5
Wyoming	466,000	482,815	701	150.4	145.2
U. S. Total	255,082,000	190,362,228	1,610,834	631.5	846.2

Comments California, Texas, Florida, and New York were the states with the most registered motor vehicles in 1992, and so it is not surprising that these same states also had the greatest number of motor vehicle thefts that year. Wyoming and Vermont had few registered vehicles and the lowest number of motor vehicle thefts.

The two rates (theft per 100,000 population and theft per 100,000 vehicles) both measure the frequency of theft but in two different ways. Although the District of Columbia had far fewer registered vehicles than any state, it had the highest frequency of motor vehicle theft when measured both against population and against registered vehicles.

Source U.S. Department of Transportation, Federal Highway Administration, *Highway Statistics 1992* (Washington, D.C.: U.S. Government Printing Office, 1993), p. 17.

U.S. Department of Justice, Federal Bureau of Investigation, *Crime in the United States, 1992* (Washington, D.C.: U.S. Government Printing Office, 1993), pp. 60–61, 68–78.

Contact U.S. Department of Transportation, Federal Highway Administration, 400 7th St. SW, Washington, D.C. 20590. Public Affairs: (202) 366-0660.

U.S. Department of Justice, Federal Bureau of Investigation, Uniform Crime Reports, Criminal Justice Information Services Division, Washington, D.C. 20535. Information Dissemination: (202) 324-5015.

How many motor vehicles are reported stolen each year?

Motor vehicle thefts in the U.S. during 1970–93, and the percent of all registered vehicles that were reported as stolen.

Year	Number of Reported Thefts	Total Vehicle Registrations	Percent of Registered Vehicles Stolen
1970	928,400	111,242,295	0.83%
1971	948,200	116,330,037	0.82%
1972	887,200	122,556,550	0.72%
1973	928,800	130,024,945	0.71%
1974	977,100	134,899,955	0.72%
1975	1,009,600	137,912,779	0.73%
1976	966,000	143,476,236	0.67%
1977	977,700	147,025,824	0.66%
1978	1,004,100	153,282,476	0.66%
1979	1,112,800	157,291,431	0.71%
1980	1,131,700	161,490,159	0.70%
1981	1,087,800	164,117,547	0.66%
1982	1,062,400	165,397,098	0.64%
1983	1,007,900	169,334,393	0.60%
1984	1,032,200	171,728,638	0.60%
1985	1,102,900	177,098,079	0.62%
1986	1,224,100	181,453,661	0.67%
1987	1,288,700	183,930,221	0.70%
1988	1,432,900	188,981,016	0.76%
1989	1,564,800	191,694,462	0.82%
1990	1,635,900	192,914,924	0.85%
1991	1,661,700	192,548,972	0.86%
1992	1,610,800	194,427,346	0.83%
1993	1,561,000	198,041,338	0.79%

Comments

The frequency of motor vehicle theft in the U.S. was about the same in 1992 as in 1970, with about 0.83% of all registered motor vehicles reported as stolen. Although the number of annual thefts has gradually climbed since 1970, the total number of registered vehicles has also increased. The percent of thefts per registered motor vehicles indicates how often a car, truck, bus, or motorcycle was stolen that year.

Since 1970, the percentage of vehicles reported stolen was at its lowest in 1983, even though the fewest number of thefts occurred in 1972. Although the annual percentage of vehicles stolen has never exceeded 1% of all vehicles, vehicle theft is still a concern for anyone who drives.

Stolen vehicles are often used to commit other crimes. A vehicle may be also be stolen for its overall value (such as an expensive car), for its purpose (such as a special purpose vehicle), or as a prank for joyriding. Vehicles that are stolen often are sent to what police call "chop shops." A "chop shop" is a garage or body shop that traffics in stolen car parts. A stolen vehicle delivered to a "chop shop" is quickly disassembled and its parts are sold or traded illegally.

Source

U.S. Department of Transportation, Federal Highway Administration, *Highway Statistics*, 1970–93 (Washington, D.C: U.S. Government Printing Office).

U.S. Department of Justice, Federal Bureau of Investigation, *Crime in the United States*, 1970–93 (Washington, D.C.: U.S. Government Printing Office).

Contact

U.S. Department of Transportation, Federal Highway Administration, 400 7th St. SW, Washington, D.C. 20590. Public Affairs: (202) 366-0660.

U.S. Department of Justice, Federal Bureau of Investigation, Uniform Crime Reports, Criminal Justice Information Services Division, Washington, D.C. 20535. Information Dissemination: (202) 324-5015.

How much shoplifting takes place?

Reported incidents of shoplifting, and shoplifting as a percentage of all larceny-theft incidents in the U.S., 1988–94.

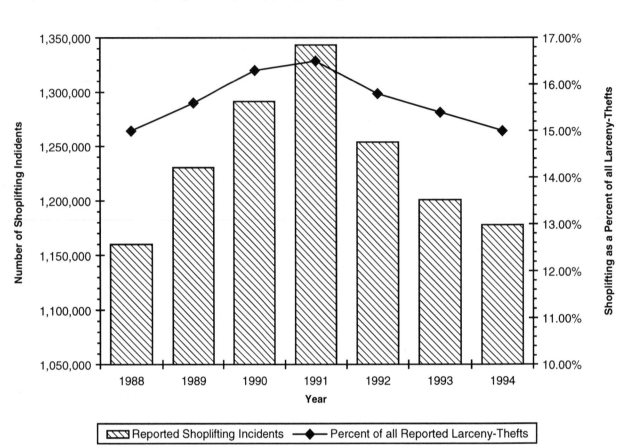

Year	Reported Shoplifting Incidents	Percent of all Reported Larceny-Thefts
1988	1,160,059	15.0%
1989	1,230,317	15.6%
1990	1,291,492	16.3%
1991	1,343,196	16.5%
1992	1,253,766	15.8%
1993	1,200,910	15.4%
1994	1,177,699	15.0%

Comments

Shoplifting involves the theft of merchandise from a retail store. Since shoplifting is a type of larceny where the potential thief has the legal right to be on the premises just like a legitimate customer, it can be difficult to prevent such a crime from happening. According to the FBI, reports of shoplifting during 1988–94 were highest in 1991, at over 1.3 million incidents (accounting for 16.5% of all larceny-thefts). It is important to remember, however, that these statistics only count the times when the shoplifter was caught and the offense was reported to a law enforcement agency.

There are two basic types of shoplifters: professionals and non-professionals. Professional shoplifters routinely steal in order to sell the merchandise. Non-professional shoplifters steal as part of a psychological or emotional problem, or because of peer pressure. Non-professional shoplifters are spur-of-the-moment thieves who often have the money to buy the item, do not intend on selling it, and may not even have a use for the stolen goods.

There are other costs involved with shoplifting besides the value of the stolen merchandise. Retail stores often must invest in costly security equipment. Security devices commonly used include cameras and special tags attached to merchandise that activate an alarm if removed from the premises. Many large department stores also hire security guards and undercover personnel to impede and detect shoplifters. Shoplifting also deprives a city, county, or state government of sales taxes that would have been generated through the legitimate sale of the stolen merchandise. The legal system also is further strained by shoplifting cases, especially the juvenile court system. In addition to these monetary costs, security procedures to prevent shoplifting often create inconveniences for paying customers, and distrust by sales personnel can make shopping unpleasant.

Source

U.S. Department of Justice, Federal Bureau of Investigation, *Crime in the United States, 1994* (Washington, D.C.: U.S. Government Printing Office, 1995), p. 107.

U.S. Department of Justice, Federal Bureau of Investigation, *Crime in the United States, 1993* (Washington, D.C.: U.S. Government Printing Office, 1994), p. 108.

U.S. Department of Justice, Federal Bureau of Investigation, *Crime in the United States, 1992* (Washington, D.C.: U.S. Government Printing Office, 1993), p. 107.

U.S. Department of Justice, Federal Bureau of Investigation, *Crime in the United States, 1991* (Washington, D.C.: U.S. Government Printing Office, 1992), p. 107.

Contact

U.S. Department of Justice, Federal Bureau of Investigation, Uniform Crime Reports, Criminal Justice Information Services Division, Washington, D.C. 20535. Information Dissemination: (202) 324-5015.

Shoplifters Alternative, 380 North Broadway, Suite 206, Jericho, NY 11753. (800) 848-9595.

What types of property are torched by arsonists?

Arson offenses in the U.S. in 1992 and 1993 according to property classification.

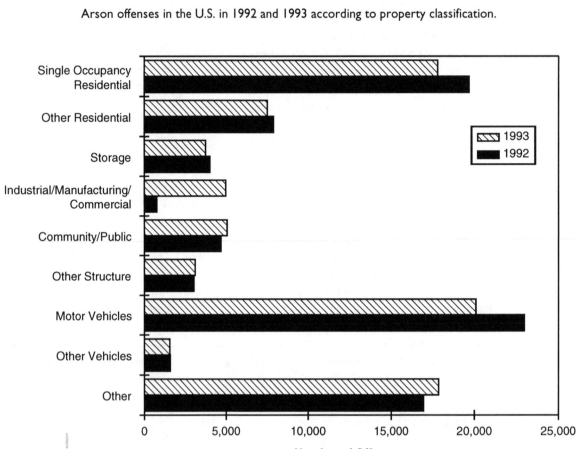

Property Classification	Number of Offenses in 1992	Percent Distribution	Number of Offenses in 1993	Percent Distribution
Structures	46,615	53.9%	42,867	52.1%
Single occupancy residential	19,682	22.7%	17,795	21.6%
Other residential	7,894	9.1%	7,516	9.1%
Storage	4,016	4.6%	3,753	4.6%
Industrial, manufacturing, commercial	747	8.5%	4,968	6.8%
Community/Public	4,685	5.4%	5,049	6.1%
Other structure	3,025	3.5%	3,105	3.8%
Mobile property	22,976	26.5%	21,617	26.3%
Motor vehicles	22,976	24.8%	20,094	24.4%
Other mobile vehicles	1,554	1.8%	1,523	1.8%
Other	16,956	19.6%	17,864	21.7%
Total	86,547	100.0%	82,348	100.0%

Comments   The most frequent targets of arsonists in 1992 and 1993 were buildings, compromising 53.9% and 52.1% of all reported incidents in 1992 and 1993, respectively. Residential property is the most frequent type of building torched by arsonists. Single occupancy homes alone accounted for 22.7% of the arsons in 1992 and 21.6% in 1993. Arson was directed at mobile property (motor vehicles, trailers, etc.) 26.5% of the time in 1992 and 26.3% in 1993.

There are many motivations behind arson. Sometimes arson can be just a malicious act with no clear monetary reward. Other times, however, arson is used by property owners to cheat insurance companies. This dangerous type of deception often occurs when the property owner has a fire insurance policy on the structure. If the condition of the structure is very poor, the owner may believe that dishonestly collecting on a fire insurance claim is better than spending a lot of money on the run-down building.

Source   U.S. Department of Justice, Federal Bureau of Investigation, *Crime in the United States, 1993* (Washington, D.C.: U.S. Government Printing Office, 1994), p. 54.

U.S. Department of Justice, Federal Bureau of Investigation, *Crime in the United States, 1992* (Washington, D.C.: U.S. Government Printing Office, 1993), p. 54.

Contact   U.S. Department of Justice, Federal Bureau of Investigation, Uniform Crime Reports, Criminal Justice Information Services Division, Washington, D.C. 20535. Information Dissemination: (202) 324-5015.

How big is the arson problem?

The estimated number of structure and vehicle fires in the U.S. caused by incendiary or suspicious means, and the number of civilian arson-related deaths, 1978–94.

Year	Structure Fires	Vehicle Fires	Civilian Deaths
1978	167,500	48,000	930
1979	160,000	63,500	675
1980	148,500	45,000	770
1981	146,000	44,500	820
1982	154,500	48,000	910
1983	129,000	48,000	970
1984	122,000	50,500	530
1985	110,500	45,500	670
1986	117,000	57,000	705
1987	111,000	51,000	730
1988	105,000	53,000	740
1989	99,500	46,000	615
1990	97,000	51,000	715
1991	98,000	49,000	490
1992	94,000	44,000	605
1993	84,500	41,500	560
1994	86,000	*	550

* Information was not available.

Comments The annual number of fires caused by arson has fallen slightly since the late 1970s, according to these statistics from the National Fire Protection Association. In 1978, there were an estimated 167,500 building fires caused by arson, but by 1994 that amount had fallen by about 50% to 84,500 fires.

Most of the arson fires were of buildings, but many vehicles also were torched. Although the number of building fires has dropped significantly in recent years, the number of vehicle fires has remained more constant. In 1978, there were 48,000 vehicle fires, and vehicle fires rose and fell slightly throughout the 1980s. In 1993, there were 41,500 vehicle fires, a drop of about 13.5% from 1978.

The most tragic destruction, however, is when people die in fires set by arsonists. In 1978, 930 people died in building fires set by arsonists, not including fatalities among firefighters. Since 1983, when there were 970 arson fatalities, the annual number of arson-related deaths has gradually declined. In 1994, 550 deaths were recorded, about 41% less than the 1978 total and 43% less than 1983.

Source Fire Analysis and Research Division, National Fire Protection Association.

Contact National Fire Protection Association, 1 Batterymarch Park, Quincy, MA 02269-9101. (617) 770-3000.

How many bombings are taking place in the U.S.?

Bombing incidents known to the police, 1980–93.

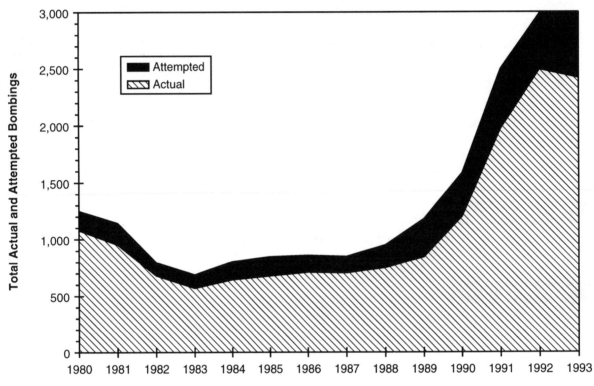

Year	Actual	Attempted	Total*	Property Damage (Millions of Dollars)	Persons Injured	Deaths
1980	1,078	171	1,249	12,562	160	34
1981	952	190	1,142	67,082	133	30
1982	679	116	795	7,203	99	16
1983	569	118	687	6,343	100	12
1984	645	158	803	5,619	112	6
1985	677	170	847	6,352	144	28
1986	709	149	858	3,405	185	14
1987	704	144	848	4,201	107	21
1988	749	201	977	2,257	145	20
1989	844	334	1,208	5,000	202	11
1990	1,198	384	1,582	9,600	222	27
1991	1,974	525	2,499	6,440	230	30
1992	2,493	496	2,989	12,500	349	26
1993	2,418	562	2,980	518,000	1,323	49

* Actual and attempted incidents may not add to total because of some incidents involving combination devices.

Comments

The FBI Bomb Data Center annually collects information about bombing incidents across the U.S. Reports of bombing incidents are gathered from state and local police agencies, the U.S. Postal Inspection Service, Military Explosive Ordnance Disposal units, and the Bureau of Alcohol, Tobacco, and Firearms. A bombing incident refers to an actual or attempted detonation of explosive or incendiary devices in violation of state, local, or federal law. Since 1990, these statistics have included hoax bomb devices, accidental explosions, and recoveries of explosive or incendiary devices.

Each year, mailboxes and other private property, as well as private homes, account for about one-half of all bombing targets. Automobiles, commercial and retail properties, and academic facilities make up most of the rest. Most of these incidents do not receive much notoriety outside the local community, and often result in relatively little damage and few injuries.

When a single large-scale bombing occurs, however, it usually receives considerable publicity. Such was the case when the World Trade Center in New York City was bombed on 26 February 1993. The World Trade Center bombing accounted for 98% of the property damage and 79% of the persons injured for 1993. More recently, the bombing of the Murrah Federal Building in Oklahoma City on 19 April 1995 resulted in 169 deaths and the total destruction of the building. Major bombings such as these usually are well planned and often linked with terrorism.

Source

U.S. Department of Justice, Bureau of Justice Statistics, *Sourcebook of Criminal Justice Statistics—1994* (Washington, D.C.: U.S. Government Printing Office, 1995), p. 366, table 3.155.

Contact

U.S. Department of Justice, Bureau of Justice Statistics Clearinghouse, Box 6000, Rockville, MD 20850. (800) 732-3277. A World Wide Web server is operated at http://ncjrs.aspensys.com:81/ncjrshome.html. Inquiries can also be sent by e-mail to askncjrs@aspensys.com.

U.S. Department of Justice, Federal Bureau of Investigation, National Press Office, Washington, D.C. 20535. (202) 324-3691.

How common are drug trafficking arrests?

Total arrests, drug-related arrests, and arrests for sale/manufacture of drugs in the U.S., 1988–93.

Year	Total Arrests	Drug-Related Arrests	Drug Sale/ Manufacture Arrests	Sale/Manufacture Arrests as Percent of Drug-Related Arrests	Sale/Manufacture Arrests as Percent of Total Arrests
1988	13,812,300	1,155,200	316,525	27.4%	2.3%
1989	14,340,900	1,361,700	441,191	32.4%	3.1%
1990	14,195,100	1,089,500	344,282	31.6%	2.4%
1991	14,211,900	1,010,000	337,340	33.4%	2.4%
1992	14,075,100	1,066,400	338,049	31.7%	2.4%
1993	14,036,300	1,126,300	334,511	29.7%	2.4%

Comments

The FBI reported that state and local police made 1,126,300 arrests for drug law violations in 1993, down from the peak of 1,361,700 in 1989 but still the third highest amount ever recorded. About 29.7% of these arrests were for the sale or manufacture of drugs. Drug sale/manufacturing arrests have held steady at about 2.4% of all arrests since 1990.

Drug production and trafficking often involve organized crime, since they are types of illegal businesses that require elaborate underground networks. Just as in a legitimate business, drug suppliers and distributors must have a means of efficiently making sales. Sales contacts, distribution routes, and credit arrangements must also be maintained.

In short, all stages of running a legal business must also be available to an illegal drug manufacturing or trafficking business. The illegal business, however, must conduct all its day-to-day business secretly in order to avoid detection by law enforcement agencies.

Source

U.S. Department of Justice, Bureau of Justice Statistics, *Drug and Crime Facts, 1994* (Washington, D.C.: U.S. Government Printing Office, June 1995), p. 11.

Contact

U.S. Department of Justice, Bureau of Justice Statistics Clearinghouse, Box 6000, Rockville, MD 20850. (800) 732-3277. A World Wide Web server is operated at http://ncjrs.aspensys.com:81/ncjrshome.html. Inquiries can also be sent by e-mail to askncjrs@aspensys.com.

How many people are arrested for prostitution each year?

Arrests for prostitution and commercialized vice in the U.S. by age group during 1990–94.

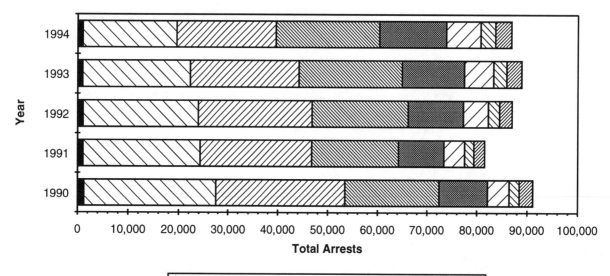

Age Group	1990	1991	1992	1993	1994
Under 18	1,281	1,075	1,095	994	1,013
18–24	26,262	23,175	22,781	21,280	18,549
25–29	25,875	22,514	22,952	21,887	20,017
30–34	18,981	17,438	19,359	20,756	20,712
35–39	9,703	9,176	11,073	12,515	13,527
40–44	4,328	4,155	4,962	5,835	6,851
45–49	2,022	1,852	2,268	2,646	2,962
50 +	2,641	2,151	2,498	2,937	3,187
Total	91,093	81,536	86,988	88,850	86,818

Statistics on Crime & Punishment

Comments In 1994, 86,818 persons were arrested for prostitution, 4,275 less than in 1990. This is about 4.7% less than in 1990, although the number of arrests has fluctuated in that period.

Although the number of arrests for prostitution fluctuated, the age distribution of arrestees consistently changed during 1991–94, becoming somewhat older. In 1990, persons ages 18–29 accounted for 57% of arrestees, but only for 56% in 1991, 53% in 1992, 49% in 1993, and 44% in 1994. Arrests of those 35 and older accounted for 20% in 1990, 21% in 1991, 24% in 1992, 27% in 1993, and 30% in 1994. Although the problem of child and teenage prostitution receives much publicity, persons under 18 fell from 1.4% of arrestees in 1990 to 1.2% in 1994.

Prostitution refers to the illegal business of selling sex in exchange for money. Females account for most prostitution arrests; less than 10% of arrestees are males, but men often work as agents for prostitutes. Prostitutes often operate in loosely formed groups rather than as independent agents, and market their services in several different ways. In some places, prostitutes gather to display themselves in public areas in order to be seen by clients, who drive them elsewhere for the transaction. In other areas, prostitutes are driven to locations or events where there is a demand for sexual services. Prostitutes also may conduct business in a brothel (such as a residence or other fixed location).

In most places across the U.S., prostitution is illegal (except in Nevada), making it a part of the large and unregulated underground economy. Consequently, prostitution is often strongly connected with the chaos and violence of the illegal drug trafficking industry and with organized crime.

Source U.S. Department of Justice, Federal Bureau of Investigation, *Crime in the United States, 1993* (Washington, D.C.: U.S. Government Printing Office, 1994), pp. 227–8.

U.S. Department of Justice, Federal Bureau of Investigation, *Crime in the United States, 1992* (Washington, D.C.: U.S. Government Printing Office, 1993), pp. 227–8.

U.S. Department of Justice, Federal Bureau of Investigation, *Crime in the United States, 1990* (Washington, D.C.: U.S. Government Printing Office, 1991), pp. 184–5.

U.S. Department of Justice, Bureau of Justice Statistics, *Sourcebook of Criminal Justice Statistics—1992* (Washington, D.C.: U.S. Government Printing Office, 1993), pp. 430–1.

Contact U.S. Department of Justice, Federal Bureau of Investigation, Uniform Crime Reports, Criminal Justice Information Services Division, Washington, D.C. 20535. Information Dissemination: (202) 324-5015.

Counterfeiting trends, 1985–94

Counterfeit plant operations put out of service for fiscal years 1985–94, by type of operation.

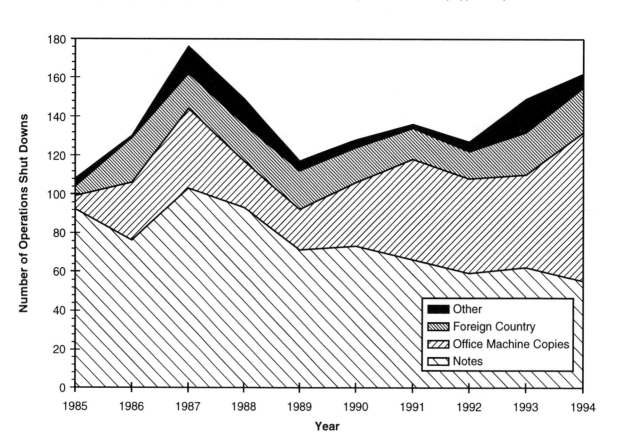

Fiscal Year	Notes	Office Machine Copies	Foreign Country	Other*	Total
1985	92	7	5	4	108
1986	76	30	23	1	130
1987	103	41	18	14	176
1988	93	24	19	13	149
1989	71	21	20	5	117
1990	73	33	18	4	128
1991	66	52	16	2	136
1992	59	49	14	5	127
1993	62	48	22	17	149
1994	55	77	23	7	162

* Includes coins, food coupons, and all other U.S. obligations.

Comments

Counterfeiting is any type of forgery that illegally produces coins, paper money, coupons, or any kind of negotiable paper or certificate. Although counterfeiting has been around for a long time, it has historically been most prominent since governments started relying on paper money.

In the U.S., the Department of the Treasury's Bureau of Engraving and Printing (BEP) is responsible for producing Federal Reserve Notes (i.e., dollar bills). The BEP uses special fibers, linen, and inks to print money. It also uses elaborate designs, seals, and miniature words concealed in the artwork to discourage counterfeiters. In 1995 the BEP changed the design of the $100 bill and added a watermark to further prevent counterfeiting.

Until recently, counterfeiting required skilled engravers and craftsmen to produce paper money that would resemble authentic currency. However, as computer and photocopying technology have greatly improved in recent years, counterfeiting today is more science than art.

Source

United States Secret Service, Office of Government Liaison and Public Affairs.

Contact

United States Secret Service, Office of Government Liaison and Public Affairs, 1800 G St. NW, Washington, DC 20223. (202) 435-5708.

How much money is counterfeited?

U.S. counterfeit notes seized and passed on to the public during fiscal years 1985–94.*

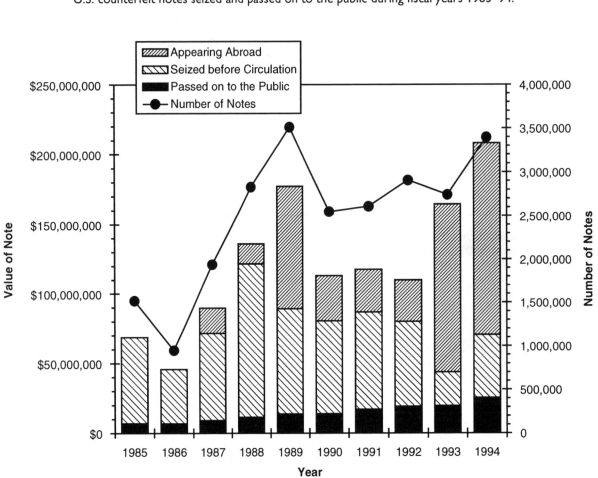

Fiscal Year	Seized before Circulation	Passed on to the Public	Appearing Abroad†	Total Value	Number of Notes	Average Value per Note
1985	$61,731,753	$6,925,756	—	$68,657,511	1,517,940	$45.23
1986	$38,848,799	$6,870,335	—	$45,719,134	949,448	$48.15
1987	$62,260,707	$9,322,348	$18,192,077	$69,755,132	1,938,759	$35.98
1988	$110,076,015	$11,562,614	$14,432,350	$136,070,979	2,829,709	$48.09
1989	$75,257,666	$13,841,983	$88,172,251	$177,271,900	3,512,622	$50.47
1990	$66,337,675	$14,021,096	$32,785,612	$113,144,383	2,548,245	$44.40
1991	$69,622,271	$17,142,926	$30,752,009	$117,517,206	2,609,372	$45.04
1992	$60,731,139	$19,145,313	$29,998,530	$109,874,982	2,905,259	$37.82
1993	$24,192,163	$19,601,697	$120,767,004	$164,560,864	2,742,381	$60.00
1994	$45,176,862	$25,285,127	$137,731,566	$208,733,575	3,394,773	$61.49

* Does not include the small amounts of counterfeit coins, which ranged from $92–$3,802 during these years.
† Figures not available prior to 1987.

Comments The total value of all counterfeit notes seized, passed on to the public, and appearing abroad increased from over $68.6 million in 1985 to $208.7 million in 1994 (an increase of over 200%). The number of counterfeit notes annually counted went from over 1.5 million to nearly 3.4 million during that time. The most popular denominations counterfeited are $20 and $100 notes. The U.S. Secret Service is in charge of detecting and arresting counterfeiters.

Counterfeiting has become more of a problem since 1985, especially the counterfeiting of U.S. currency outside the country. U.S. currency is often popular for use in foreign countries, especially those with unstable currencies or an active black market.

Counterfeit production varies from year to year. During some years, many notes of smaller denominations are manufactured. In other years, the value is greater because high denomination notes are made. For example, the number of counterfeit notes produced in 1992 was about 3% more than in 1988, but the value of the 1988 notes was about 23% higher.

Source United States Secret Service, Office of Government Liaison and Public Affairs.

Contact United States Secret Service, Office of Government Liaison and Public Affairs, 1800 G St. NW, Washington, DC 20223. (202) 435-5708.

What kinds of electronic crimes are committed?

Types of financial crime cases closed and the number of arrests made by the U.S. Secret Service in fiscal year 1994.

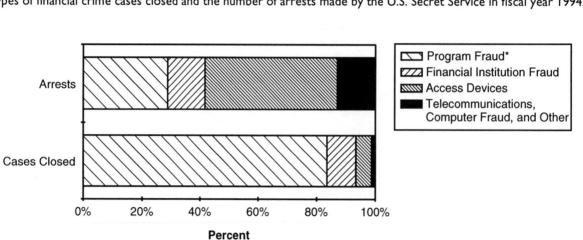

Type of Financial Crime	Cases Closed	Arrests
Program fraud*	52,451	1,600
Financial institution fraud	6,171	727
Access devices (such as ATM cards)	3,319	2,526
Telecommunications	299	161
Computer fraud	48	25
Other	470	536
Total	62,758	5,775

* Includes forgery, electronic funds transfers, and food coupon fraud cases.

Comments

The Secret Service is in charge of catching criminals who commit various financial crimes. A financial crime typically involves forgery, fraud, or unauthorized money transfers through the use of computers and telecommunications devices. By illegally accessing corporate or personal records and accounts, a financial criminal can steal money or change private records.

In 1994, the Secret Service closed 62,758 financial crimes cases. About 84% of these cases were program fraud cases. Program fraud involves forgery of records, electronic funds transfers, and food coupon fraud.

Although program fraud accounted for the largest percentage of all closed cases, financial crimes involving access devices (such as ATM cards) resulted in the largest percentage of arrests (44%). One explanation may be because one category is measured in cases and the other in people. One case may involve several arrests, and one arrested person may be involved in several cases.

Source

United States Secret Service, Office of Government Liaison and Public Affairs.

Contact

United States Secret Service, Office of Government Liaison and Public Affairs, 1800 G St. NW, Washington, DC 20223. (202) 435-5708.

Hate crimes in 1994

Number of hate crime offenses, victims, and offenders by offense category, 1994.

Type of Crime	Offenses*	Victims	Known Offenders
Total Hate Crimes	7,144	7,379	6,473
Crimes against persons	5,115	5,115	5,357
Murder	13	13	18
Forcible rape	7	7	12
Aggravated assault	998	998	1,512
Simple assault	1,305	1,305	1,776
Intimidation	2,792	2,792	2,039
Crimes against property	2,023	2,255	1,110
Robbery	126	160	285
Burglary	58	61	48
Larceny-theft	40	42	27
Motor vehicle theft	2	8	6
Arson	63	82	38
Destruction/Damage/Vandalism	1,734	1,902	706
Other	6	9	6

* Will not equal the number of victims or offenders because some offenses involve multiple victims while other offenses involve multiple offenders. Some of the offenders also are unapprehended.

Comments Crimes against persons accounted for 72% of the hate crimes reported in 1994. Intimidation was the most frequently reported hate crime, accounting for 39% of the total, and 55% of crimes against persons. Simple assault constituted 18% of all hate crimes; aggravated assault, 14%.

Damage/destruction/vandalism of property was the most frequent property crime, accounting for 24% of all hate crimes and 86% of property hate crimes.

Most crimes are motivated to some extent by selfishness and hatred. Offenses that are labeled as hate crimes, however, have different motivations than other types of violent and property crimes. Hate crimes are motivated entirely by personal bias and intolerance, rather than by greed or bad temper. The FBI classifies hate crimes by four bias motivations: race, religion, sexual orientation, and ethnicity.

Source U.S. Department of Justice, Federal Bureau of Investigation, Criminal Justice Information Services, Uniform Crime Reports, "Hate Crime—1994" (Washington, D.C.: U.S. Government Printing Office, 1995).

Contact U.S. Department of Justice, Federal Bureau of Investigation, Uniform Crime Reports, Criminal Justice Information Services Division, Washington, D.C. 20535. Information Dissemination: (202) 324-5015.

Hate crimes and race

Racially-biased hate crime offenders and victims for the U.S. in 1993 and 1994.

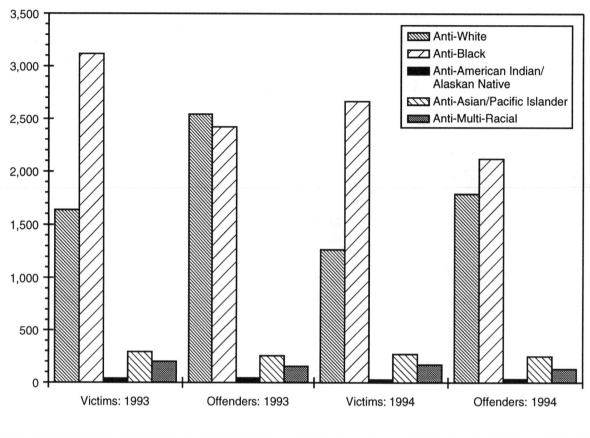

Bias Motivation	Known Offenders 1993	Known Offenders 1994	Victims of Racial Bias 1993	Victims of Racial Bias 1994
Anti-White	2,544	1,786	1,637	1,268
Anti-Black	2,421	2,120	3,117	2,666
Anti-American Indian/Alaskan Native	45	31	40	27
Anti-Asian/Pacific Islander	254	248	293	270
Anti-Multi-Racial	155	130	201	170
Total	5,419	4,315	5,288	4,408

Comments The reported number of racially-motivated hate crime victims dropped from 5,288 in 1993 to 4,408 in 1994, while the number of racially-motivated offenders declined from 5,419 to 4,315.

There were 2,544 anti-white offenders in 1993 and 1,786 in 1994, but victims of anti-white hate crimes numbered just 1,637 in 1993 and 1,268 in 1994. Clearly, during both years the number of anti-white offenders was greater than the number of victims. This implies that anti-white hate crimes often involve more than one offender for each victim (for example, an assault on an individual by a group of people).

On the other hand, anti-black offenders numbered 2,421 in 1993 and 2,120 in 1994, while victims of anti-black hate crimes amounted to 3,117 in 1993 and 2,666 in 1994.

The trend for anti-black hate crimes is the reverse of anti-white hate crimes. The number of victims exceeds the number of offenders for anti-black hate crimes, implying that anti-black hate crimes often involve more than one victim for each offender (for example, a household victimized by a single arsonist).

It is important to remember that these statistics do not neccessarily identify the race of the offender or victim, only the motivation behind the crime. The intuitive assumption would be that most anti-white hate crimes are committed against whites but not by whites, most anti-black hate crimes are committed against blacks but not by blacks, etc. However, this might not be true for every racially-motivated hate crime.

Source U.S. Department of Justice, Federal Bureau of Investigation, Criminal Justice Information Services, Uniform Crime Reports, "Hate Crime—1994" (Washington, D.C.: U.S. Government Printing Office, 1995).

U.S. Department of Justice, Federal Bureau of Investigation, Criminal Justice Information Services, Uniform Crime Reports, "Hate Crime—1993" (Washington, D.C.: U.S. Government Printing Office, June 1994).

Contact U.S. Department of Justice, Federal Bureau of Investigation, Uniform Crime Reports, Criminal Justice Information

Services Division, Washington, D.C. 20535. Information Dissemination: (202) 324-5015.

What kinds of violent hate crimes are most common?

The of violent incidents and offenses motivated by bias in the U.S. in 1993.

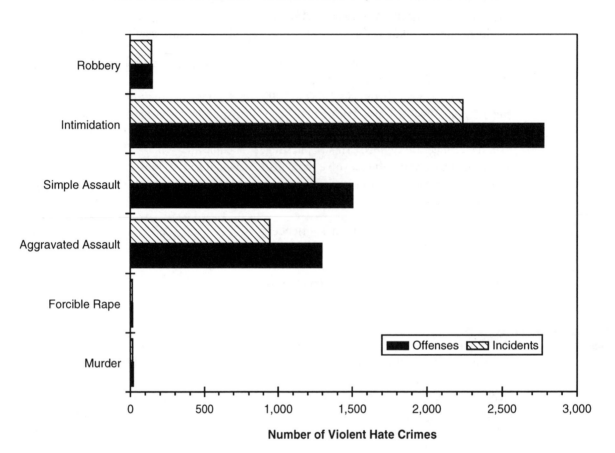

Number of Violent Hate Crimes

Type of Offense	Offenses	Incidents	Offenses per Incident
Murder	20	15	1.33
Forcible rape	15	13	1.15
Aggravated assault	1,296	944	1.37
Simple assault	1,504	1,249	1.20
Intimidation	2,776	2,239	1.24
Total crimes against persons	5,611	4,460	1.26
Robbery*	148	144	1.03

* Although robbery is a property crime rather than a personal crime, it is still treated as a violent crime because of the use of force or threat of using force.

Comments The definition of an incident differs from that of an offense. An offense refers to each individual crime committed, regardless of whether there was a single offender and multiple victims, or multiple offenders and a single victim. A single hate crime incident may involve multiple offenses. In the case of a multiple-offense incident, the incident was categorized by the most serious offense.

In 1993, the difference between the number of violent hate crime incidents and offenses varied depending on the type of crime. Hate crimes against persons in 1993 numbered 4,460 incidents and 5,611 offenses,

for a ratio of 1.26 offenses for every hate crime against persons. These totals do not include robbery, which is a violent type of property crime.

Aggravated assault had the highest ratio of offenses per hate crime incident in 1993, at 1.37. This means that multiple offenses most frequently happened during aggravated assault incidents (for example, when an individual is assaulted by a group of people). Murder had the next highest ratio of offenses per incident (1.33), followed by intimidation (1.24), simple assault (1.20), forcible rape (1.15), and then robbery (1.03).

Source U.S. Department of Justice, Federal Bureau of Investigation, Criminal Justice Information Services, Uniform Crime Reports, "Hate Crime—1993" (Washington, D.C.: U.S. Government Printing Office, June 1994).

Contact U.S. Department of Justice, Federal Bureau of Investigation, Uniform Crime Reports, Criminal Justice Information Services Division, Washington, D.C. 20535. Information Dissemination: (202) 324-5015.

What was the racial composition of robbers in 1992?

Victimizations and arrests for robbery in the U.S. for 1992, by perceived race of offender.

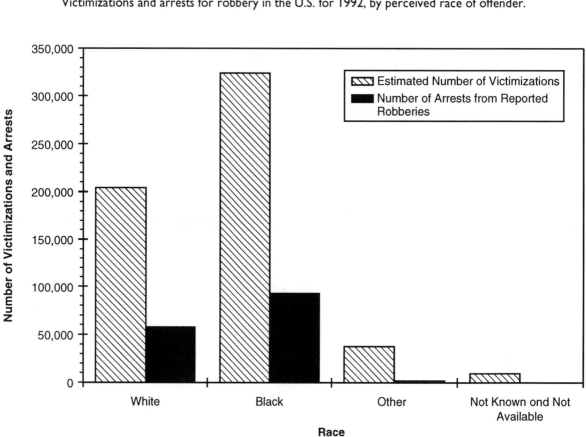

Perceived Race of Offender	Estimated Number of Victimizations	Number of Arrests from Reported Robberies
White	204,220	57,837
Black	324,110	93,392
Other*	37,770	2,017
Not Known or Not Available	9,520	—
Total	575,620	153,246

* This group is composed mainly of Asian and Pacific Islanders, and Native Americans, Alaskans, or Aleuts.

Comments The majority of robberies in 1992 were committed by blacks, but the chance of being arrested for a robbery was about the same for blacks and whites, according to data from the National Crime Victimization Survey (NCVS) and the FBI. The NCVS is a nationwide survey which measures both reported and unreported crimes, while the FBI records information on arrests.

According to the 1992 NCVS, 56.3% of robbery offenders were black, 35.5% were white, 6.7% were of another racial group, and the race of the others was unknown or not available. The FBI reported that 60.1% of robbery offenders were black, 37.7% were white,

and 1.3% were of another racial group. The FBI's statistics did not include an "unknown" racial category. Blacks account for about 12.5% of the U.S. population; whites, 83%; and persons of other races, 4.5%.

By comparing the ratio of arrests to victimizations, we can see if the chances of arrest differ for the various racial groups. Robberies committed by blacks resulted in arrest 28.3% of the time; by whites, 28.8% of the time; and by other races, 5.3% of the time. Robberies committed by all races resulted in arrest 26.6% of the time. Remember, however, that not all of these robberies were reported to police.

Source U.S. Department of Justice, Bureau of Justice Statistics. *Criminal Victimization in the United States, 1992* (Washington, D.C.: U.S. Government Printing Office, 1994), p. 62.

U.S. Department of Justice, Federal Bureau of Investigation, *Crime in the United States, 1992* (Washington, D.C.: U.S. Government Printing Office, 1993), p. 235.

Contact U.S. Department of Justice, Bureau of Justice Statistics Clearinghouse, Box 6000, Rockville, MD 20850. (800) 732-3277. A World Wide Web server is operated at http://ncjrs.aspensys.com:81/ncjrshome.html. Inquiries can also be sent by e-mail to askncjrs@aspensys.com.

U.S. Department of Justice, Federal Bureau of Investigation, Uniform Crime Reports, Criminal Justice Information Services Division, Washington, D.C. 20535. Information Dissemination: (202) 324-5015.

How old are violent offenders?

Percent distribution of nonfatal violent victimizations involving only one offender, by type of crime and perceived age of offender, 1992.

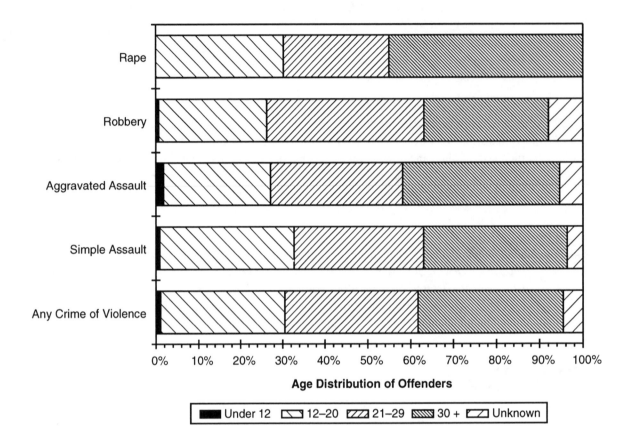

Age Distribution of Offenders

■ Under 12   ⌐⌐ 12–20   ⧸⧸ 21–29   ⧵⧵ 30 +   ⌐⌐ Unknown

Type of Crime	Under 12	12–20	21–29	30 +	Unknown
Rape	0.0%	30.2%	24.7%	45.1%	0.0%
Robbery	0.7%	25.6%	36.7%	29.0%	7.9%
Aggravated assault	1.8%	25.4%	30.9%	36.5%	5.4%
Simple assault	0.9%	31.8%	30.3%	33.3%	3.7%
Any crime of violence	1.1%	29.4%	31.2%	33.7%	4.6%

Comments Victims of violent crimes identified 33.7% of the assailants as age 30 or older, 31.2% as ages 21-29, 29.4% as ages 12-20, and 1.1% as under 12, according to a 1992 national survey. These statistics involve victimizations where there was only one offender.

Reports on persons age 12-20 were most often for simple assault (31.8%), followed by rape (30.2%), robbery (25.6%), and aggravated assault (25.4%). The highest percentage for those age 21-29 was for robbery (36.7%), followed by aggravated assault (30.9%), simple assault (33.3%), and then rape (26.7%). As for persons age 30 and older, the highest percentage was for rape (45.1%), followed by aggravated assault (36.5%), simple assault (33.3%), and then robbery (29.0%). Offenders under age 12 were most likely to be involved in aggravated assault (1.8%), followed by simple assault (0.9%), and then robbery (0.7%).

It is important to remember that the percentages only indicate how often persons within certain age groups were offenders and not how many offenses occurred. Also, the unknown cases can affect the total distribution, because the unknown cases may not have the same proportions as the known cases.

These statistics are based on a national survey, and therefore indicate the age distribution for both reported and unreported crimes in 1992. As for reported crimes, the FBI states that there were more than 100,000 children arrested for felonies in 1994. The arrest rate for juveniles for violent crime increased from 17.9 per 100,000 children in 1990 to 23.5 in 1994. The age at which a juvenile commits the first offense is a good indicator of future criminal behavior. The younger the age, the more likely it is that the juvenile will commit additional offenses. The FBI indicates that for those who were first convicted at the age of 10 or younger, 61% committed additional offenses, while only 16% of those whose first conviction was at age 17 or older committed new offenses.

Source U.S. Department of Justice, Bureau of Justice Statistics, *Criminal Victimization in the United States, 1992* (Washington, D.C.: U.S. Government Printing Office, 1994), p. 59.

Contact U.S. Department of Justice, Bureau of Justice Statistics Clearinghouse, Box 6000, Rockville, MD 20850. (800) 732-3277. A World Wide Web server is operated at http://ncjrs.aspensys.com:81/ncjrshome.html. Inquiries can also be sent by e-mail to askncjrs@aspensys.com.

How common is juvenile delinquency ?

Delinquency cases (in thousands) disposed to juvenile courts, by reason of referral, 1983–91.

Reason for Referral	1983	1984	1985	1986	1987	1988	1989	1990	1991
Violent offenses	55	61	67	73	67	70	77	94	103
Criminal homicide	1	1	1	2	1	2	2	3	3
Forcible rape	3	3	4	5	4	4	4	4	5
Robbery	24	22	26	26	22	22	23	28	30
Aggravated assault	27	35	36	40	39	43	49	59	66
Property offenses	451	442	489	496	498	498	524	538	577
Burglary	145	129	139	140	131	128	131	141	149
Larceny	270	276	307	308	314	309	318	321	351
Motor vehicle theft	31	31	36	42	47	54	68	69	70
Arson	5	6	7	6	6	7	7	7	7
Delinquency offenses	524	530	555	583	590	596	606	642	658
Simple assault	81	73	92	95	100	103	108	121	130
Vandalism	64	69	84	84	83	81	83	93	103
Drug law violations	57	65	76	73	73	82	78	69	59
Obstruction of justice	55	63	68	76	79	79	82	85	79
Other	268	260	235	255	256	251	257	275	286
Total	1,030	1,034	1,112	1,151	1,154	1,164	1,207	1,274	1,338

Comments

From 1983 to 1991, the annual number of juvenile delinquency cases rose from about 1 million to over 1.3 million, an increase of nearly 30%. Of the 1,338,000 juvenile delinquency cases reported in 1991, 49% were delinquency offenses, 43% were property crimes, and 8% were violent crimes.

Delinquency offenses accounted for the largest growth in case numbers during these years. Delinquency offenses increased from 524,000 cases in 1983 to 658,000 cases in 1991, accounting for about 13% of the 30% increase in delinquency cases during those years.

Although violent offenses made up only 8% of all delinquency cases in 1991, violent offenses grew at a faster rate during 1983–91 than did property or delinquency offenses. The annual number of violent crimes increased by 87%, while property crimes increased by 28%, and delinquency offenses by 26%.

Rising numbers of aggravated assaults accounted for most of the increase in violent offenses. Aggravated assault offenses grew by 144% from 1983 to 1991.

Source

U.S. Department of Justice, Office of Juvenile Justice and Delinquency Programs, *Juvenile Court Statistics, 1991* (Washington, D.C.: U.S. Government Printing Office, 1994) as cited by *The American Almanac 1994–1995: Statistical Abstract of the United States* (Austin, Tex.: The Reference Press, Inc., 1994), p. 213.

Contact

U.S. Department of Justice, Juvenile Justice Clearinghouse, P.O. Box 6000, Rockville MD 20849. (800) 638-8736. A World Wide Web server is operated at http://ncjrs.aspensys.com:81/ncjrshome.html. Inquiries can also be sent by e-mail to askncjrs@aspensys.com.

How frequently is a child murdered, and how frequently is a child the murderer?

The rate (per 100,000 persons in each group) of murder committed against children and by children, by age group, 1983–93.

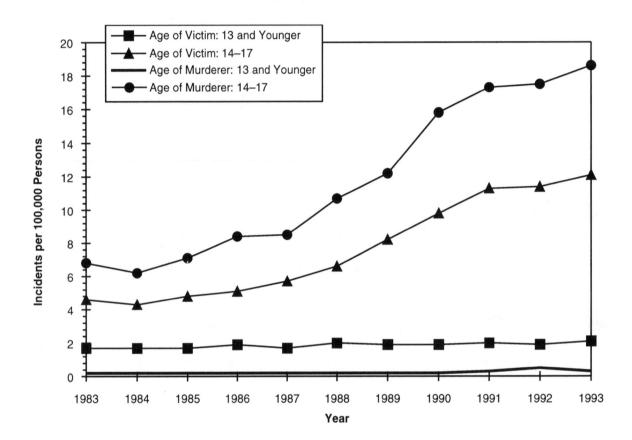

Year	Age of victim: 13 and younger	Age of victim: 14–17	Age of murderer: 13 and younger	Age of murderer: 14–17
1983	1.7	4.6	0.2	6.8
1984	1.7	4.3	0.2	6.2
1985	1.7	4.8	0.2	7.1
1986	1.9	5.1	0.2	8.4
1987	1.7	5.7	0.2	8.5
1988	2.0	6.6	0.2	10.7
1989	1.9	8.2	0.2	12.2
1990	1.9	9.8	0.2	15.8
1991	2.0	11.3	0.3	17.3
1992	1.9	11.4	0.5	17.5
1993	2.1	12.1	0.3	18.6

Comments

Children under the age of 13 are more likely to be murder victims than murderers, but children between the ages of 14 and 17 are more likely to be murderers than murder victims. These rates follow the frequency of murder (per 100,000 persons in that age group) committed against children and committed by children during the years 1983–93.

During 1983–93, the rates for children age 13 and younger changed very little. In the early 1980s, 1.7 children per 100,000 age 13 and younger were murdered in the U.S., and that rate advanced slightly to 2.1 by 1993. Throughout the 1980s only about 0.2 children per 100,000 in that age group were murderers, but that rate increased a little to peak at 0.5 in 1992.

The statistics for children between the ages of 14 and 17 were very different. The rates of murder committed against and by children in that age group have been steadily rising since the early 1980s. In 1984, only 4.3 children per 100,000 ages 14–17 were murder victims, but that rate had climbed to 12.1 by 1993. The rate with the sharpest increase, however, was the rate of murder committed by

14–17 year-olds. In 1984, only 6.2 children per 100,000 in that age group were murderers, but that rate had tripled to 18.6 murderers per 100,000 persons ages 14–17 by 1993.

There are several possible reasons explaining the changes in these rates. The rates of murder committed against and committed by children age 13 and younger changed very little, while the rates for 14–17 year-olds both increased. This trend indicates that there is now more lethal violence committed against and by children in the 14–17 age group than in the recent past, but that those age 13 and younger have been relatively unaffected by that trend. Another interesting fact to gain from this information is that the rate of murder committed by 14–17 year-olds has consistently been higher than the rate of murder committed against them. In order for this to happen, either the 14–17 year-olds are committing multiple murders within their own age group, or they are frequently murdering people outside of their age group. A single murderer can be responsible for multiple incidents, but a single murder victim can only be killed once.

Source

U.S. Department of Justice, Bureau of Justice Statistics, *Sourcebook of Criminal Justice Statistics—1994* (Washington,

D.C.: U.S. Government Printing Office, 1995), p. 339 table 3.116, p. 342 table 3.121.

Contact

U.S. Department of Justice, Juvenile Justice Clearinghouse, P.O. Box 6000, Rockville MD 20849. (800) 638-8736. A World Wide Web server is operated at

http://ncjrs.aspensys.com:81/ncjrshome.html. Inquiries can also be sent by e-mail to askncjrs@aspensys.com.

Juveniles and gang-related killings

Juvenile gang killings and adult gang killings, 1987–94.

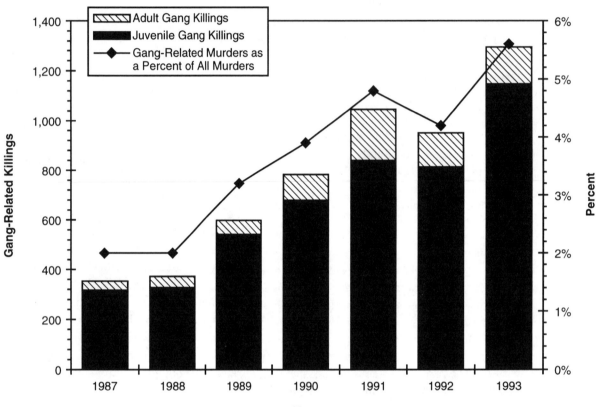

Year	Juvenile Gang Killings	Adult Gang Killings	Gang-related Murders as a Percent of all Murders
1987	317	36	2.0%
1988	327	45	2.0%
1989	542	56	3.2%
1990	679	104	3.9%
1991	840	206	4.8%
1992	813	137	4.2%
1993	1,147	147	5.6%
1994	1,157	111	5.7%

Comments

In 1987, law enforcement agencies reported 353 gang-related killings, of which 317 (90%) were juvenile gang killings. By 1993, the annual number of gang-related killings had increased by about 250% over the 1987 level. Juvenile gang killings typically accounted for 85–90% of all gang-related killings during this period. Although juveniles and adults in gangs have some dealings together, the FBI separates juvenile gang killings from gangland killings, which involve adults or adult gangs.

A juvenile gang killing involves juveniles murdering other youths, usually from rival gangs. Juvenile gang killings are often caused by feuds over territorial claims, personal disputes, or acts of revenge for previous attacks. Juvenile gang killings have received much publicity in recent years because of their rising numbers. Also, juvenile gang shootings (particularly driveby shootings) have often injured or killed bystanders who were caught in the crossfire.

Street gangs have existed throughout U.S. history and are different from more sophisticated organized crime groups. Historically, most street gangs formed along racial or ethnic lines. This still applies in attracting members to gangs. Researchers began studying gangs in the 1920s, when most of the problems associated with gangs were in delinquent acts, minor crimes, and fights with other gangs. Gang activities since then have become increasingly violent and malicious. Today's gangs typically traffic in drugs, terrorize neighborhoods, and commit shootings, assaults, robbery, extortion, and other felonies. The most ambitious urban gangs have begun "colonizing" in other cities by establishing drug trafficking syndicates.

Source

U.S. Department of Justice, Federal Bureau of Investigation, *Crime in the United States, 1994* (Washington, D.C.: U.S. Government Printing Office, 1995), p. 21.

U.S. Department of Justice, Federal Bureau of Investigation, *Crime in the United States, 1993* (Washington, D.C.: U.S. Government Printing Office, 1994), p. 21.

U.S. Department of Justice, Federal Bureau of Investigation, *Crime in the United States, 1992* (Washington, D.C.: U.S. Government Printing Office, 1993), p. 21.

U.S. Department of Justice, Federal Bureau of Investigation, *Crime in the United States, 1991* (Washington, D.C.: U.S. Government Printing Office, 1992), p. 21.

Contact

U.S. Department of Justice, Federal Bureau of Investigation, Uniform Crime Reports, Criminal Justice Information Services Division, Washington, D.C. 20535. Information Dissemination: (202) 324-5015.

For what crimes are minors usually arrested?

Total arrests and the percent of persons under 18 years of age arrested for selected offenses in 1993.

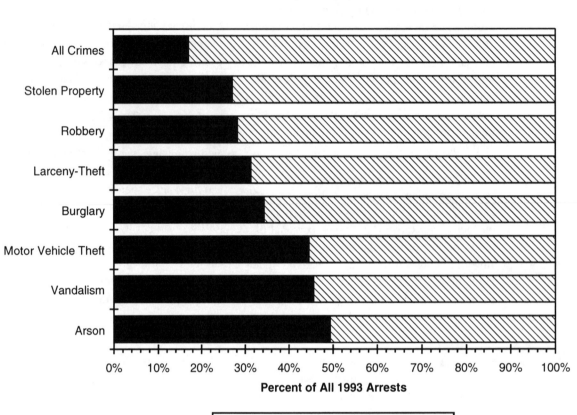

Type of Crime	Total Arrests	Under 18 Arrests	Percent of Total Under 18
Arson	16,113	7,949	49.3%
Vandalism	261,282	119,142	45.6%
Motor vehicle theft	168,795	75,315	44.6%
Burglary	338,238	116,024	34.3%
Larceny-theft	1,251,277	391,950	31.3%
Robbery	153,533	43,340	28.2%
Stolen property (buying, receiving, selling)	134,864	36,440	27.0%
All crimes (includes all other arrests)	11,765,764	2,014,472	17.1%

Comments Persons under 18 are more likely to be arrested for certain crimes, according to 1993 arrest information from the FBI. Minors accounted for 17.1% of all arrests in 1993.

Almost half of all arrestees for arson, vandalism, and motor vehicle theft were under 18. Although arson was less frequent than vandalism or motor vehicle theft, the percentage of arrests involving minors was highest, at 49.3%. Vandalism was next (45.6%), followed by motor vehicle theft (44.6%).

Of the crimes listed here, minors were arrested in greatest numbers for larceny-theft (391,950), followed by vandalism (119,142) and burglary (116,024). These three offenses made up 31.1% of all arrests among persons under 18, but only 15.7% of arrests among persons of all ages. This finding indicates that since these arrests were more common among minors, it is likely that these crimes were more frequently committed by minors than by adults.

Source U.S. Department of Justice, Federal Bureau of Investigation, *Crime in the*

United States, 1993 (Washington, D.C.: U.S. Government Printing Office, 1994), p. 233.

Contact U.S. Department of Justice, Federal Bureau of Investigation, Uniform Crime Reports, Criminal Justice Information

Services Division, Washington, D.C. 20535. Information Dissemination: (202) 324-5015.

pUniShmeNt

What portion of all arrests are from cities or rural areas?

The total number of U.S. arrests in 1993, and the percentage of urban (city) and rural arrests.

Unit	Total	Percent from Cities	Percent from Rural Areas
Population counted	214,099,000	68.0%	32.0%
Total arrests	11,753,628	76.7%	23.3%
Offense	**Total Arrests**	**Percent from Cities**	**Percent from Rural Areas**
Curfew and loitering laws	85,354	95.0%	5.0%
Prostitution and commercialized vice	88,850	94.5%	5.5%
Vagrancy	24,806	91.1%	8.9%
Robbery	153,533	88.7%	11.3%
Disorderly conduct	607,472	87.4%	12.6%
Gambling	15,336	86.3%	13.7%
Larceny-theft	1,251,277	84.2%	15.8%
Drunkenness	604,979	83.9%	16.1%
Suspicion (not included in totals)	12,136	82.6%	17.4%
Weapons; carrying, possessing, etc.	224,395	81.2%	18.8%
Vandalism	261,282	80.3%	19.7%
Stolen property; buying, receiving, possessing	134,864	80.2%	19.8%
Motor vehicle theft	168,795	79.6%	20.4%
Liquor laws	419,082	79.5%	20.5%
Runaways	152,132	78.9%	21.1%
Drug abuse violations	968,606	78.7%	21.3%
Other assaults	965,318	78.2%	21.8%
Murder and nonnegligent manslaughter	20,285	77.6%	22.4%
Aggravated assault	442,075	77.0%	23.0%
Forgery and counterfeiting	89,487	75.0%	25.0%
All other offenses (except traffic)	2,935,490	74.4%	25.6%
Arson	16,113	74.1%	25.9%
Forcible rape	32,523	74.0%	26.0%
Burglary	338,238	73.7%	26.3%
Sex offenses (except forcible rape and prostitution)	87,712	72.5%	27.5%
Embezzlement	10,916	72.1%	27.9%
Fraud	335,580	61.3%	38.7%
Driving under the influence	1,229,971	61.3%	38.7%
Offenses against family and children	89,157	55.6%	44.4%

Comments

Cities recorded 76.7% of all arrests but accounted for only 68% of the population in 1993, according to the FBI. A total population of 214 million was served by 10,512 law enforcement agencies, of which 7,446 were in cities.

Since the urban population was 68% of the total, then urban arrests should be about the same percentage if arrest trends were only a matter of population size. Location, however, is a factor. Law enforcement agencies serving cities make the bulk of arrests (76.7%).

Cities accounted for a disproportionate amount of arrests for most types of crime. Cities accounted for almost all arrests for curfew and loitering violations (95.0%), prostitution and commercialized vice (94.5%), and vagrancy (91.1%). Only arrests for three crimes were disproportionately low in cities and high in rural areas (although cities still accounted for the majority of arrests). The frequency of rural arrests for fraud (38.7%), driving under the influence (38.7%), and offenses against family and children (44.4%) was higher than in the cities since rural inhabitants were only 32.0% of the population.

Source

U.S. Department of Justice, Federal Bureau of Investigation, *Crime in the United States, 1993* (Washington, D.C.: U.S. Government Printing Office, 1994), pp. 219–220.

Contact

U.S. Department of Justice, Federal Bureau of Investigation, Uniform Crime Reports, Criminal Justice Information Services Division, Washington, D.C. 20535. Information Dissemination: (202) 324-5015.

How often are arrests made for crimes that are reported?

Violent and property crime offenses reported, the number of arrests, and the ratio (percentage) of arrests to offenses in 1993 for the fifty states and the District of Columbia.

State	Violent Crime Offenses	Violent Crime Arrests	Ratio of Arrests to Violent Offenses	Property Crime Offenses	Property Crime Arrests	Ratio of Arrests to Property Offenses
Alabama	32,676	11,347	34.7%	171,598	23,595	13.8%
Alaska	4,557	1,606	35.2%	28,795	6,694	23.2%
Arizona	28,142	9,657	34.3%	264,371	45,378	17.2%
Arkansas	14,381	5,123	35.6%	102,231	18,353	18.0%
California	336,381	146,320	43.4%	1,678,884	276,476	16.5%
Colorado	20,229	8,760	43.3%	176,856	36,540	20.7%
Connecticut	14,949	8,803	58.9%	137,443	30,898	22.5%
Delaware	4,801	762	15.9%	29,304	1,543	5.3%
District of Columbia	16,888	5,485	32.5%	51,091	6,191	12.1%
Florida	164,975	52,229	31.7%	977,363	119,648	12.2%
Georgia	50,019	20,208	40.4%	378,348	49,968	13.2%
Hawaii	3,061	1,233	40.3%	70,505	11,399	16.2%
Idaho	3,097	1,147	37.0%	39,161	7,578	19.4%
Illinois	112,260	*	—	544,869	*	—
Indiana	27,941	8,501	30.4%	227,149	23,703	10.4%
Iowa	9,159	2,638	28.9%	99,080	10,815	10.9%
Kansas	12,564	*	—	113,360	*	—
Kentucky	17,530	7,716	44.0%	105,979	14,770	13.9%
Louisiana	45,600	11,266	24.7%	248,461	28,627	11.5%
Maine	1,558	826	53.0%	37,519	7,531	20.1%
Maryland	49,540	14,433	29.1%	253,647	50,059	19.7%
Massachusetts	48,393	16,450	34.0%	245,831	22,146	9.0%
Michigan	75,021	22,759	30.3%	441,767	49,187	11.1%
Minnesota	14,778	8,533	57.7%	183,347	33,980	18.5%
Mississippi	11,467	2,153	18.8%	105,308	10,418	10.0%
Missouri	38,963	10,251	26.3%	227,731	35,016	15.4%
Montana	1,489	194	13.0%	38,699	1,544	4.0%
Nebraska	5,450	1,499	27.5%	60,712	11,598	19.1%
Nevada	12,157	3,003	24.7%	73,685	13,758	18.7%
New Hampshire	1,550	583	37.6%	31,131	3,748	12.0%
New Jersey	49,390	20,757	42.0%	328,867	63,678	19.4%
New Mexico	15,024	1,851	12.3%	86,236	8,667	10.5%
New York	195,352	67,467	34.5%	814,824	102,846	12.6%
North Carolina	47,178	27,195	57.6%	345,377	58,415	16.9%
North Dakota	522	173	33.1%	17,387	3,800	21.9%

[Continued]

How often are arrests made for crimes that are reported?

[Continued]

State	Violent Crime Offenses	Violent Crime Arrests	Ratio of Arrests to Violent Offenses	Property Crime Offenses	Property Crime Arrests	Ratio of Arrests to Property Offenses
Ohio	55,915	13,981	25.0%	441,550	43,499	9.9%
Oklahoma	20,512	5,868	28.6%	150,546	21,047	14.0%
Oregon	15,254	4,533	29.7%	159,558	35,507	22.3%
Pennsylvania	50,295	21,480	42.7%	343,841	54,507	15.9%
Rhode Island	4,017	2,395	59.6%	40,973	5,804	14.2%
South Carolina	37,281	10,092	27.1%	177,779	25,043	14.1%
South Dakota	1,490	578	38.8%	19,661	4,656	23.7%
Tennessee	39,047	8,876	22.7%	228,117	24,848	10.9%
Texas	137,419	39,526	28.6%	1,023,612	149,731	14.6%
Utah	5,599	2,592	46.3%	91,816	25,762	28.1%
Vermont	658	185	28.1%	22,223	956	4.3%
Virginia	24,160	12,771	52.9%	242,975	50,772	20.9%
Washington	27,040	6,672	24.7%	285,753	44,308	15.5%
West Virginia	3,793	1,506	39.7%	42,300	7,787	18.4%
Wisconsin	13,321	7,947	59.7%	190,923	60,095	31.5%
Wyoming	1,345	481	35.8%	18,221	2,540	13.9%

* Data unavailable.

Comments   California led the states in the number of violent and property crimes in 1993, as well as in the number of arrests for such crimes. New York, Florida, and Texas were also leading states in number of crimes and arrests reported. These same states are also the most populous, and so it is expected that they would account for a large share of crimes. Some states with small populations, such as Wyoming, Vermont, and North Dakota had the fewest crimes and arrests.

However, by looking at the ratio of arrests to crimes, we can see how often arrests are made for violent and property crimes while accounting for population differences. For example, Wisconsin, Rhode Island, Connecticut, and Minnesota had the highest arrest percentages for violent crimes. Wisconsin also had the highest arrest percentage for property crimes, followed by Utah, South Dakota, and Alaska.

Source   U.S. Department of Justice, Federal Bureau of Investigation, *Crime in the United States, 1993* (Washington, D.C.: U.S. Government Printing Office, 1994), pp. 68–78, 274–280.

Contact   U.S. Department of Justice, Federal Bureau of Investigation, Uniform Crime Reports, Criminal Justice Information Services Division, Washington, D.C. 20535. Information Dissemination: (202) 324-5015.

Which regions have the highest arrest rates for aggravated assault?

Arrest rates (per 100,000 inhabitants) for aggravated assault by U.S. region, 1971–93.

Year	Northeast*	Midwest†	South‡	West¤
1971	81.2	59.0	119.5	111.3
1972	83.7	63.1	125.0	134.4
1973	96.5	58.8	120.0	134.7
1974	108.6	74.7	134.1	164.7
1975	109.1	64.1	139.2	145.2
1976	106.3	62.5	135.6	136.9
1977	117.3	59.5	137.1	154.7
1978	149.2	57.9	144.7	152.1
1979	114.3	67.7	151.9	174.4
1980	118.1	64.5	147.0	170.5
1981	115.2	69.7	148.5	163.5
1982	129.6	82.5	158.7	161.3
1983	127.7	77.8	155.1	148.5
1984	139.4	84.9	141.4	143.5
1985	136.1	85.5	143.7	145.8
1986	154.1	93.2	151.3	191.3
1987	161.1	94.6	140.8	207.2
1988	171.5	115.1	138.9	226.7
1989	182.2	131.0	152.3	252.6
1990	182.7	131.1	186.9	272.6
1991	188.3	128.6	183.4	265.0
1992	186.9	129.5	210.0	267.7
1993	190.8	131.4	213.0	270.3

*The Northeast consists of Connecticut, Maine, Massachusetts, New Hampshire, New Jersey, New York, Pennsylvania, Rhode Island, and Vermont.
†The Midwest consists of Illinois, Indiana, Iowa, Kansas, Michigan, Minnesota, Missouri, Nebraska, North Dakota, Ohio, South Dakota, and Wisconsin.
‡The South consists of Alabama, Arkansas, Delaware, the District of Columbia, Florida, Georgia, Kentucky, Louisiana, Maryland, Mississippi, North Carolina, Oklahoma, South Carolina, Tennessee, Texas, Virginia, and West Virginia.
¤The West consists of Alaska, Arizona, California, Colorado, Hawaii, Idaho, Montana, Nevada, New Mexico, Oregon, Utah, Washington, and Wyoming.

Comments Each year, aggravated assaults account for the majority of all reported violent crimes, outnumbering murders, rapes, and robberies. As the number of reported aggravated assaults has increased, so has the annual number of arrests.

However, just because a crime occurs does not necessarily mean that an arrest will happen. The gap between crimes and arrests may fluctuate considerably from one year to the next. A rise in the number of arrests could mean increased crime, increased law enforcement efforts, or some combination of the two.

The arrest rate indicates how frequently an arrest occurs within a given region. Here the U.S. is divided into four geographic regions: Northeast, Midwest, South, and West. In 1971, the South had the highest arrest rate for aggravated assault (119.5 arrests per 100,000 inhabitants), narrowly above that of the West (111.3). However, by 1993, the West's rate of 270.3 had surpassed the 213.0 of the South.

Source U.S. Department of Justice, Bureau of Justice Statistics, *Sourcebook of Criminal Justice Statistics—1992* (Washington, D.C.: U.S. Government Printing Office, 1993), p. 449, table 4.16.

U.S. Department of Justice, Federal Bureau of Investigation, *Crime in the United States, 1993* (Washington, D.C.: U.S. Government Printing Office, 1994), p. 218.

U.S. Department of Justice, Federal Bureau of Investigation, *Crime in the United States, 1992* (Washington, D.C.: U.S. Government Printing Office, 1993), p. 218.

Contact U.S. Department of Justice, Federal Bureau of Investigation, Uniform Crime Reports, Criminal Justice Information Services Division, Washington, D.C. 20535. Information Dissemination: (202) 324-5015.

How often are minors arrested for certain offenses compared to adults?

The number of persons under and over 18 years of age arrested for violent and property offenses in the U.S. during 1993, and the percent distribution of arrests for each age group.

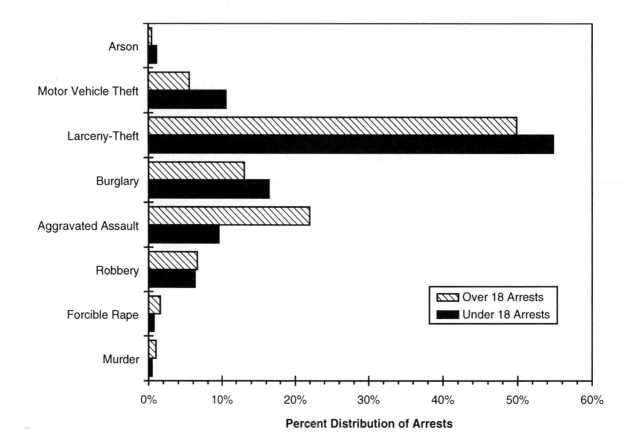

Offense	Under 18	Percent	Over 18	Percent
Violent Crimes	114,592	17.03%	505,431	31.09%
Murder*	3,150	0.47%	16,266	1.00%
Forcible rape	5,026	0.75%	25,716	1.58%
Robbery	42,011	6.24%	106,469	6.55%
Aggravated assault	64,405	9.57%	356,980	21.96%
Property Crimes	558,376	82.97%	1,120,504	68.91%
Burglary	110,512	16.42%	212,572	13.07%
Larceny-theft	368,907	54.81%	810,809	49.87%
Motor vehicle theft	71,444	10.62%	89,466	5.50%
Arson	7,513	1.12%	7,657	0.47%
Total	672,968	100.00%	1,625,935	100.00%

*Includes nonnegligent manslaughter.

Comments   In 1993, the FBI reported that among persons under 18, 82.97% of the arrests were for property crimes and 17.03% were for violent crimes. As for individuals over 18, 68.91% of the arrests were for property crimes and 31.09% were for violent crimes.

These percentages indicate that when a minor is arrested, it is more likely for a property crime than if an adult were arrested. By the same token, when an adult is arrested, it is more likely for a violent crime than if a minor were arrested. Arrests made for burglary, larceny-theft, motor vehicle theft, and arson were all more frequent for minors than for adults. Arrests for murder, forcible rape, robbery, and aggravated assault were all more frequent among adults than for minors.

It is important to remember that these statistics only show how frequently arrests for different offenses occurred among the two groups (minors and adults). The total number of adult arrests exceeded arrests of minors.

Source   U.S. Department of Justice, Federal Bureau of Investigation, *Crime in the United States, 1993* (Washington, D.C.: U.S. Government Printing Office, 1994), p. 225.

Contact   U.S. Department of Justice, Federal Bureau of Investigation, Uniform Crime Reports, Criminal Justice Information Services Division, Washington, D.C. 20535. Information Dissemination: (202) 324-5015.

Male and female arrests for violent and property offenses

Total 1993 arrests in the U.S. for violent and property crimes, by gender.

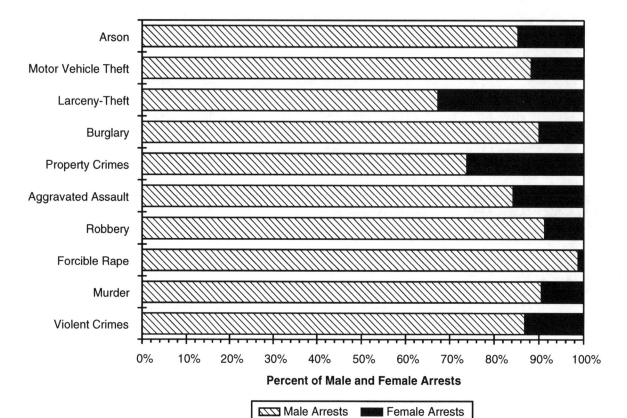

Percent of Male and Female Arrests

Type of Offense	Male Arrests	Female Arrests
Violent Crimes	538,523	81,500
Murder	17,585	1,831
Forcible rape	30,363	379
Robbery	135,525	12,955
Aggravated assault	355,050	66,335
Property Crimes	1,239,889	438,991
Burglary	290,798	32,286
Larceny-theft	794,164	385,552
Motor vehicle theft	141,989	18,921
Arson	12,938	2,232

Comments Males made up the overwhelming majority of persons arrested for violent or property crimes in 1993. Males accounted for 86.9% of violent crime arrests (murder, forcible rape, robbery, and aggravated assault), and 73.9% of property crime arrests (burglary, larceny-theft, motor vehicle theft, and arson).

Males were most often arrested for every crime listed. The percentages were higher for violent crimes than for property crimes. Males accounted for 98.8% of forcible rape arrests, 91.3% of robbery arrests, and 90.1% of murder arrests. As for property crimes, the percentage of male arrests was highest for burglary (90%) and motor vehicle theft (88.2%).

Females were not most often arrested for any of the crimes listed, but were more likely arrested for some crimes than others. For example, among violent crime arrests, aggravated assault had the highest percent of female arrestees (15.7%).

Property crimes had a higher percentage of female arrests than violent crimes. Females accounted for about 32.7% of all larceny-theft arrests and 14.7% of all arson arrests in 1993.

Source U.S. Department of Justice, Federal Bureau of Investigation, *Crime in the United States, 1993* (Washington, D.C.: U.S. Government Printing Office, 1994), p. 226.

Contact U.S. Department of Justice, Federal Bureau of Investigation, Uniform Crime Reports, Criminal Justice Information Services Division, Washington, D.C. 20535. Information Dissemination: (202) 324-5015.

What is the racial diversity of arrested persons?

Percent distribution* of U.S. arrests by race in 1993, by offense charged.

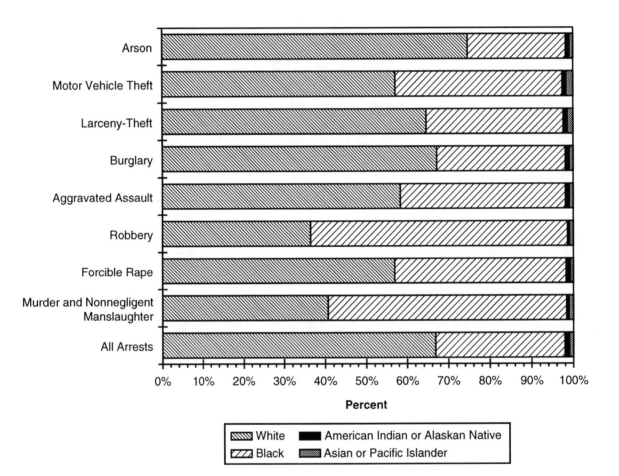

Offense Charged	Number of Arrests	White	Black	American Indian or Alaskan Native	Asian or Pacific Islander
All arrests	11,741,751	66.9%	31.1%	1.1%	1.0%
Murder and nonnegligent manslaughter	20,243	40.7%	57.6%	0.6%	1.1%
Forcible rape	32,469	56.9%	41.3%	1.0%	0.8%
Robbery	153,281	36.5%	62.1%	0.4%	1.0%
Aggravated assault	441,455	58.4%	39.8%	0.9%	1.0%
Burglary	337,810	67.2%	30.9%	0.9%	1.0%
Larceny-theft	1,249,303	64.6%	33.0%	1.0%	1.4%
Motor vehicle theft	168,591	57.1%	40.3%	0.9%	1.7%
Arson	16,073	74.6%	23.5%	0.9%	0.9%

* Rows may not add to exactly 100% because of rounding.

Comments In 1993, law enforcement agencies across the U.S. arrested over 11.7 million persons. The racial diversity of those arrests was as follows: 66.9% were white, 31.1% were black, 1.1% were American Indian or Alaskan Native, and 1.0% were Asian or Pacific Islander.

Arrests for certain crimes had different racial proportions. For example, whites accounted for 74.6% of arson arrests, but only for 36.5% of robbery arrests. Blacks made up 62.1% of robbery arrests, while accounting for just 23.5% of arson arrests. The crime with the highest percentage of arrested American Indians and Alaskan Natives was larceny-theft (1.0%); the highest percentage of arrested Asians and Pacific Islanders was for motor vehicle theft (1.7%).

It is important to remember that these percentages only indicate racial diversity of arrestees, and not how many offenses occurred. Some crimes were more frequent than others, with consequently more arrests. For example, although 74.6% of arson arrestees were white, this was only about 12,000 persons. At the same time, 68,000 blacks were arrested for motor vehicle theft, even though blacks were only arrested 40.3% of the time for that crime. This is because there were about ten times as many arrests for motor vehicle theft as for arson, but that is not apparent by only looking at these percentages.

Source U.S. Department of Justice, Federal Bureau of Investigation, *Crime in the United States, 1993* (Washington, D.C.: U.S. Government Printing Office, 1994), p. 235.

Contact U.S. Department of Justice, Federal Bureau of Investigation, Uniform Crime Reports, Criminal Justice Information Services Division, Washington, D.C. 20535. Information Dissemination: (202) 324-5015.

Arrests in the U.S., 1990–94

Total estimated number of arrests for violent, property, and other offenses in the U.S. during 1990–94.

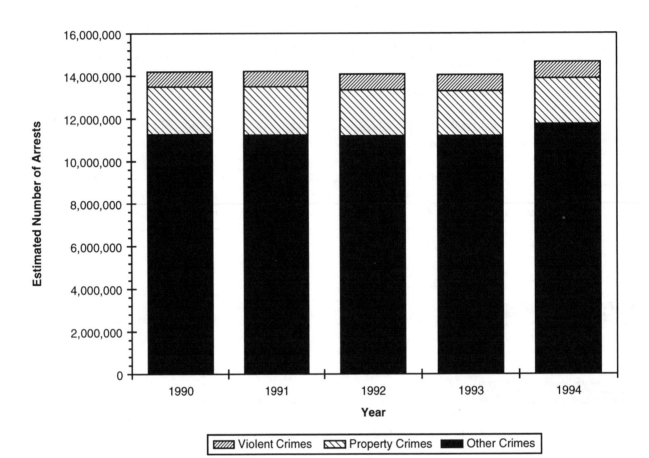

Type of Offense	1990	1991	1992	1993	1994
Violent crimes	705,500	718,890	742,130	754,110	778,730
Property crimes	2,217,800	2,252,500	2,146,000	2,094,300	2,131,700
Other crimes	11,271,800	11,240,500	11,186,900	11,187,900	11,738,300
Total*	14,195,100	14,211,900	14,075,100	14,036,300	14,648,700

* May not add to total due to rounding.

Comments   During 1990–94, the annual number of arrests in the U.S. varied between about 14 and 14.6 million. Approximately 80% of all arrests during those years were for offenses other than violent or property crimes. Property crimes accounted for about 15% of all arrests; violent crimes, 5%.

Although violent crimes accounted for the smallest proportion of all arrests, violent crime arrests increased by about 7% during 1990–94. During those same years, arrests for property crimes decreased by nearly 6%, and arrests for other crimes dropped by almost 1%.

Violent crimes are offenses of murder, forcible rape, robbery, and aggravated assault. Property crimes include offenses of burglary, larceny-theft, motor vehicle theft, and arson. The category "other crimes" includes the fol-

lowing: simple assaults, forgery and counter-feiting, fraud, embezzlement, dealing or possessing stolen property, vandalism, weapons violations, prostitution and commercialized vice, sex offenses (except rape and prostitution), drug abuse violations, gambling, offenses against family and children, driving under the influence, liquor laws, drunkenness, disorderly conduct, vagrancy, suspicion, curfew and loitering law violations, and runaways.

It is important to remember that these records only indicate the number of arrests, and not the number of offenses. A single offense may result in multiple arrests. Or, an individual arrested for one crime may be responsible for others as well. Also, arrests may be more difficult to make for some crimes than others.

Source   U.S. Department of Justice, Federal Bureau of Investigation, *Crime in the United States, 1994* (Washington, D.C.: U.S. Government Printing Office, 1995), p. 217.

U.S. Department of Justice, Federal Bureau of Investigation, *Crime in the United States, 1993* (Washington, D.C.: U.S. Government Printing Office, 1994), p. 217.

U.S. Department of Justice, Federal Bureau of Investigation, *Crime in the United*

States, 1992 (Washington, D.C.: U.S. Government Printing Office, 1993), p. 217.

U.S. Department of Justice, Federal Bureau of Investigation, *Crime in the United States, 1991* (Washington, D.C.: U.S. Government Printing Office, 1992), p. 213.

U.S. Department of Justice, Federal Bureau of Investigation, *Crime in the United States, 1990* (Washington, D.C.: U.S. Government Printing Office, 1991), p. 173.

Contact   U.S. Department of Justice, Federal Bureau of Investigation, Uniform Crime Reports, Criminal Justice Information Services Division, Washington, D.C. 20535. Information Dissemination: (202) 324-5015.

Arrests in the U.S. during 1993

Total estimated number of arrests for violent, property, and other offenses in the U.S. during 1993.

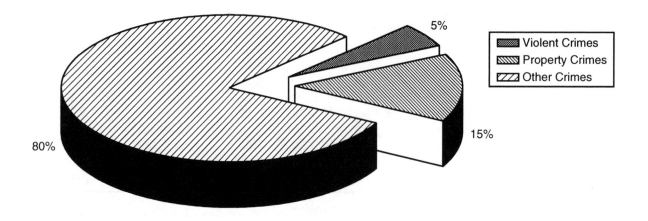

Type of Offense	Number of Arrests
Violent Crimes	754,110
Murder	23,400
Forcible rape	38,420
Robbery	173,620
Aggravated assault	518,670
Property Crimes	2,094,300
Burglary	402,700
Larceny-theft	1,476,300
Motor vehicle theft	195,900
Arson	19,400
Other Crimes	11,187,900
Total	14,036,300

Comments In 1993, the FBI estimated the total number of arrests in the U.S. at 14,036,000. Only 2,848,400 (20%) of those arrests were for violent or property crimes.

Property crimes accounted for 15% of all arrests. The most common property crimes were larceny-theft (10.5%) and burglary (2.9%). Together, these accounted for 90% of all property crime arrests.

Arrests for violent crimes accounted for only 5% of all arrests. The most common violent crimes were aggravated assault (3.7%) and robbery (1.2%). Together, these accounted for nearly 92% of all violent crime arrests.

It is important to remember that these records only indicate the number of arrests, and not the number of offenses. A single offense may result in multiple arrests. Or, an individual arrested for one crime may be responsible for others as well. Also, arrests may be more difficult to make for some crimes than others.

Source U.S. Department of Justice, Federal Bureau of Investigation, *Crime in the United States, 1993* (Washington, D.C.: U.S. Government Printing Office, 1994), p. 217.

Contact U.S. Department of Justice, Federal Bureau of Investigation, Uniform Crime Reports, Criminal Justice Information Services Division, Washington, D.C. 20535. Information Dissemination: (202) 324-5015.

Arrests for economic crimes

Estimated arrests for selected economically-related crimes in the U.S., 1990–94.

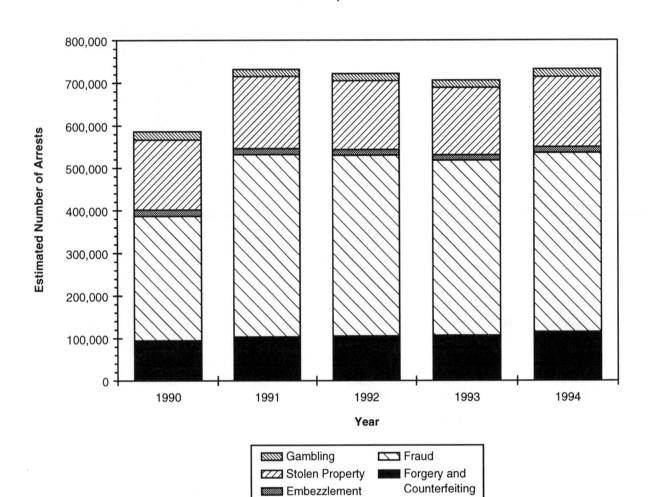

Offense	1990	1991	1992	1993	1994
Forgery and counterfeiting	94,800	103,700	105,400	106,900	115,300
Fraud	291,600	427,800	424,200	410,700	419,800
Embezzlement	15,300	14,000	13,700	12,900	14,300
Stolen property*	165,200	170,000	161,500	158,100	164,700
Gambling	19,300	16,600	17,100	17,300	18,500

* Includes buying, receiving, and possessing stolen property.

Comments Crimes such as forgery and counterfeiting, fraud, embezzlement, dealing with stolen property, and illegal gambling are often difficult for law enforcement agencies to detect. Such crimes may often have no direct victim, but are designed to take advantage of society in general. From 1991 to 1994, over 700,000 persons were arrested annually in the U.S. for one of these economically-motivated crimes. In 1991, the number of fraud arrests increased 145% over 1990.

Forgery and counterfeiting, fraud, and embezzlement are crimes that are often not detected until long after the damage has been done. These crimes rely on deception or deceit, making it difficult to find the criminal. Sometimes such crimes may not be detected at all.

Buying, receiving, and possessing stolen property can also be difficult to trace, because the buyers and sellers of stolen property each stand to gain from the transaction and want to avoid detection. When thefts take place, the criminal may only keep a small portion of the stolen merchandise for personal use. The rest of the stolen property is then "fenced," which means that the criminal finds someone to buy or receive the stolen goods in exchange for money, goods, or services. Stolen property can circulate through many sellers and buyers long after the original theft.

Illegal gambling also can be difficult to detect. Legal gambling is regulated to insure fairness, and is subject to taxation according to state laws. When gambling occurs illegally, there is no way to make sure the game or contest is fair, and the government does not collect any revenue.

Source U.S. Department of Justice, Federal Bureau of Investigation, *Crime in the United States, 1994* (Washington, D.C.: U.S. Government Printing Office, 1995), p. 217.

U.S. Department of Justice, Federal Bureau of Investigation, *Crime in the United States, 1993* (Washington, D.C.: U.S. Government Printing Office, 1994), p. 217.

U.S. Department of Justice, Federal Bureau of Investigation, *Crime in the United States, 1992* (Washington, D.C.: U.S. Government Printing Office, 1993), p. 217.

U.S. Department of Justice, Federal Bureau of Investigation, *Crime in the United States, 1991* (Washington, D.C.: U.S. Government Printing Office, 1992), p. 213.

U.S. Department of Justice, Federal Bureau of Investigation, *Crime in the United States, 1990* (Washington, D.C.: U.S. Government Printing Office, 1991), p. 174.

Contact U.S. Department of Justice, Federal Bureau of Investigation, Uniform Crime Reports, Criminal Justice Information Services Division, Washington, D.C. 20535. Information Dissemination: (202) 324-5015.

How often does a crime result in an arrest?

Offenses known to police and percent cleared by arrest in the U.S., 1980–93

Year	Total Offenses Known to Police	Percent of Total Offenses Cleared by Arrest	Violent Offenses Known to Police	Percent of Violent Offenses Cleared by Arrest	Property Crime Offenses Known to Police	Percent of Property Crime Offenses Cleared by Arrest
1980	12,483,083	19.2%	1,242,511	43.6%	11,240,527	16.5%
1981	12,715,894	19.5%	1,275,135	42.9%	11,440,759	16.9%
1982	11,932,744	20.1%	1,195,533	45.4%	10,737,211	17.3%
1983	11,403,141	20.6%	1,166,888	46.5%	10,236,253	17.7%
1984	11,121,418	21.0%	1,172,616	47.7%	9,948,802	17.9%
1985	11,762,540	20.9%	1,240,134	47.6%	10,522,406	17.8%
1986	12,734,405	20.7%	1,445,965	46.3%	11,288,440	17.5%
1987	12,502,268	20.9%	1,354,012	47.7%	11,148,256	17.7%
1988	12,059,648	20.7%	1,355,693	45.7%	10,703,955	17.5%
1989	12,124,462	21.1%	1,364,705	45.8%	10,759,757	18.0%
1990	13,468,228	21.6%	1,700,303	45.6%	11,767,925	18.1%
1991	13,334,099	21.2%	1,682,487	44.7%	11,651,612	17.8%
1992	13,644,294	21.4%	1,854,630	44.6%	11,789,664	17.7%
1993	12,863,631	21.1%	1,772,279	44.2%	11,091,352	17.4%

Comments

The percent of reported crimes resulting in arrest rose from 19.2% in 1980 to 21.6% in 1990 before falling back to 21.1% in 1993. However, the arrest rate for violent crimes was much higher than for property crimes. During 1980-93, the arrest rate for violent crimes ranged from a low of 42.9% in 1981 to a high of 47.7% in 1984 and 1987. The arrest rate for property crimes ranged from a low of 16.5% in 1980 to a high of 18.1% in 1990.

The arrest percentage overall is closer to the property crime rate than the violent crime rate because of the large number of property crime offenses. Each year during the period, there were about ten times as many property crimes reported as violent crimes. This volume pulls the overall rate close to the property crime percentage.

The percent of violent crimes resulting in arrest may be higher than for property crimes, but the number of property crime arrests exceeded that of violent crimes. For example, in 1993, about 44.2% of 1,772,279 violent crimes resulted in an arrest, or around 783,000 arrests. That same year, only about 17.4% of 11,091,352 property crimes resulted in an arrest, but that was nearly 1,930,000 arrests.

Source

U.S. Department of Justice, Bureau of Justice Statistics, *Sourcebook of Criminal Justice Statistics—1992* (Washington, D.C.: U.S. Government Printing Office, 1993), p. 452, table 4.20.

U.S. Department of Justice, Federal Bureau of Investigation, *Crime in the United States, 1992* (Washington, D.C.: U.S. Government Printing Office, 1993), p. 208.

U.S. Department of Justice, Federal Bureau of Investigation, *Crime in the United States, 1993* (Washington, D.C.: U.S. Government Printing Office, 1994), p. 208.

Contact

U.S. Department of Justice, Federal Bureau of Investigation, Uniform Crime Reports, Criminal Justice Information Services Division, Washington, D.C. 20535. Information Dissemination: (202) 324-5015.

How often do economically-motivated crimes result in prison sentences?

Number of reported crimes, arrests, convictions, and prison sentences for specific economically-motivated felony crimes in 1992.

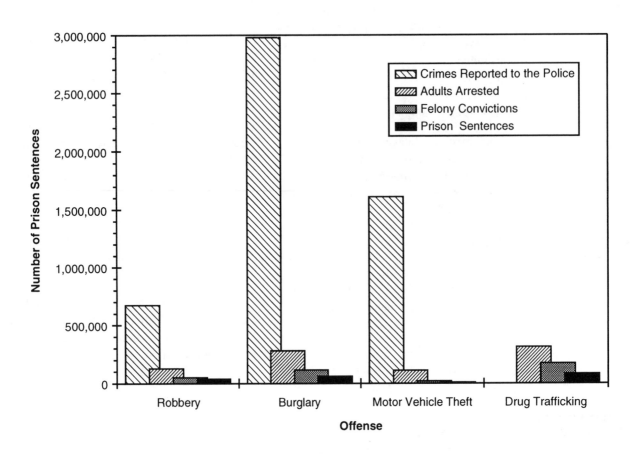

Offense	Crimes Reported to the Police	Adults Arrested	Felony Convictions	Prison Sentences
Robbery	672,480	127,729	51,878	38,390
Burglary	2,979,900	279,416	114,630	59,608
Motor vehicle theft	1,610,800	110,063	19,332	7,926
Drug trafficking	*	311,005	170,806	81,987

* Data not available.

Comments Robbery, burglary, motor vehicle theft, and drug trafficking are four types of crime that are usually motivated by the hope of acquiring cash or valuables. Burglary and motor vehicle theft are classified as property crimes, i.e., no force is used and the completion of the crime requires deception or stealth. Drug trafficking is the commerce in illegal substances, and is operated much like a legitimate business (suppliers, distributors, customers, etc.). Robbery, however, is classified as a violent crime, because of the use or intention to use force (such as a gun or knife).

The Bureau of Justice Statistics' National Judicial Reporting Program (NJRP) compiles detailed information on the sentences and characteristics of convicted felons. Using data from the NJRP and the FBI's Uniform Crime Reports (UCR) on arrests, we can compare reported crimes, arrests, and convictions.

When known, reported offenses dwarfed the number of arrests for these crimes. Arrests resulted from about 19% of robberies, 9.3% of burglaries, and 6.8% of motor vehicle thefts. Data for the number of drug trafficking offenses is unavailable, probably because there are no unwilling victims filing reports with the police.

The conviction rate per arrest was somewhat higher. Convictions resulted from 41% of robbery arrests, 41% of burglary arrests, 18% of motor vehicle theft arrests, and 55% of drug trafficking arrests.

Once convicted, the chance of being sent to prison varies with the severity of the crime. Prison sentences resulted from 31% of robbery convictions, 21% of burglary convictions, and 7% of motor vehicle theft convictions. The 26% of drug trafficking convictions resulting in a sentence could be a sign of exasperation with the drug problem in American society.

It is important to remember that these numbers are totals and should not be interpreted as representing individual cases. Actually, a person arrested for a specific crime may end up being convicted of a different crime. Also, a single crime can sometimes involve more than one arrest, and a single individual is often responsible for more than one crime. Also, someone arrested in 1992 may have been convicted in a different year. In spite of that, these comparisons illustrate the approximate odds of being convicted and going to prison if one is arrested for an economically-motivated crime.

Source U.S. Department of Justice, Bureau of Justice Statistics, "Felony Sentences in State Courts, 1992" (Washington, D.C.: U.S. Government Printing Office, January 1995).

Contact U.S. Department of Justice, Bureau of Justice Statistics Clearinghouse, Box 6000, Rockville, MD 20850. (800) 732-3277. A World Wide Web server is operated at http://ncjrs.aspensys.com:81/ncjrshome.html. Inquiries can also be sent by e-mail to askncjrs@aspensys.com.

During one year, how many people are convicted of felonies by state courts?

The number of felony convictions in state courts throughout the U.S. during 1992, by offense and type of conviction.*

Offense	Jury Trial	Bench Trial	Guilty Plea	Total for Offense
Murder†	4,076	1,046	7,427	12,549
Rape	3,023	929	17,703	21,655
Robbery	3,860	2,225	45,794	51,879
Aggravated assault	4,409	3,053	51,507	58,969
Other violent‡	1,312	1,404	17,333	20,049
Burglary	3,759	3,652	107,218	114,630
Larceny¤	2,668	4,049	112,283	119,000
Fraud**	1,045	980	61,839	63,864
Drug possession	1,839	8,039	99,548	109,426
Drug trafficking	6,728	4,624	159,453	170,805
Weapons offenses	1,205	1,126	24,091	26,422
Other offenses††	3,668	4,249	116,465	124,382
Total for conviction type	37,593	35,376	820,662	893,630

* Detail may not equal total because of rounding. Data on type of conviction was available for 707,787 cases. Table figures include estimates for cases missing a designation on type of conviction.
† Includes nonnegligent manslaughter.
‡ Includes offenses such as negligent manslaughter, sexual assault, and kidnapping.
¤ Includes motor vehicle theft.
** Includes forgery and embezzlement.
†† Composed of nonviolent offenses such as receiving stolen property and vandalism.

Comments In 1992, state courts convicted 893,630 adults of a felony. About 91.8% (820,662) of the felony convictions were the result of a guilty plea. The remainder were found guilty by a jury (4.2%) or by a judge in a bench trial (4.0%).

Drug traffickers (19.1%) and drug possessors (12.2%) together made up 31.3% of felons convicted in state courts during 1992. Drug trafficking was the felony most frequently decided by juries, accounting for 18% (6,728 cases) of all jury convictions.

Violent offenders made up about 18.4% of all convicted felons. Murderers accounted for 1.4% of all convictions; rapists, 2.4%; robbers, 5.8%; assaulters, 6.6%; and others,

2.2%. Burglars (12.8%) and larcenists (13.3%) made up most of the remaining convictions.

Persons convicted of murder were the least likely to have pleaded guilty (59%) and the most likely to have been convicted by a jury (33%).

Contrary to popular belief, neither murder nor violent crime generally accounts for most jury trials. Of all felony convictions by juries in 1992, 44% (16,680 cases) were for violent crime, and 56% (20,913 cases) were for nonviolent crime. Murder cases only comprised 11% (4,076 cases) of all felony convictions by juries, and only 1.4% (12,549 cases) of all convictions.

Source U.S. Department of Justice, Bureau of Justice Statistics, "Felony Sentences in State Courts, 1992" (Washington, D.C.: U.S. Government Printing Office, January 1995).

Contact U.S. Department of Justice, Bureau of Justice Statistics Clearinghouse, Box 6000, Rockville, MD 20850. (800) 732-3277. A World Wide Web server is operated at http://ncjrs.aspensys.com:81/ncjrshome.html. Inquiries can also be sent by e-mail to askncjrs@aspensys.com.

How many adults are part of the correctional population?

The number of adults on probation, in jail or prison, or on parole in the U.S., 1980–92.

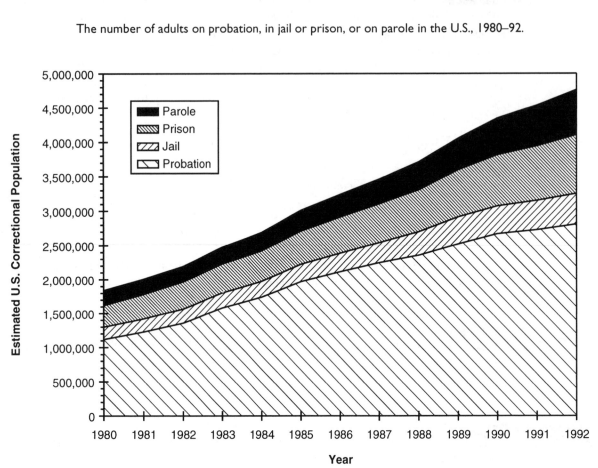

Year	Probation	Jail	Prison	Parole	Total Estimated Correctional Population*
1980	1,118,097	182,288	319,598	220,438	1,840,400
1981	1,225,934	195,085	360,029	225,539	2,006,600
1982	1,357,264	207,853	402,914	224,604	2,192,600
1983	1,582,947	221,815	423,898	246,440	2,475,100
1984	1,740,948	233,018	448,264	266,992	2,689,200
1985	1,968,712	254,986	487,593	300,203	3,011,400
1986	2,114,621	272,735	526,436	325,638	3,239,400
1987	2,247,158	294,092	562,814	355,505	3,459,600
1988	2,356,483	341,893	607,766	407,977	3,714,100
1989	2,522,125	393,303	683,367	456,803	4,055,600
1990	2,670,234	403,019	743,382	531,407	4,348,100
1991	2,729,322	424,129	792,353	590,198	4,536,200
1992	2,811,611	441,781	851,205	658,601	4,763,200

* Columns do not add to estimated total because a small number of individuals may have more than one correctional status. Therefore, the total may be an overestimate.

Comments The number of persons in the correctional population increased by almost 150% from 1980 to 1992. Individuals on probation made up the largest portion, accounting for about 59% of the total correctional population in 1992. Inmates of jails and prisons accounted for 9.3% and 17.9%, respectively. Persons on parole made up 13.8% of the correctional population in 1992.

There are four main categories in the correctional population. Probation is often used for someone sentenced for a misdemeanor or some felonies. Instead of confinement, the offender is put under the surveillance of a probation agency. The probationer remains free but is subject to certain restrictions, and must periodically report to a probation officer.

Jails are operated by city and county governments to hold persons awaiting trial, and usually those sentenced to less than one year of confinement. In a few states, the jails are operated by the authority that operates the prisons.

Prisons are operated by the federal and state governments. Their function is to hold criminals sentenced to more than one year of confinement. Prisons are the most restrictive of all the correctional categories.

Parole is the early release of a prisoner by the decision of a paroling authority. A parole officer then supervises the offender, making sure that he obeys the rules imposed by the parole board. Violations of these rules can mean return to prison to complete the sentence.

Not included in these statistics are public and private community-based facilities that hold individuals for less than 24 hours a day. This part-time restriction allows the individual to work, go to school, or make contacts in the community. These facilities are often used as a transition for prisoners who will soon receive a parole. They are also used to assist drug and alcohol treatment programs.

Source U.S. Department of Justice, Bureau of Justice Statistics, *Correctional Populations in the United States, 1992* (Washington, D.C.: U.S. Government Printing Office, 1995), p. 5.

U.S. Department of Justice, Bureau of Justice Statistics, *Report to the Nation on Crime and Justice* (Washington, D.C.: U.S. Government Printing Office, 1988), pp. 100, 106.

Contact U.S. Department of Justice, Bureau of Justice Statistics Clearinghouse, Box 6000, Rockville, MD 20850. (800) 732-3277. A World Wide Web server is operated at

http://ncjrs.aspensys.com:81/ncjrshome.html. Inquiries can also be sent by e-mail to askncjrs@aspensys.com.

What proportion of the adult correctional population is on probation, in jail or prison, or on parole?

The percentage of the adult correctional population on probation, in jail or prison, or on parole in the U.S., 1980–93. Percentages may not add to 100% because of rounding.

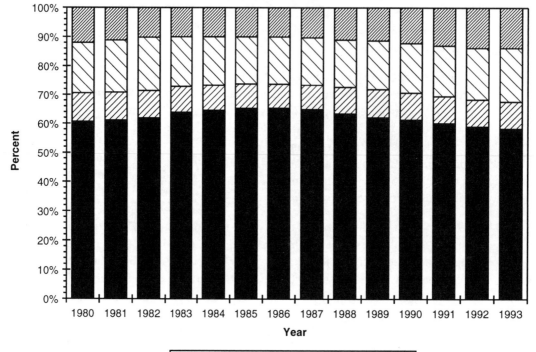

Year	Total estimated correctional population	Probation	Jail	Prison	Parole
1980	1,840,400	60.7	9.9	17.4	12.0
1981	2,006,600	61.1	9.7	17.9	11.2
1982	2,192,600	61.9	9.5	18.4	10.2
1983	2,475,100	63.9	9.0	17.1	10.0
1984	2,689,200	64.7	8.7	16.7	10.0
1985	3,011,400	65.4	8.5	16.2	10.0
1986	3,239,400	65.3	8.4	16.2	10.0
1987	3,459,600	65.0	8.5	16.3	10.3
1988	3,714,100	63.4	9.2	16.3	11.0
1989	4,055,600	62.2	9.7	16.8	11.3
1990	4,348,100	61.4	9.3	17.1	12.2
1991	4,536,200	60.2	9.3	17.5	13.0
1992	4,763,200	59.0	9.3	17.9	13.8
1993	4,879,600	58.3	9.3	18.6	13.8

Comments   Although the number of adults in the U.S. correctional population increased by over 2.5 times during 1980–93, the ratios of those on probation, in jail or prison, and on parole remained fairly steady during those years.

Persons on probation account for the majority of the correctional population. During 1980–93, the percentage of the correctional population on probation was lowest in 1993, at 58.3%, and highest in 1985, at 65.4%. The prison population made up the second largest percentage, and ranged between 16.2% in 1985 to 18.6% in 1993. The proportion on parole was next, with values between 10% and 13.8% during 1980–93. The percentage of the correctional population in jail ranged from 8.4% in 1986 to 9.9% in 1980.

The percentage changes between the categories may indicate general trends in the correctional population. For example, the rise in the parole percentage may be a result of state governments trying to reduce prison costs and overcrowding by making paroles more available. The gradual rise in the prison percentage may be related to the drop in the probation percentage, because persons already on probation are more likely to receive a prison sentence for a repeat offense.

Source   U.S. Department of Justice, Bureau of Justice Statistics, *Correctional Populations in the United States, 1993* (Washington, D.C.: U.S. Government Printing Office, 1995), p. 5.

Contact   U.S. Department of Justice, Bureau of Justice Statistics Clearinghouse, Box 6000, Rockville, MD 20850. (800) 732-3277. A World Wide Web server is operated at http://ncjrs.aspensys.com:81/ncjrshome.html. Inquiries can also be sent by e-mail to askncjrs@aspensys.com.

How many adults are on probation?

The number of adults on probation in the 50 states and the District of Columbia as of 31 December 1992.
Also shown is the ratio of adults on probation per 100,000 adult residents.

State	Probation Population	Number on Probation per 100,000 Adult Residents
Alabama	32,778	1,071
Alaska	3,764	936
Arizona	34,879	1,252
Arkansas	15,364	868
California	302,754	1,349
Colorado	36,002	1,406
Connecticut	48,567	1,935
Delaware	14,887	2,879
District of Columbia	10,262	2,174
Florida	198,615	1,913
Georgia	153,154	3,093
Hawaii	10,962	1,264
Idaho	4,075	548
Illinois	76,125	885
Indiana	78,818	1,876
Iowa	13,912	670
Kansas	23,820	1,291
Kentucky	10,750	385
Louisiana	30,533	1,001
Maine	8,942	963
Maryland	82,948	2,253
Massachusetts	48,312	1,047
Michigan	142,384	2,055
Minnesota	69,288	2,116
Mississippi	10,664	571
Missouri	34,565	899
Montana	3,930	657
Nebraska	15,386	1,318
Nevada	8,533	863
New Hampshire	4,104	494
New Jersey	97,828	1,651
New Mexico	6,881	619
New York	152,165	1,111
North Carolina	86,371	1,667
North Dakota	1,931	416
Ohio	88,515	1,080
Oklahoma	25,929	1,101

[Continued]

How many adults are on probation?

[Continued]

State	Probation Population	Number on Probation per 100,000 Adult Residents
Oregon	39,019	1,765
Pennsylvania	89,944	981
Rhode Island	16,710	2,165
South Carolina	35,896	1,350
South Dakota	2,959	584
Tennessee	39,520	1,046
Texas	355,233	2,823
Utah	6,671	576
Vermont	6,034	1,416
Virginia	23,510	488
Washington	101,132	2,675
West Virginia	6,163	449
Wisconsin	35,532	966
Wyoming	3,265	995
U.S. Total	2,806,197	1,485

Comments

About 1.5% (2,806,197) of the adult U.S. population was on probation at the end of 1992, according to the Bureau of Justice Statistics.

Probation is often used for someone sentenced for a misdemeanor or certain felonies. Instead of going to jail, the offender is placed under the supervision of a probation agency. The probationer remains free but is subject to certain restrictions, and must periodically report to a probation officer.

Texas, California, and Florida led the country in number of probationers at the end of 1992. Wyoming, South Dakota, and North Dakota had the fewest. This trend generally follows population levels; the more residents in a state, the higher the number of people on probation.

Georgia, Delaware, and Texas, had the highest rates of probation per population. Kentucky, North Dakota, and West Virginia had the lowest.

Source

U.S. Department of Justice, Bureau of Justice Statistics. *Correctional Populations in the United States, 1992* (Washington, D.C.: U.S. Government Printing Office, 1995), p. 25.

Contact

U.S. Department of Justice, Bureau of Justice Statistics Clearinghouse, Box 6000, Rockville, MD 20850. (800) 732-3277. A World Wide Web server is operated at http://ncjrs.aspensys.com:81/ncjrshome.html. Inquiries can also be sent by e-mail to askncjrs@aspensys.com.

Who is on probation?

Characteristics of adults on probation, 1992.

Characteristics	Adults on Probation from State or Federal Courts	Percent of Those with a Known Status
Type of offense	2,203,480	100%
Felony	1,070,602	49%
Misdemeanor	703,369	32%
Driving while intoxicated	394,373	18%
Other infractions	35,136	2%
Sex	2,017,910	100%
Male	1,620,270	80%
Female	397,640	20%
Race	1,755,525	100%
White	1,151,829	66%
Black	584,344	33%
American Indian/Alaska Native	14,624	1%
Asian/Pacific Islander	4,728	*
Hispanic origin	1,073,459	100%
Hispanic	77,199	7%
Non-Hispanic	996,260	93%

* Less than 0.5%.

Comments As of 31 December 1992, there were 2,806,197 adults on probation in the U.S., or about 1.5% of the total adult population. The U.S. Department of Justice's Bureau of Justice Statistics annually monitors the number and characteristics of adults on probation.

Nearly half (49%) of all adults on probation in 1992 were under supervision because of a felony, while 32% were on probation because of a misdemeanor. Persons convicted of driving while intoxicated accounted for 18% of all probation cases, and other infractions comprised the remaining 2%.

About 80% of probationers were male and 20% were female. Whites accounted for approximately 66% of probationers; blacks, 33%; American Indian/Alaska Natives, 1%; and Asians/Pacific Islanders, less than 0.5%. About 7% of probationers were of Hispanic origin.

These percentages only indicate the characteristics of the probation population when this information was known. Incomplete information on some of the questionnaires used made it so that the type of offense, sex, race, or Hispanic status for some of the 2,806,197 probationers was unknown.

Source U.S. Department of Justice, Bureau of Justice Statistics, *Correctional Populations in the United States, 1992* (Washington, D.C.: U.S. Government Printing Office, 1995).

Contact U.S. Department of Justice, Bureau of Justice Statistics Clearinghouse, Box 6000, Rockville, MD 20850. (800) 732-3277. A World Wide Web server is operated at http://ncjrs.aspensys.com:81/ncjrshome.html. Inquiries can also be sent by e-mail to askncjrs@aspensys.com.

What proportion of the population is in prison?

The number of sentenced prisoners per 100,000 residents in the U.S. during 1925–94.

Year	Rate	Year	Rate	Year	Rate
1925	79	1949	109	1972	93
1926	83	1950	109	1973	96
1927	91	1951	107	1974	102
1928	96	1952	107	1975	111
1929	98	1953	108	1976	120
1930	104	1954	112	1977	126
1931	110	1955	112	1978	132
1932	110	1956	112	1979	133
1933	109	1957	113	1980	138
1934	109	1958	117	1981	153
1935	113	1959	117	1982	170
1936	113	1960	117	1983	179
1937	118	1961	119	1984	187
1938	123	1962	117	1985	200
1939	137	1963	114	1986	216
1940	131	1964	111	1987	228
1941	124	1965	108	1988	244
1942	112	1966	102	1989	271
1943	103	1967	98	1990	292
1944	100	1968	94	1991	310
1945	98	1969	97	1992	332
1946	99	1970	96	1993	359
1947	105	1971	95	1994	387
1948	106				

Comments

Relative to U.S. population, the number of prisoners in state and federal prisons rose from 79 per 100,000 residents in 1925 to 387 in 1994. This represents a 390% increase between those years.

Much of that growth, however, only occurred since the early 1970s. In 1972, there were 93 prisoners per 100,000 residents, only 17% higher than the 1925 level. From 1972 to 1994 though, there was a gain of 316%.

The only other period to experience a similar rise was during 1925–39. During those years, the rate of prisoners increased from 79 to 137 per 100,000 population, a gain of about 74%. Throughout much of the 1940s and 1950s, the ratio of prisoners to population remained pretty stable. During most of the 1960s, the prisoner population rate declined.

Source

U.S. Department of Justice, Bureau of Justice Statistics, "Prisoners in 1994" (Washington, D.C.: U.S. Government Printing Office, August 1995).

U.S. Department of Justice, Bureau of Justice Statistics, "Prisoners in 1993" (Washington, D.C.: U.S. Government Printing Office, June 1994).

U.S. Department of Justice, Bureau of Justice Statistics, *Sourcebook of Criminal Justice Statistics—1992* (Washington, D.C.: U.S. Government Printing Office, 1993), p. 608.

Contact

U.S. Department of Justice, Bureau of Justice Statistics Clearinghouse, Box 6000, Rockville, MD 20850. (800) 732-3277. A World Wide Web server is operated at http://ncjrs.aspensys.com:81/ncjrshome.html. Inquiries can also be sent by e-mail to askncjrs@aspensys.com.

What type of criminals are in state prisons?

The estimated number of inmates in U.S. state prisons, by most serious offense, 1979–93.

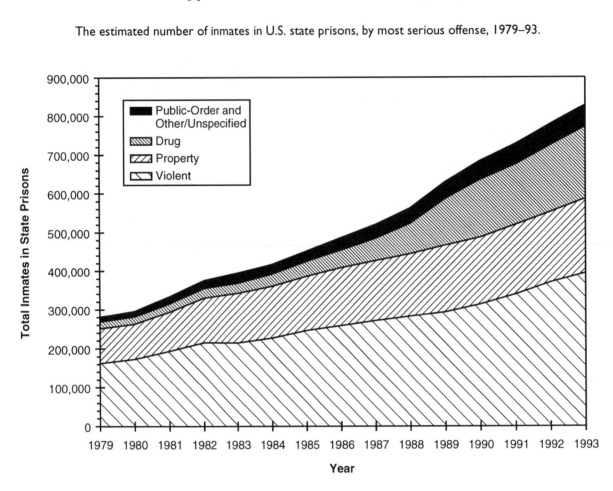

Year	Violent	Property	Drug	Public-Order	Other/Unspecified	Total*
1979	162,800	88,300	18,000	11,200	800	281,233
1980	173,300	89,300	19,000	12,400	1,800	295,819
1981	193,300	100,500	21,700	14,600	3,100	333,251
1982	215,300	114,400	25,300	17,800	2,900	375,603
1983	214,600	127,100	26,600	24,400	2,300	394,953
1984	227,300	133,100	31,700	21,900	3,400	417,389
1985	246,200	140,100	38,900	23,000	3,200	451,812
1986	258,600	150,200	45,400	28,800	3,600	486,655
1987	271,300	155,500	57,900	31,300	4,400	520,336
1988	282,700	161,600	79,100	35,000	4,100	562,605
1989	293,900	172,700	120,100	39,500	3,800	629,995
1990	313,600	173,700	148,600	45,500	3,100	684,544
1991	339,500	180,700	155,200	49,500	2,900	728,605
1992	370,300	182,400	172,300	51,100	3,100	778,495
1993	394,500	192,200	186,000	52,100	3,500	828,371

* Columns do not add to totals because of rounding.

Comments The number of inmates in state prisons more than doubled during 1979–93. The majority of prisoners during any year were violent offenders (serving for murder, rape, robbery, or aggravated assault).

In 1979, violent offense inmates accounted for 57.9% of state prisoners. By 1993, however, only 47.6% of state prisoners were violent offense inmates. The reason why the percentage of violent offense inmates declined was not because the number of violent offense inmates diminished. The number of violent offense inmates grew, but the substantial increases in drug offense inmates made that growth small in comparison.

Source U.S. Department of Justice, Bureau of Justice Statistics, *Correctional Populations in the United States, 1992* (Washington, D.C.: U.S. Government Printing Office, 1995), p. 53.

U.S. Department of Justice, Bureau of Justice Statistics, "Prisoners in 1994" (Washington, D.C.: U.S. Government Printing Office, August 1995).

Contact U.S. Department of Justice, Bureau of Justice Statistics Clearinghouse, Box 6000, Rockville, MD 20850. (800) 732-3277. A World Wide Web server is operated at http://ncjrs.aspensys.com:81/ncjrshome.html. Inquiries can also be sent by e-mail to askncjrs@aspensys.com.

State and federal prisoners in 1994

The number of prisoners under the jurisdiction of state or federal authorities at the end of 1994 in each state, and the number of prisoners per 100,000 resident population.

State	Prisoners	Prisoners per 100,000 Residents†
Alabama	19,573	450
Alaska	3,292	317
Arizona	19,746	459
Arkansas	8,836	353
California*	125,605	384
Colorado	10,717	289
Connecticut	14,380	321
Delaware	4,411	393
District of Columbia	10,943	1,583
Florida*	57,139	406
Georgia*	33,425	456
Hawaii	3,333	202
Idaho	2,964	258
Illinois*	36,351	310
Indiana	15,014	258
Iowa*	5,437	192
Kansas	6,373	249
Kentucky	11,066	288
Louisiana	24,092	530
Maine	1,537	118
Maryland	20,998	395
Massachusetts	11,282	171
Michigan*	40,775	428
Minnesota	4,572	100
Mississippi	11,274	408
Missouri	17,898	338
Montana	1,680	194
Nebraska	2,633	159
Nevada	7,122	460
New Hampshire	2,021	177
New Jersey	24,632	310
New Mexico	3,866	220
New York	66,750	367
North Carolina	23,639	322
North Dakota	536	78
Ohio	41,913	377
Oklahoma	16,631	508

[Continued]

State and federal prisoners in 1994

[Continued]

State	Prisoners	Prisoners per 100,000 Residents†
Oregon	6,936	175
Pennsylvania	28,302	235
Rhode Island	2,919	186
South Carolina	18,999	494
South Dakota	1,734	240
Tennessee	14,474	277
Texas	118,195	636
Utah	3,016	155
Vermont	1,301	168
Virginia	26,192	395
Washington	10,833	201
West Virginia*	1,930	106
Wisconsin	10,020	187
Wyoming	1,217	254
Total, state prisons	958,704	356
Total, federal prisons	95,034	30
U.S. Total	1,053,738	387

Note: Italics indicate prisons and jails form one integrated system
* Population figures are based on custody counts.
† Among prisoners with a sentence of more than one year.

Comments At the end of 1994, California, Texas, New York, Florida, and Ohio had the largest number of state prisoners, according to the Bureau of Justice Statistics. These five states together accounted for nearly 43% of all state prisoners that year. North Dakota, Wyoming, Vermont, Maine, and Montana had the lowest number of state prisoners.

The District of Columbia, Texas, Louisiana, Oklahoma, South Carolina, and Nevada had the largest number of prisoners per 100,000 population. This rate indicates the frequency for someone in a given state to be in one of its state prisons. North Dakota, Minnesota, West Virginia, Maine, and Utah had the lowest number per 100,000 population.

Source U.S. Department of Justice, Bureau of Justice Statistics, "Prisoners in 1994" (Washington, D.C.: U.S. Government Printing Office, August 1995).

Contact U.S. Department of Justice, Bureau of Justice Statistics Clearinghouse, Box 6000, Rockville, MD 20850. (800) 732-3277. A World Wide Web server is operated at http://ncjrs.aspensys.com:81/ncjrshome.html. Inquiries can also be sent by e-mail to askncjrs@aspensys.com.

How fast are the numbers of state and federal prisoners growing?

The percent change in the number of prisoners (sentenced to one year or more)
during 1993–94, 1989–94, and 1984–94.

State	Percent Change, 1993–94	Percent Change, 1989–94	Percent Change, 1984–94
Alabama	5.0	40.5	86.2
Alaska	–1.0	1.4	49.6
Arizona	10.8	49.3	148.6
Arkansas	9.1	33.1	94.4
California	4.8	43.6	190.7
Colorado	13.3	55.1	231.7
Connecticut	–0.1	66.4	79.8
Delaware	0.3	22.1	80.3
District of Columbia	0.6	34.8	141.0
Florida	8.0	42.9	113.5
Georgia	20.1	65.8	122.8
Hawaii	2.7	36.1	79.8
Idaho*	13.7	NA	NA
Illinois	5.9	47.8	113.5
Indiana	3.9	22.1	64.7
Iowa	11.0	51.7	91.7
Kansas	11.3	13.5	50.2
Kentucky	6.0	33.5	129.6
Louisiana	2.2	33.0	68.1
Maine	1.2	2.2	72.8
Maryland	3.8	29.1	59.6
Massachusetts*	1.9	NA	NA
Michigan	3.7	28.9	179.2
Minnesota	8.9	47.3	111.0
Mississippi	12.1	42.2	83.3
Missouri	10.6	28.6	104.1
Montana	9.0	26.5	74.3
Nebraska	5.0	13.7	65.3
Nevada	12.0	34.5	97.2
New Hampshire	13.9	73.3	247.8
New Jersey*	3.0	26.3	NA
New Mexico	9.1	17.9	92.8
New York	3.4	30.3	100.6
North Carolina	7.6	38.2	51.0
North Dakota	12.3	24.0	33.6
Ohio	3.1	37.2	125.1
Oklahoma	1.4	43.3	111.3

[Continued]

How fast are the numbers of state and federal prisoners growing?

[Continued]

State	Percent Change, 1993–94	Percent Change, 1989–94	Percent Change, 1984–94
Oregon*	6.8	NA	NA
Pennsylvania	8.6	38.3	117.7
Rhode Island	7.8	26.1	108.0
South Carolina	1.5	22.7	95.0
South Dakota	11.7	38.1	91.8
Tennessee	12.9	36.2	98.1
Texas	28.3	60.5	230.1
Utah	4.4	26.6	101.0
Vermont	9.9	56.7	159.5
Virginia	14.9	59.9	143.9
Washington	4.0	56.4	58.8
West Virginia	6.9	25.7	22.2
Wisconsin	13.0	40.5	91.4
Wyoming	7.9	18.6	68.1
Total, state prisons	8.7	40.6	124.8
Total, federal prisons	7.3	69.2	189.1
U.S. Total	8.6	42.5	128.8

* The methods or guidelines for counting prisoners changed during the time period analyzed here, making comparisons unsuitable.

Comments According to the Bureau of Justice Statistics, the growth in the state and federal prison population during 1994 averaged about 1,542 new prisoners per week.

Between 1993 and 1994, 16 states had increases of at least 10%. Texas, Georgia, Virginia, New Hampshire, and Idaho had the greatest percentage increases. In five states (Delaware, Maine, Oklahoma, South Carolina, and Massachusetts) and the District of Columbia, the number of sentenced prisoners increased by less than 2% during 1994. In Alaska and Connecticut, the number of sentenced prisoners declined. Remember that the percentage changes over one, five, or ten years for various states can vary significantly.

Source U.S. Department of Justice, Bureau of Justice Statistics, "Prisoners in 1994" (Washington, D.C.: U.S. Government Printing Office, August 1995).

Contact U.S. Department of Justice, Bureau of Justice Statistics Clearinghouse, Box 6000, Rockville, MD 20850. (800) 732-3277. A World Wide Web server is operated at http://ncjrs.aspensys.com:81/ncjrshome.html. Inquiries can also be sent by e-mail to askncjrs@aspensys.com.

How many people are in local jails?

Local jail inmates and their number per 100,000 U.S. residents, midyear 1983–94.

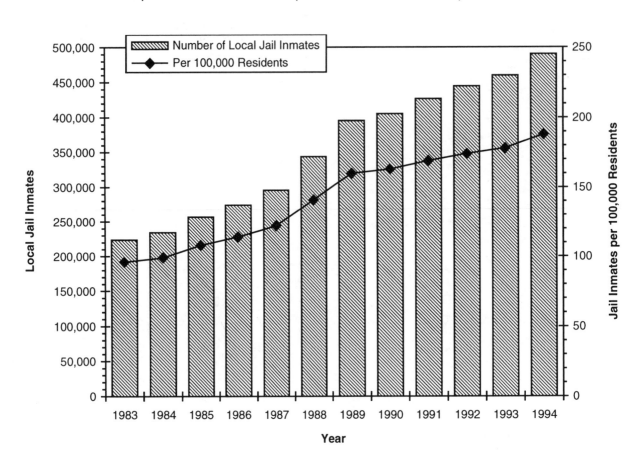

Year	Number of Local Jail Inmates	Per 100,000 Residents
1983	223,551	96
1984	234,500	99
1985	256,615	108
1986	274,444	114
1987	295,873	122
1988	343,569	141
1989	395,553	160
1990	405,320	163
1991	426,479	169
1992	444,584	174
1993	459,804	178
1994	490,442	188

Comments   The number of inmates held in local jails across the U.S. reached a record high of 490,442 in mid-1994. Local jails are operated by counties or municipalities, and are administered by local government agencies. As of mid-1994, inmates in local jails accounted for about one-third of all prisoners in the U.S.; the others were in state or federal prisons.

Between 1983 and 1994, the number of jail inmates increased by 119%. The annual average rate of increase was 7.5%. Between 1 July 1993 and 30 June 1994, the jail population grew by 30,638 inmates, the third largest annual increase recorded since 1983. This 12-month increase was the equivalent of a 6.7% rate of growth. In mid-1994 about 1 in every 398 adult U.S. residents was in a local jail.

There are several factors that have caused the jail population to increase so rapidly in recent years. There has been an increase in the annual number of adults arrested since the early 1980s. Also, there are now more felons sentenced to serve time in local jails. A rise in the number of convicted drug offenders has also expanded the jail population. Finally, more inmates are now held in local jails because of crowding in state or federal prisons.

Source   U.S. Department of Justice, Bureau of Justice Statistics, "Jails and Jail Inmates, 1993–94" (Washington, D.C.: U.S. Government Printing Office, April 1995).

Contact   U.S. Department of Justice, Bureau of Justice Statistics Clearinghouse, Box 6000, Rockville, MD 20850. (800) 732-3277. A World Wide Web server is operated at http://ncjrs.aspensys.com:81/ncjrshome.html. Inquiries can also be sent by e-mail to askncjrs@aspensys.com.

Which states have the highest concentrations of jail inmates?

Local jail facilities, inmates, and the number of inmates per 100,000 population for the 50 states and the District of Columbia, midyear 1993.

State	Number of Facilities	Number of Inmates	Inmates per 100,000 Population
Alabama	129	7,072	169
Alaska†	5	31	N/A
Arizona	33	7,231	184
Arkansas	83	2,846	117
California	136	69,298	222
Colorado	61	6,316	177
Connecticut	*	*	*
Delaware	*	*	*
District of Columbia	1	1,687	292
Florida	100	34,183	250
Georgia	202	22,663	328
Hawaii	*	*	*
Idaho	39	1,485	135
Illinois	93	14,549	124
Indiana	88	8,297	145
Iowa	90	1,602	57
Kansas	96	2,797	111
Kentucky	81	6,813	180
Louisiana	96	16,208	377
Maine	15	704	57
Maryland	33	9,358	188
Massachusetts	20	7,878	131
Michigan	89	12,479	132
Minnesota	75	3,654	81
Mississippi	95	4,851	184
Missouri	127	5,030	96
Montana	44	680	81
Nebraska	64	1,680	105
Nevada	20	2,987	215
New Hampshire	11	1,127	100
New Jersey	25	15,122	192
New Mexico	34	3,058	189
New York	78	29,809	164
North Carolina	104	8,939	129
North Dakota	25	361	57
Ohio	120	11,695	105
Oklahoma	100	4,102	127

[Continued]

Which states have the highest concentrations of jail inmates?

[Continued]

State	Number of Facilities	Number of Inmates	Inmates per 100,000 Population
Oregon	43	3,777	125
Pennsylvania	79	19,231	160
Rhode Island	*	*	*
South Carolina	55	5,713	157
South Dakota	28	623	87
Tennessee	111	14,375	282
Texas	267	55,395	307
Utah	25	1,895	102
Vermont	*	*	*
Virginia	93	14,623	225
Washington	56	7,435	141
West Virginia	41	1,771	97
Wisconsin	72	7,879	156
Wyoming	22	495	105
U.S. Total	3,304	459,804	178

* These states have jail systems that are integrated with the state prison system and were excluded from the report.
† Except for five locally operated jails, Alaska has an integrated jail-prison system.

Comments As of mid-1993, there were 459,804 inmates in 3,304 jails across the U.S. The ratio of jail inmates to population was 178 for every 100,000 residents. These figures include all but five states, where the jails are integrated with the state prison systems.

From the reporting states, Texas, Georgia, California, Alabama, and Missouri had the most jail facilities. These five states together had 26% of the nation's jails. California, Texas, Florida, New York, and Georgia had the most jail inmates. About 46% of all jail inmates were in one of those five states. Alaska, North Dakota, Wyoming, South Dakota, Montana, and Maine had the fewest inmates, together accounting for about 6.3% of all jail inmates.

The number of jails and inmates generally are higher in states with large populations, and lower in states with small populations. However, comparing number of inmates to state population shows that Louisiana, Georgia, and Texas have the largest ratios; Iowa, Maine, and North Dakota, the smallest.

Source U.S. Department of Justice, Bureau of Justice Statistics, "Jails and Jail Inmates, 1993–94" (Washington, D.C.: U.S. Government Printing Office, April 1995).

Contact U.S. Department of Justice, Bureau of Justice Statistics Clearinghouse, Box 6000, Rockville, MD 20850. (800) 732-3277. A World Wide Web server is operated at http://ncjrs.aspensys.com:81/ncjrshome.html. Inquiries can also be sent by e-mail to askncjrs@aspensys.com.

How frequently does someone convicted of a homicide receive a life in prison or death sentence?

New court commitments to state prisons in 1992: inmates sentenced to life in prison or to death, by homicide offense.

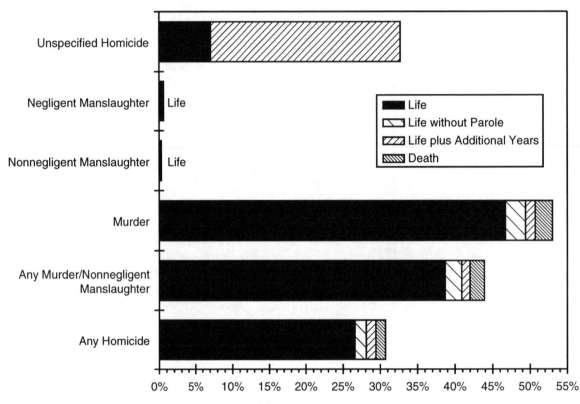

Percent of Inmates Sentenced to Prison

Type of Homicide Offense	Number of Inmates Sentenced	Life	Life Without Parole	Life Plus Additional Years	Death
Unspecified homicide	211	7.1%	0.0%	25.6%	0.0%
Negligent manslaughter	3,199	0.6%	0.0%	0.0%	0.0%
Nonnegligent manslaughter	1,241	0.3%	0.0%	0.0%	0.0%
Murder	5,970	46.7%	2.7%	1.3%	2.3%
Any murder/nonnegligent manslaughter	7,211	38.7%	2.2%	1.1%	1.9%
Any homicide	10,621	26.6%	1.5%	1.3%	1.3%

Comments The type of sentence that a person convicted of a homicide receives depends upon the type of homicide. Murder and non-negligent manslaughter is the willful killing of one person by another. Manslaughter is the unlawful killing of one person by another, but not as a result of hostility. Negligent manslaughter is the killing of another person through gross negligence.

Of all those who were convicted of a homicide and sentenced to state prisons in 1992, 26.6% received life sentences, 1.5% received life without parole, 1.3% received life plus additional years, and 1.3% received death sentences. The remaining 69.4% were sentenced to serve a fixed number of months in prison.

Murder was the type of homicide where severe punishment was most commonly issued. Over half (53%) of those sentenced to state prisons in 1992 for murder received some type of life in prison or death sentence. Life sentences accounted for 46.7%; life without parole, 2.7%; life plus additional years, 1.3%; and death sentences, 2.3%.

Source U.S. Department of Justice, Bureau of Justice Statistics, *National Corrections Reporting Program, 1992* (Washington, D.C.: U.S. Government Printing Office, 1994), p. 24.

Contact U.S. Department of Justice, Bureau of Justice Statistics Clearinghouse, Box 6000, Rockville, MD 20850. (800) 732-3277. A World Wide Web server is operated at http://ncjrs.aspensys.com:81/ncjrshome.html. Inquiries can also be sent by e-mail to askncjrs@aspensys.com.

How often do murderers receive a life sentence or death sentence?

Percent distribution of 12,549 murder convictions by state courts in 1992, by type of sentence imposed.

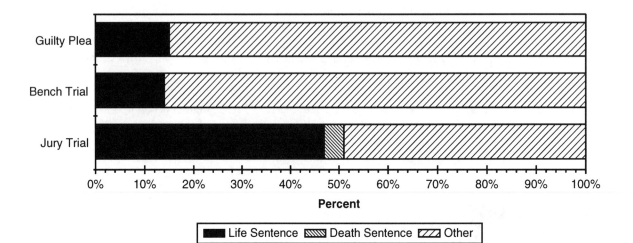

Type of Conviction	Life Sentence	Death Sentence	Other*
Jury Trial	47%	4%	49%
Bench Trial	14%	†	86%
Guilty Plea	15%	†	85%

* Includes all prison sentences of a fixed duration, and a small number of jail and probation sentences.
† Less than 0.5%.

Comments Death sentences and life sentences are the most severe forms of punishment that a legal justice system can give to convicted felons.

A death sentence places the felon into a state prison to await execution, but a lengthy appeals process usually delays the execution for several years. A life sentence is given frequently to murderers, especially to repeat offenders or for especially vicious murders occurring in states that do not have a death penalty.

In 1992, murderers convicted by a jury were the most likely to have received the death penalty (4%) or a life prison sentence (47%). Murderers convicted by a judge in a bench trial were given life sentences 14% of the time, and murderers who pleaded guilty were given life sentences 15% of the time. It may seem odd that people who pleaded guilty were given life sentences a little more frequently than those who went to trial, but some of these murderers may have pleaded guilty in order to avoid a death sentence.

Source U.S. Department of Justice, Bureau of Justice Statistics, "Felony Sentences in State Courts, 1992" (Washington, D.C.: U.S. Government Printing Office, January 1995).

Contact U.S. Department of Justice, Bureau of Justice Statistics Clearinghouse, Box 6000, Rockville, MD 20850. (800) 732-3277. A World Wide Web server is operated at http://ncjrs.aspensys.com:81/ncjrshome.html. Inquiries can also be sent by e-mail to askncjrs@aspensys.com.

How many people enter and leave prison within a year?

Prisoners admitted and released from a state or federal jurisdiction in the U.S. during 1992.

Type of Admission or Release	Admissions	Releases
New court commitments	334,301	—
Parole or other conditional release violators returned	141,961	—
Escapees and AWOLs returned	10,031	—
Returns from appeal or bond	1,054	—
Transfers from other jurisdictions	5,049	—
Other admissions	3,360	—
Conditional releases	—	357,731
Unconditional releases	—	58,425
Escapees and AWOLs	—	10,706
Out on appeal or bond	—	1,203
Transfers to other jurisdictions	—	6,201
Deaths	—	2,088
Other releases	—	10,751
Totals	495,756	447,105

Comments   In 1992, there were 495,756 admissions and 447,105 prisoner releases occurring at state and federal prisons across the U.S. The cycle of releasing some prisoners while admitting others resulted in a net gain of 48,651 prisoners (about 11%) during 1992.

The majority of admissions were due to new court commitments (recently convicted individuals who received a prison sentence), accounting for 67% of all admissions. Prisoners often will receive a conditional release (such as a parole), which requires them to follow certain rules of conduct and to frequently report their status to a parole officer. Individuals who had previously been conditionally released but then violated the terms of that release accounted for about 29% of the 1992 admissions. Escapees and prisoners AWOL (absent without leave) who were caught accounted for about 2% of the admissions. Prisoners returning from an appeal or bond, transfers from other jurisdictions, and other admissions accounted for the remaining 2%.

Conditional releases accounted for 357,731 of the 447,105 releases (80%). Conditional releases include paroles, probations, and supervised mandatory releases. Unconditional releases (such as expirations of sentences and commutations) numbered 58,425 and comprised 13% of all releases. Over 2% of the releases in 1992 occurred illegally, due to 10,706 prisoners escaping or remaining AWOL. Prisoners who were out on an appeal or bond, transferred to another jurisdiction, or who died in prison together accounted for just over 2% of the releases. Other releases accounted for the remaining 3%.

Source   U.S. Department of Justice, Bureau of Justice Statistics, *Correctional Populations in the United States, 1992* (Washington, D.C.: U.S. Government Printing Office, 1995), pp. 73, 74.

Contact   U.S. Department of Justice, Bureau of Justice Statistics Clearinghouse, Box 6000, Rockville, MD 20850. (800) 732-3277. A World Wide Web server is operated at http://ncjrs.aspensys.com:81/ncjrshome.html. Inquiries can also be sent by e-mail to askncjrs@aspensys.com.

Annual turnover of state prisoners

Turnover rates* of sentenced prisoners under state jurisdiction, and percentage of admissions to state prisons due to probation/parole violation, 1980–92.

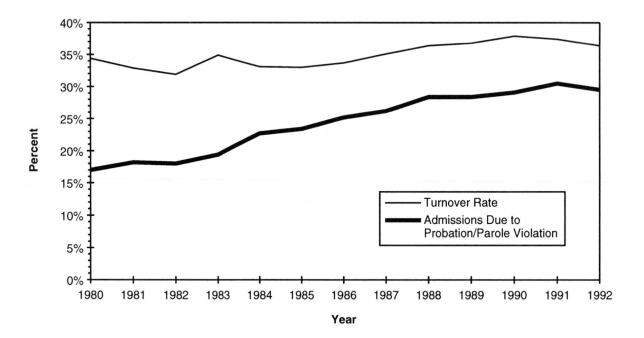

Year	Turnover Rate*	Admissions Due to Probation/parole Violation
1980	34.4%	17.0
1981	32.9%	18.2
1982	31.9%	18.0
1983	34.9%	19.4
1984	33.1%	22.7
1985	33.0%	23.4
1986	33.7%	25.2
1987	35.1%	26.2
1988	36.4%	28.4
1989	36.8%	28.4
1990	37.9%	29.1
1991	37.4%	30.5
1992	36.4%	29.5

* Releases as a percent of the number of inmates at the beginning of the year plus admissions. The turnover rate is calculated by dividing the number of sentenced prisoners released during the year by the number of inmates present at the beginning of the year plus the number of inmates admitted during the year.

Comments The Bureau of Justice Statistics calculates the turnover rate among state prisoners to examine the flow at which criminals enter and leave state prisons. The turnover rate shows the percentage of prisoners who were released during the year compared to the number present and admitted during that year. This means that in 1992, out of all the state prisoners present and admitted, 36.4% were released.

The turnover rate of prisoners in state prisons increased from 34.4% in 1980 to 36.4% in 1992. The turnover rate was at its highest in 1990, at 37.9%. Admissions to state prisons due to probation or parole violation also have increased since the early 1980s. In 1980, only 17% of all the inmates entering state prisons were probation/parole violators, but this rate climbed to 30.5% by 1991 and remained at 29.5% in 1992. A probation or parole violator is someone who was convicted of a crime but permitted to remain in society as long as certain restrictions and rules of conduct are obeyed (probation allows the criminal to remain free without serving any time in prison, while parole is an early release from prison).

There probably is a relationship between these two rates, although it is not possible to tell from these statistics which rate affects the other. In general, these rates indicate that a higher turnover rate also involves a higher rate of admissions due to probation/parole violation. This situation may be because turnover involves releasing prisoners through parole. So if more prisoners receive parole, it is logical to assume that more violations and consequent re-admissions will also occur. This does not necessarily mean, however, that a higher proportion of prisoners released on parole are later becoming parole violators.

Source U.S. Department of Justice, Bureau of Justice Statistics, *Correctional Populations in the United States, 1992* (Washington, D.C.: U.S. Government Printing Office, 1995), p. 56.

Contact U.S. Department of Justice, Bureau of Justice Statistics Clearinghouse, Box 6000, Rockville, MD 20850. (800) 732-3277. A World Wide Web server is operated at http://ncjrs.aspensys.com:81/ncjrshome.html. Inquiries can also be sent by e-mail to askncjrs@aspensys.com.

Admissions and first releases of violent prisoners

Violent offenders in state prisons: new court commitments and first releases, 1994.

State	Violent New Court Commitments to State Prison	Violent First Releases from State Prison	Net Gain (Loss)
Alaska	464	228	236
Arizona	1,383	917	466
Arkansas	1,031	978	53
California	10,308	9,939	369
Colorado	1,052	600	452
Connecticut	965	343	622
Delaware	351	388	(37)
District of Columbia	354	344	10
Florida	6,931	6,486	445
Georgia	2,621	1,420	1,201
Hawaii	251	170	81
Idaho	115	75	40
Illinois	5,581	4,674	907
Iowa	532	558	(26)
Kansas	395	38	357
Kentucky	945	780	165
Louisiana	1,248	1,190	58
Maine	197	188	9
Maryland	2,233	2,421	(188)
Massachusetts	1,268	1,684	(416)
Michigan	3,241	1,828	1,413
Minnesota	356	177	179
Mississippi	1,112	746	366
Missouri	2,116	1,167	949
Montana	256	189	67
Nebraska	377	337	40
New Hampshire	253	138	115
New Jersey	2,406	2,380	26
New York	7,715	5,533	2,182
North Carolina	2,521	1,882	639
North Dakota	112	66	46
Ohio	3,879	2,585	1,294
Oklahoma	1,634	867	767
Oregon	682	608	74
Pennsylvania	2,250	1,247	1,003
South Carolina	1,450	1,205	245
South Dakota	236	160	76

[Continued]

Admissions and first releases of violent prisoners

[Continued]

State	Violent New Court Commitments to State Prison	Violent First Releases from State Prison	Net Gain (Loss)
Tennessee	905	992	(87)
Texas	4,440	3,201	1,239
Utah	209	172	37
Vermont	66	70	(4)
Washington	1,507	1,219	288
West Virginia	202	147	55
Wisconsin	1,254	932	322
Wyoming	99	13	86
Total*	81,535	61,282	20,253

* Among all participating states. Complete data was not available for Alabama, Indiana, Nevada, New Mexico, Rhode Island, and Virginia.

Comments

During the 1990s, state prisons across the U.S. have been admitting over 80,000 violent offenders per year. At the same time, state prisons have also been releasing about 60,000 violent offenders per year. In 1994, reporting state agencies recorded 81,535 admissions and 61,282 first releases of violent offenders, for a net gain of 20,253 persons. State-by-state data varied substantially between 1992 and 1994.

Violent crimes involve personal injury, threat of injury, and theft or attempted theft by force or threat of force. The releases in these statistics count prisoners who were released for the first time on the current sentence, and exclude prisoners who had previously been released on parole, readmitted on the same sentence, and then released again.

The average violent prisoner who was admitted during 1992–94 received a sentence of about ten years, but expected to serve slightly less than five years. Among released prisoners, the average sentence for a violent crime was eight years, and the average time served was less than four years.

Source

U.S. Department of Justice, Bureau of Justice Statistics, "Violent Offenders in State Prison: Sentences and Time Served" (Washington, D.C.: U.S. Government Printing Office, July 1995).

Contact

U.S. Department of Justice, Bureau of Justice Statistics Clearinghouse, Box 6000, Rockville, MD 20850. (800) 732-3277. A World Wide Web server is operated at http://ncjrs.aspensys.com:81/ncjrshome.html. Inquiries can also be sent by e-mail to askncjrs@aspensys.com.

What happens to those leaving parole?

Characteristics of adults who left parole in 1992.

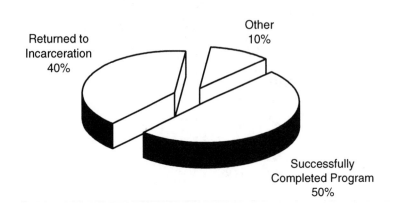

Parole Status	Number of Adults on Parole from State or Federal Courts
Successfully completed program	163,296
Returned to incarceration	133,738
With new sentence	40,706
With parole revoked	87,083
With revocation or charges pending	5,949
Other*	34,585
Total	331,619

* Includes discharged absconders, 1,925; discharged to detainers/warrants, 4,435; transferred to another state, 4,043; death, 3,931; and all other conditions, 20,251.

Comments In 1992, state and federal courts recorded 634,255 adults on parole. That year, 363,110 adults entered and 331,619 adults left parole programs.

Of those who left parole, however, only 50% did so through a successful completion, and 40% returned to prison. The remaining 10% consisted of individuals who were absent, transferred, or who died during the year. An "absconder" refers to a parolee who failed to report to the parole authority or left the area without permission. A discharged absconder is a parolee who was formally dismissed from the parole authority even if no arrest warrant was issued. Parolees discharged to a detainer or warrant include those who are wanted in another jurisdiction, or those who are released to a noncorrectional agency (such as a mental hospital or half-way house).

Source U.S. Department of Justice, Bureau of Justice Statistics, *Correctional Populations in the United States, 1992* (Washington, D.C.: U.S. Government Printing Office, 1995) p. 104.

Contact U.S. Department of Justice, Bureau of Justice Statistics Clearinghouse, Box 6000, Rockville, MD 20850. (800) 732-3277. A World Wide Web server is operated at http://ncjrs.aspensys.com:81/ncjrshome.html. Inquiries can also be sent by e-mail to askncjrs@aspensys.com.

How long does a criminal usually stay in prison before receiving a parole?

First entries to parole supervision from state prison in 1992: sentence length, time served, and percent of sentence served, by offense.

Offense	Average Sentence Length* (Months)	Average Time Served (Months)	Percent of Sentence Served in Prison†
Violent offenses	117	36	31.1%
Homicide	173	58	33.6%
Murder/nonnegligent manslaughter	215	74	34.4%
Murder	256	82	32.1%
Nonnegligent manslaughter	150	61	40.8%
Negligent manslaughter	114	36	31.2%
Unspecified homicide	108	29	26.9%
Kidnapping	171	44	25.6%
Rape	148	60	40.3%
Other sexual assault	91	32	35.1%
Robbery	126	37	29.5%
Assault	83	23	27.9%
Other violent	69	22	32.1%
Property offenses	93	18	19.0%
Burglary	109	22	19.9%
Larceny-theft	76	13	17.4%
Motor vehicle theft	64	14	21.5%
Arson	101	28	27.7%
Fraud	82	14	16.8%
Stolen property	109	15	14.1%
Other property	74	13	18.0%
Drug offenses	79	16	20.4%
Possession	71	14	19.6%
Trafficking	85	18	20.8%
Other/unspecified	69	14	19.6%
Public order offenses	51	12	24.1%
Weapons	66	17	25.6%
Driving while intoxicated	33	9	26.0%
Other public order	58	13	22.0%
Other offenses	88	15	17.5%
All offenses	90	21	23.5%

* Excludes sentences of life without parole, life plus additional years, life, and death.
† Calculated by dividing time served in prison by total sentence.

Comments

In 1992, there were 198,009 prisoners released from state prisons (from 36 reporting states) and placed on parole. The majority were male, minority group members, and in their late twenties. Of all those released to parole for the first time, the average prison sentence was 90 months (7.5 years), of which the average time served was just 21 months (1.75 years). Thus, the average state prisoner served 23.5% of the sentence before being released.

Some crimes receive harsher sentences, but those crimes are not always the ones which result in the longest time in prison or the highest percentage of time served before parole. The highest average sentence lengths among those who were released on parole were for the following offenses (in months):

murder, 256; kidnapping, 171; nonnegligent manslaughter, 150; and rape, 148.

The highest average time actually served was 82 months for murder, 61 months for nonnegligent manslaughter, 60 months for rape, and 44 months for kidnapping. However, the highest percentage of time actually served was for nonnegligent manslaughter (40.8% of sentence), followed by rape (40.3%), other sexual assault (35.1%), and then murder (32.1%).

Keep in mind that these averages do not include death or life sentences where no parole was possible. Obviously, such inclusion would raise the average sentence and time-served lengths for the most serious crimes.

Source

U.S. Department of Justice, Bureau of Justice Statistics, *National Corrections Reporting Program, 1992* (Washington, D.C.: U.S. Government Printing Office, 1994), p. 61.

Contact

U.S. Department of Justice, Bureau of Justice Statistics Clearinghouse, Box 6000, Rockville, MD 20850. (800) 732-3277. A World Wide Web server is operated at http://ncjrs.aspensys.com:81/ncjrshome.html. Inquiries can also be sent by e-mail to askncjrs@aspensys.com.

Historical trends in U.S. executions from the 1890s to the mid-1990s

The number of executions per decade under civil authority (local or state) and illegal lynchings.

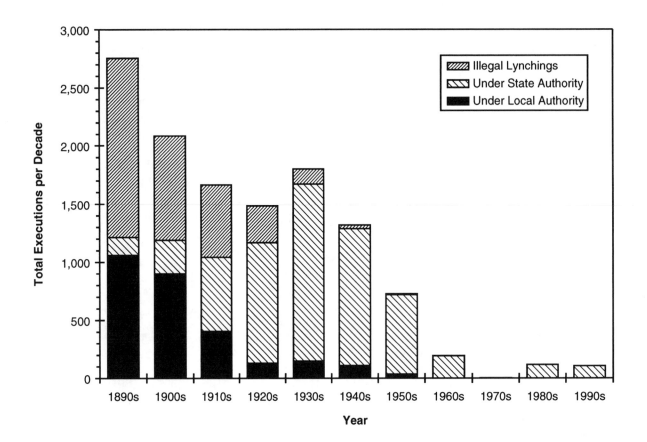

Decade	Under Local Authority	Under State Authority	Illegal Lynchings	Total per Decade (Legal and Illegal)
1890s	1,060	155	1,540	2,755
1900s	901	289	895	1,995*
1910s	406	636	621	1,663
1920s	131	1,038	315	1,484
1930s	147	1,523	130	1,800
1940s	110	1,177	33	1,292*
1950s	35	684	8	721*
1960s	0	192	1	192*
1970s	0	3	0	3
1980s	0	117	0	117
1990s†	0	106	0	106

* The total shown is less than the sum of the categories because of inconsistencies among the data sources. The difference between the total shown and the sum of the categories for the 1900s is 90; for the 1940s, 28; for the 1950s, 6; and for the 1960s, 1.

† Includes only the data for 1990, 1991, 1992, and 1993.

Comments The earliest recorded execution committed in the U.S. under state authority was in 1864. During 1864–90, 57 persons were executed under state authority. In the 1890s, executions performed under state authority accounted for 12.8% of all legal executions and 5.6% of all executions (legal and illegal). Since the 1960s, 100% of the executions performed under civil authority have been state executions.

Executions performed under the local authorities made up the majority of all legal executions in the U.S. during the 1890s and 1900s. The power for local governments to perform executions, however, greatly diminished during this century. Perhaps the transfer of death penalty power from local to state governments was partially due to increased technology. Improved communications made it easier to centralize the decision-making about executions with state governments.

Illegal lynchings (hangings) were commonplace in the U.S. during the late 1800s. Rural areas often had small numbers of law enforcement officers trying to cover large jurisdictions. When crimes occurred in these remote areas, local groups of citizens would often bypass the legal justice system. This spur-of-the-moment form of "justice" denied the accused of the right to a fair and impartial trial. As a result, these illegal executions were often performed in haste. No one will ever know how many of the people that were illegally lynched would have been found guilty by the legal justice system.

Blacks were disproportionately often the victims of lynchings, either as scapegoats (innocent victims that were the object of ridicule) or because of vengeance. As the number of illegal lynchings declined, the percentage involving black victims increased. In the 1880s, blacks accounted for 44% of lynching victims, but that figure gradually rose to 94% by the 1950s.

Source U.S. Department of Justice, Bureau of Justice Statistics, *Historical Corrections Statistics in the United States, 1850–1984* (Washington, D.C.: U.S. Government Printing Office, 1986), p. 10.

U.S. Department of Justice, Bureau of Justice Statistics, "Capital Punishment 1993" (Washington, D.C.: U.S. Government Printing Office, December 1994).

Barnes, H.E., and Teeters, N.K., *New Horizons in Criminology* (Englewood Cliffs, N.J.: Prentice-Hall, 1942), p. 425.

Bedau, *The Death Penalty in America* (New York: Anchor Press, 1967), p. 35.

Bowers, William; Pierce, Glen; and McDevitt, John, *Legal Homicide: Death as Punishment in America 1864–1967* (Boston: Northeastern University Press, 1984).

Bye, R.T., *Capital Punishment in the United States* (Philadelphia: The Committee of Philanthropic Labor of Philadelphia Yearly Meeting of Friends, 1919), pp. 57–58.

Ploski, Harry, and Williams, James, *The Negro Almanac: A Reference Work on the Afro-American* (New York: Wiley, 1983), p. 218.

Sellin, T., "A Note on Capital Executions in the U.S." (*British Journal of Delinquency* 1:6, 1950), p. 7.

Contact U.S. Department of Justice, Bureau of Justice Statistics Clearinghouse, Box 6000, Rockville, MD 20850. (800) 732-3277. A World Wide Web server is operated at

http://ncjrs.aspensys.com:81/ncjrshome.html. Inquiries can also be sent by e-mail to askncjrs@aspensys.com.

How many prisoners have been executed in the U.S.?

Prisoners executed under civil authority, 1930–93.

Year	Executions	Year	Executions	Year	Executions
1930	155	1952	83	1973	0
1931	153	1953	62	1974	0
1932	140	1954	81	1975	0
1933	160	1955	76	1976	0
1934	168	1956	65	1977	1
1935	199	1957	65	1978	0
1936	195	1958	49	1979	2
1937	147	1959	49	1980	0
1938	190	1960	56	1981	1
1939	160	1961	42	1982	2
1940	124	1962	47	1983	5
1941	123	1963	21	1984	21
1942	147	1964	15	1985	18
1943	131	1965	7	1986	18
1944	120	1966	1	1987	25
1945	117	1967	2	1988	11
1946	131	1968	0	1989	16
1947	153	1969	0	1990	23
1948	119	1970	0	1991	14
1949	119	1971	0	1992	31
1950	82	1972	0	1993	38
1951	105				

Comments

The legal killing of a criminal by carrying out a death sentence is a type of punishment called "capital punishment." By taking away the criminal's life, capital punishment is the ultimate penalty. From 1930 to 1993, 4,085 prisoners were executed in the U.S., mostly during the 1930s and 1940s.

In 1972, the Supreme Court ruled that laws regulating the death penalty in various states were defined as being unconstitutional in the form in which they existed at the time. This ruling prevented any executions from taking place. In 1976, however, the Supreme Court upheld revised state laws regarding capital punishment, which made it legally possible again for states to carry out death sentences. From 1977 to 1993, 226 prisoners were executed.

Capital punishment offenses differ between the states, and not all states have a death penalty. Most states with a death penalty option cite first-degree murder as a capital offense. In some states, certain types of murders (usually one committed during the course of a felony) also qualify as capital offenses. Some federal crimes also can be capital offenses, such as certain crimes involving contract killing, killing an on-duty law enforcement officer, espionage, or assassination of the President, Vice President, a member of Congress, or a Supreme Court Justice.

Source

U.S. Department of Justice, Bureau of Justice Statistics, *Sourcebook of Criminal Justice Statistics—1992* (Washington, D.C.: U.S. Government Printing Office, 1993), p. 680.

U.S. Department of Justice, Bureau of Justice Statistics, "Capital Punishment 1992" (Washington, D.C.: U.S. Government Printing Office, 1993).

U.S. Department of Justice, Bureau of Justice Statistics, "Capital Punishment 1993" (Washington, D.C.: U.S. Government Printing Office, 1994).

Contact

U.S. Department of Justice, Bureau of Justice Statistics Clearinghouse, Box 6000, Rockville, MD 20850. (800) 732-3277. A World Wide Web server is operated at http://ncjrs.aspensys.com:81/ncjrshome.html. Inquiries can also be sent by e-mail to askncjrs@aspensys.com.

How frequently are persons serving a death sentence executed?

The number of persons under sentence of death, the number of executions, and the percentage of the death sentence population executed in the U.S. during 1953–93.

Year	Number of Persons Under Sentence of Death	Number of Executions	Percentage of Death Sentence Population Executed
1953	131	62	47.3%
1954	147	81	55.1%
1955	125	76	60.8%
1956	146	65	44.5%
1957	151	65	43.0%
1958	147	49	33.3%
1959	164	49	29.9%
1960	210	56	26.7%
1961	257	42	16.3%
1962	267	47	17.6%
1963	297	21	7.0%
1964	315	15	4.8%
1965	331	7	2.1%
1966	406	1	0.2%
1967	435	2	0.5%
1968	517	0	0.0%
1969	575	0	0.0%
1970	631	0	0.0%
1971	642	0	0.0%
1972	334	0	0.0%
1973	134	0	0.0%
1974	244	0	0.0%
1975	488	0	0.0%
1976	420	0	0.0%
1977	423	1	0.2%
1978	483	0	0.0%
1979	595	2	0.3%
1980	697	0	0.0%
1981	863	1	0.1%
1982	1,073	2	0.2%
1983	1,216	5	0.4%
1984	1,421	21	1.5%
1985	1,589	18	1.1%
1986	1,800	18	1.0%
1987	1,964	25	1.3%

[Continued]

How frequently are persons serving a death sentence executed?

[Continued]

Year	Number of Persons Under Sentence of Death	Number of Executions	Percentage of Death Sentence Population Executed
1988	2,111	11	0.5%
1989	2,232	16	0.7%
1990	2,346	23	0.1%
1991	2,466	14	0.6%
1992	2,575	31	1.2%
1993	2,716	38	1.4%

Comments   In 1972, the U.S. Supreme Court ruled that laws regulating the death penalty in various states were unconstitutional. This ruling prevented any executions from taking place. In the years immediately preceding this ruling, the number of prisoners serving under sentence of death declined, partly because of questions over the lawfulness of capital punishment. In 1976, however, the Supreme Court upheld revised state laws regarding capital punishment, which made it legally possible again for states to carry out death sentences.

Ever since the Supreme Court made that ruling, the number of prisoners serving under sentence of death has soared. In 1973, there were only 134 prisoners sentenced to death, but by 1993 that number had risen to 2,716, a twenty-fold increase.

The number of executions has also risen since the mid-1970s, but not nearly at the same rate as with the death sentence population. The result is that within any recent year, only a small percentage of all the prisoners serving under sentence of death were executed. For example, in 1955, there were 125 prisoners serving under sentence of death and 76 executions, for an execution rate of 60.8%. In 1993, there were 38 executions among the 2,716 serving under sentence of death, for an execution rate of 1.4%. It is important to remember that this rate only indicates how frequently executions were performed, and does not follow individual cases since prisoners are added and subtracted from death sentence lists every year for various reasons.

Source   U.S. Department of Justice, Bureau of Justice Statistics. *Correctional Populations in the United States, 1992* (Washington, D.C.: U.S. Government Printing Office, 1995).

U.S. Department of Justice, Bureau of Justice Statistics, "Capital Punishment 1993" (Washington, D.C.: U.S. Government Printing Office, December 1994), p. 12.

Contact   U.S. Department of Justice, Bureau of Justice Statistics Clearinghouse, Box 6000, Rockville, MD 20850. (800) 732-3277. A World Wide Web server is operated at

http://ncjrs.aspensys.com:81/ncjrshome.html. Inquiries can also be sent by e-mail to askncjrs@aspensys.com.

Which states executed prisoners most frequently in 1994?

Executions in states with a death penalty during 1994, and the percentage of each state's death row population executed.

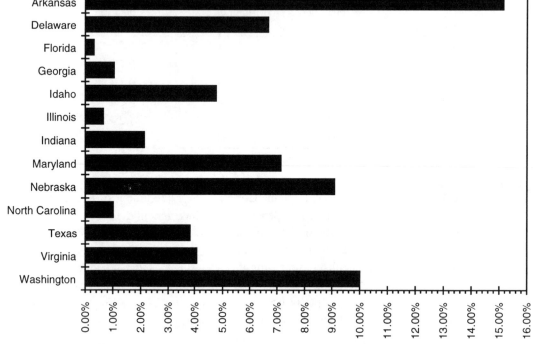

Percentage of Death Row Populations Executed in 1994

State	Prisoners under sentence of death at the start of 1994	Prisoners executed during 1994	Percent of state's death sentence prisoners executed	Method of execution authorized
Arkansas	33	5	15.15%	lethal injection*
Delaware	15	1	6.67%	lethal injection
Florida	325	1	0.31%	electrocution
Georgia	96	1	1.04%	electrocution
Idaho	21	1	4.76%	lethal injection*
Illinois	151	1	0.66%	lethal injection
Indiana	47	1	2.13%	electrocution
Maryland	14	1	7.14%	lethal gas
Nebraska	11	1	9.09%	electrocution
North Carolina	99	1	1.01%	lethal gas*
Texas	366	14	3.83%	lethal injection
Virginia	49	2	4.08%	electrocution
Washington	10	1	10.00%	lethal injection*

* The state authorizes two methods of execution.

Comments In 1994, 13 different states executed 31 persons. The average time that the offender served in prison before being executed in 1994 was about 10.2 years. As of 1994, 37 states had some form of capital punishment authorized. Lethal injection was the most common method of execution (authorized in 27 states), electrocution was next (12 states), followed by lethal gas (7), hanging (4), and firing squad (1). Several states authorize more than one type of execution, and may even allow the condemned prisoner to select the method. The jurisdictions without a death penalty include the following: Alaska, the District of Columbia, Hawaii, Iowa, Maine, Massachusetts, Michigan, Minnesota, New York, North Dakota, Rhode Island, Vermont, West Virginia, and Wisconsin.

Texas led the nation in the number of executions in 1994, at 14, followed by Arkansas (5) and Virginia (2). Each of the other states had only a single execution in 1994. Although those three states accounted for about 68% of the persons executed in 1994, the frequency of execution among the states for that year varied. The frequency of executions refers to the percentage of each state's death row population that was put to death during that year. For example, Arkansas had the highest frequency of executions in 1994. Out of the 33 Arkansas death row prisoners at the beginning of 1994, there were five executed during the course of the year, for a frequency of 15.15%. These percentages do not take into account prisoners new to death row in 1994. Also excluded are any prisoners that were removed from death row by a means other than execution (such as death by natural causes or suicide). After Arkansas, the states with the highest frequency of execution in 1994 were Washington (10%) and Nebraska (9.09%).

It is important to remember that these figures cover only one year. The year-to-year percentages can vary significantly, especially in states that typically might have only one execution per year or a small number of prisoners on death row. The laws in some states might emphasize the initial placement of prisoners on death row, but not necessarily on executing them. That emphasis might result in a state having a low frequency of execution. Other states' laws might focus more on the execution itself rather than on death row placement; such an emphasis might result in a state having a higher frequency of execution.

Source U.S. Department of Justice, Bureau of Justice Statistics, "Capital Punishment 1994" (Washington, D.C.: U.S. Government Printing Office, February 1996).

Contact U.S. Department of Justice, Bureau of Justice Statistics Clearinghouse, Box 6000, Rockville, MD 20850. (800) 732-3277. A World Wide Web server is operated at http://ncjrs.aspensys.com:81/ncjrshome.html. Inquiries can also be sent by e-mail to askncjrs@aspensys.com.

How often does someone accused of a felony have a prior conviction?

The number of prior felony convictions of felony defendants in the 75 most populous U.S. counties during 1992.
Defendants are classified by the most serious current arrest charge.

Most Serious Current Arrest Charge	Number of Defendants	No Prior Convictions	Non-Felony Conviction Only	1 Prior Felony Conviction	2–4 Prior Felony Convictions	5–9 Prior Felony Convictions	10 or More Prior Felony Convictions
All Offenses	49,923	45%	17%	15%	17%	5%	1%
Murder	552	53%	12%	15%	14%	5%	0%
Rape	725	56%	18%	13%	12%	1%	0%
Robbery	4,434	42%	15%	15%	21%	5%	2%
Assault	6,146	50%	17%	14%	13%	5%	1%
Burglary	5,926	35%	18%	16%	23%	7%	2%
Theft	6,251	44%	17%	14%	17%	7%	2%
Drug sales/trafficking	8,333	44%	17%	18%	16%	5%	1%
Weapons	1,418	49%	17%	16%	15%	3%	0%
Driving-related	604	26%	39%	15%	15%	4%	1%

In 1992, the 75 largest counties in the U.S. accounted for 37% of the nation's population and about half of all reported crimes, arrests, and felony convictions. The Bureau of Justice Statistics' National Pretrial Reporting Program (NPRP) tracks felony cases to collect criminal history information on felony defendants in these counties. According to the 1992 NPRP, about 38% of all defendants had at least one prior felony conviction, 17% had a prior non-felony (e.g., misdemeanor) conviction, and 45% had no prior convictions.

Burglary (47%) and robbery (43%) defendants were the most likely to have a prior felony conviction at the time of their most recent arrest. About 39% of theft and drug trafficking defendants and 35% of murder and driving-related defendants had a felony conviction record. Defendants charged with a weapons felony had at least one prior felony conviction 34% of the time, and 33% of assault defendants had a prior felony conviction. Rape defendants (26%) were the least likely to have a prior felony conviction.

Crimes with the objective of stealing cash or property were consistently the most common offenses among convicted habitual felons. Defendants with more than two prior felony convictions were most often those currently charged with burglary (32%), robbery (28%), or theft (26%).

Source U.S. Department of Justice, Bureau of Justice Statistics, *Felony Defendants in Large Urban Counties, 1992* (Washington, D.C.: U.S. Government Printing Office, 1995), p. 13.

Contact U.S. Department of Justice, Bureau of Justice Statistics Clearinghouse, Box 6000, Rockville, MD 20850. (800) 732-3277. A World Wide Web server is operated at http://ncjrs.aspensys.com:81/ncjrshome.html. Inquiries can also be sent by e-mail to askncjrs@aspensys.com.

What types of civil cases are most common?

Number of civil cases and percent that went to a jury trial (by case type) in state courts of the nation's 75 largest counties during 1992.

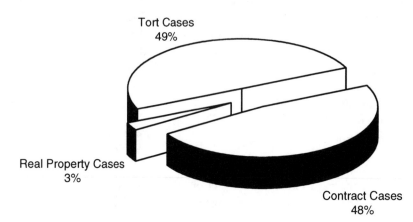

Tort Cases
49%

Real Property Cases
3%

Contract Cases
48%

Case Type	All Civil Cases Disposed	Percent of Cases Disposed by a Jury Trial
Tort cases	377,421	2.3%
Automobile	277,087	1.6%
Premises liability	65,372	3.3%
Medical malpractice	18,396	6.4%
Intentional tort	10,879	2.7%
Product liability	12,763	2.6%
Toxic substance	6,045	2.8%
Professional malpractice	6,827	3.2%
Slander/libel	3,159	1.9%
Other tort	26,891	2.6%
Contract cases	365,263	0.7%
Seller plaintiff	188,761	0.5%
Buyer plaintiff	44,592	1.1%
Fraud	15,917	2.0%
Employment	8,064	4.0%
Rental/lease	20,587	0.4%
Mortgage foreclosure	68,811	1.1%
Other contract	18,531	1.3%
Real property cases	19,235	2.1%
Eminent domain	4,595	4.3%
Other real property	14,650	1.4%
Total civil cases	761,919	1.5%

According to this study of the nation's 75 most populous counties, there were 761,919 civil cases handled over a year-long period ending in June 1992. Of that total, juries decided the outcomes of only about 12,000 cases (1.5%). Tort cases accounted for 49% of all civil cases, and were the most frequent type to be disposed by a jury trial (2.3%). Contract cases accounted for 48% of all civil cases, but only 0.7% of all contract cases were settled by a jury trial. Real property cases only comprised 3% of all civil cases, and 2.1% were decided by a jury trial.

Civil cases are another method of seeking justice through the legal system. Unlike criminal cases, civil cases do not involve prosecution by a governmental agency. Civil cases are lawsuits where one individual or group disputes another, and the government's legal system acts as a referee between the two.

Civil cases fall into one of three categories: torts, contracts, or real property. Torts involve claims arising from personal injury or property damage caused by the negligent or intentional act of another person or business (such as automobile accidents, injuries caused by dangerous conditions of residential or commercial premises, and malpractice). Contract cases include all accusations of someone breaking a contract (such as sellers seeking to collect money owed, and buyers seeking the return of their money). Real property cases involve claims regarding ownership of material property (excluding mortgage foreclosures, which are included under contracts).

Source U.S. Department of Justice, Bureau of Justice Statistics, "Civil Jury Cases and Verdicts in Large Counties" (Washington, D.C.: U.S. Government Printing Office, July 1995).

Contact U.S. Department of Justice, Bureau of Justice Statistics Clearinghouse, Box 6000, Rockville, MD 20850. (800) 732-3277. A World Wide Web server is operated at http://ncjrs.aspensys.com:81/ncjrshome.html. Inquiries can also be sent by e-mail to askncjrs@aspensys.com.

How much money is usually awarded to civil lawsuit winners?

Final award amounts for civil jury cases with plaintiff winners in state courts
from the nation's 75 largest counties during 1992.

Case Type	Number of Cases with a Plaintiff Winner	Total Amount Awarded to Plaintiff Winners	Average Award	Median Award	Percent of Plaintiff Winner Cases with Final Awards over $250,000
Tort cases	4,584	$1,869,699,000	$408,000	$51,000	21.2%
Toxic substance	202	106,306,000	526,000	101,000	30.4%
Automobile	2,280	502,602,000	220,000	29,000	12.7%
Professional malpractice	92	97,308,000	1,057,000	156,000	38.4%
Intentional tort	199	105,466,000	530,000	54,000	21.5%
Other tort	393	154,032,000	391,000	65,000	23.5%
Premises liability	845	196,207,000	232,000	57,000	22.0%
Slander/libel	27	6,284,000	229,000	25,000	18.4%
Product liability	142	103,346,000	727,000	260,000	50.5%
Medical malpractice	403	598,148,000	1,484,000	201,000	47.1%
Contract cases	1,322	820,098,000	620,000	56,000	22.6%
Rental/lease	85	159,734,000	1,881,000	71,000	17.7%
Seller plaintiff	417	88,368,000	212,000	35,000	17.9%
Buyer plaintiff	363	173,95,000	479,000	45,000	20.8%
Employment	170	249,206,000	1,462,000	141,000	39.8%
Fraud	173	117,209,000	678,000	70,000	26.5%
Other contract	113	31,616,000	280,000	49,000	17.9%
Real property cases*	43	13,886,000	325,000	55,000	16.1%
All civil jury cases	5,949	$2,703,683,000	$455,000	$52,000	21.5%

* Eminent domain cases are not included in final awards because they always entail an award; the issue is how much the defendant will receive for the property.

Comments

Juries in the 75 most populous counties of the U.S. awarded over $2.7 billion in compensatory and punitive damages to plaintiff winners in 1992. Justice in civil cases is usually reached when the plaintiff is awarded some kind of cash settlement that the defendant must pay. In civil cases, the plaintiff must prove the key elements of the case by a "preponderance of the evidence." This standard is less restrictive than "beyond a reasonable doubt," the standard used in criminal cases. The mean (average) award was $455,000, while the median award was $52,000.

A *mean* is a type of statistic that indicates what the typical case should be, and is calculated by dividing the sum of all the cases by the number of cases. A *median* is another type of statistic, but it indicates the actual midpoint of all the cases. The median is the value where half of the cases have greater values, and the other half have smaller values. In this example, a median of $52,000 indicates that out of 5,949 cases, 2,974 cases had awards greater than $52,000, and 2,974 cases had awards less than $52,000 (this adds to 5,948 cases—the final case is the $52,000 case itself).

The mean is much greater than the median for all the categories listed. This happened because there were a few cases that received very high awards, which drove up the mean. In fact, 21.5% of all cases were awarded over $250,000. This percentage, however, varied greatly depending upon the type of jury case.

Both tort and contract cases typically involve a compensatory award for economic damages. Tort cases can also include a compensatory award for non-economic damages, which include awards for pain and suffering and emotional distress. Distinct from compensatory damages are punitive damages, which are almost exclusively reserved for tort claims in which the defendant's conduct was grossly negligent or intentional.

Source

U.S. Department of Justice, Bureau of Justice Statistics, "Civil Jury Cases and Verdicts in Large Counties" (Washington, D.C.: U.S. Government Printing Office, July 1995).

Contact

U.S. Department of Justice, Bureau of Justice Statistics Clearinghouse, Box 6000, Rockville, MD 20850. (800) 732-3277. A World Wide Web server is operated at http://ncjrs.aspensys.com:81/ncjrshome.html. Inquiries can also be sent by e-mail to askncjrs@aspensys.com.

The costs of crime to victims

Total economic loss to victims of crime in the U.S., 1992.

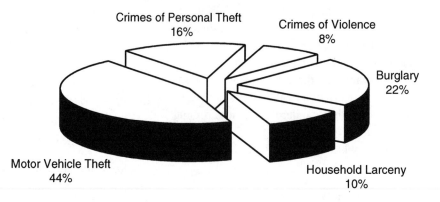

Crimes of Personal Theft 16%

Crimes of Violence 8%

Burglary 22%

Motor Vehicle Theft 44%

Household Larceny 10%

Victims with Losses	$ Millions
Household crimes	$13,536
Burglary	3,970
Household larceny	1,750
Motor vehicle theft	7,816
Crimes of personal theft	2,748
Crimes of violence	1,362
Rape	33
Robbery	680
Assault	649
Total	$17,646

Comments Crime victims in 1992 lost about $17.6 billion in direct costs, according to the National Crime Victimization Survey (NCVS). The NCVS is a nationwide survey of over 100,000 residents which measures both reported and unreported crimes. These costs included losses from property theft or damage, cash losses, medical expenses, and amount of pay lost due to injuries or activities related to the crime. The crimes included in the NCVS are rape, robbery, assault, personal and household theft, burglary, and motor vehicle theft. Crimes include attempts as well as completed offenses. Murders are not included by the NCVS because the victims cannot be surveyed.

Household crimes accounted for over 76% of all economic losses in 1992, with motor vehicle theft contributing 44%; burglary, 22%; and household larceny, 10%. Crimes of personal theft comprised 16% of all economic losses to crime victims. Crimes of personal theft involve stealing cash or property by stealth without the use of force and include thefts of articles from cars, pocket picking, and purse snatching.

Violent crimes accounted for the remaining 8% of economic losses. Economic losses from robbery made up about 4% of all losses; assault, nearly 4%; and rape, less than 1%.

Source U.S. Department of Justice, Bureau of Justice Statistics, "The Costs of Crime to Victims" (Washington, D.C.: U.S. Government Printing Office, February 1994).

Contact U.S. Department of Justice, Bureau of Justice Statistics Clearinghouse, Box 6000, Rockville, MD 20850. (800) 732-3277. A World Wide Web server is operated at http://ncjrs.aspensys.com:81/ncjrshome.html. Inquiries can also be sent by e-mail to askncjrs@aspensys.com.

Average amounts stolen during economically-motivated crimes

Average value of loss from various economically-motivated crimes in the U.S., 1990–94.

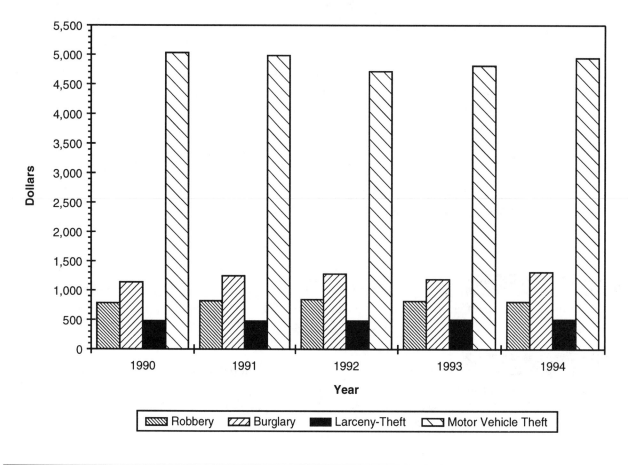

Type of Crime	1990	1991	1992	1993	1994
Robbery	$783	$817	$840	$815	$801
Burglary	$1,133	$1,246	$1,278	$1,185	$1,311
Larceny-theft	$480	$478	$483	$504	$505
Motor vehicle theft	$5,032	$4,983	$4,713	$4,808	$4,940

Comments The FBI annually collects statistics from state and local law enforcement agencies regarding the value of cash and property stolen during crimes. Most stealing occurs as the result of a robbery, burglary, larceny-theft, or motor vehicle theft, although some occurs with other types of crime.

Among these four main types of crime usually motivated by money, motor vehicle thefts typically yield the highest monetary loss to the victim. The average motor vehicle theft had a value of $5,032 in 1990, which declined by about 2% to $4,940 in 1994. Meanwhile, the average value of a burglary increased by about 15%, from $1,133 in 1990 to $1,311 in 1994. The average value of a larceny-theft also increased from $480 in 1990 to $505 in 1994 (about 5%).

Source U.S. Department of Justice, Federal Bureau of Investigation, *Crime in the United States, 1994* (Washington, D.C.: U.S. Government Printing Office, 1995), p 205.

U.S. Department of Justice, Federal Bureau of Investigation, *Crime in the United States, 1993* (Washington, D.C.: U.S. Government Printing Office, 1994), p. 205.

U.S. Department of Justice, Federal Bureau of Investigation, *Crime in the United States, 1992* (Washington, D.C.: U.S. Government Printing Office, 1993), p. 205.

U.S. Department of Justice, Federal Bureau of Investigation, *Crime in the United States, 1991* (Washington, D.C.: U.S. Government Printing Office, 1992), p. 201.

U.S. Department of Justice, Federal Bureau of Investigation, *Crime in the United States, 1990* (Washington, D.C.: U.S. Government Printing Office, 1991), p. 162.

Contact U.S. Department of Justice, Federal Bureau of Investigation, Uniform Crime Reports, Criminal Justice Information Services Division, Washington, D.C. 20535. Information Dissemination: (202) 324-5015.

How much is stolen in a typical robbery?

Average value stolen during a robbery, by location of the incident, 1993.

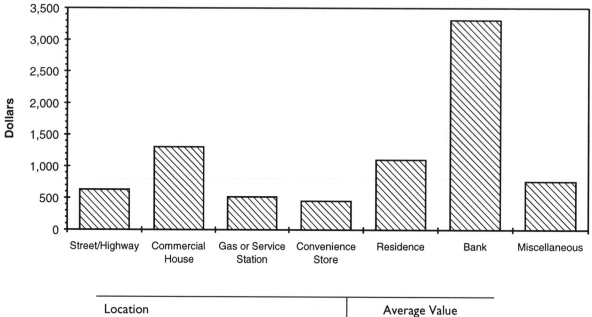

Location	Average Value
Street/highway	628
Commercial house	1,304
Gas or service station	515
Convenience store	449
Residence	1,104
Bank	3,308
Miscellaneous	759
Total	$815

Comments The average value of cash and property stolen in the course of a robbery was $815 in 1993. There were 577,925 robberies in 1993 where the value of the loss was reported.

Bank robberies were by far the most profitable type of robberies, with an average value of $3,308 per offense in 1993. Bank robberies on average resulted in over twice the amount of loot as the second most profitable type of robbery, commercial house robbery ($1,304). Commercial houses include businesses that are open to the public, such as restaurants, retail stores, and shops. Robberies of private residences cleared the next highest average amount ($1,104), followed by street/highway robberies ($628), gas or service station robberies ($515), and convenience store robberies ($449). Robberies of all other types of establishments averaged $759 per offense in 1993.

Source U.S. Department of Justice, Federal Bureau of Investigation, *Crime in the United States, 1993* (Washington, D.C.: U.S. Government Printing Office, 1994), p. 205.

U.S. Department of Justice, Federal Bureau of Investigation, *Crime in the United States, 1992* (Washington, D.C.: U.S. Government Printing Office, 1993), p. 205.

U.S. Department of Justice, Federal Bureau of Investigation, *Crime in the United States, 1991* (Washington, D.C.: U.S. Government Printing Office, 1992), p. 201.

U.S. Department of Justice, Federal Bureau of Investigation, *Crime in the United States, 1990* (Washington, D.C.: U.S. Government Printing Office, 1991), p. 162.

Contact U.S. Department of Justice, Federal Bureau of Investigation, Uniform Crime Reports, Criminal Justice Information Services Division, Washington, D.C. 20535. Information Dissemination: (202) 324-5015.

How much is stolen in a typical burglary?

Average value of cash and property stolen during a burglary, by time and location of the incident, 1993.

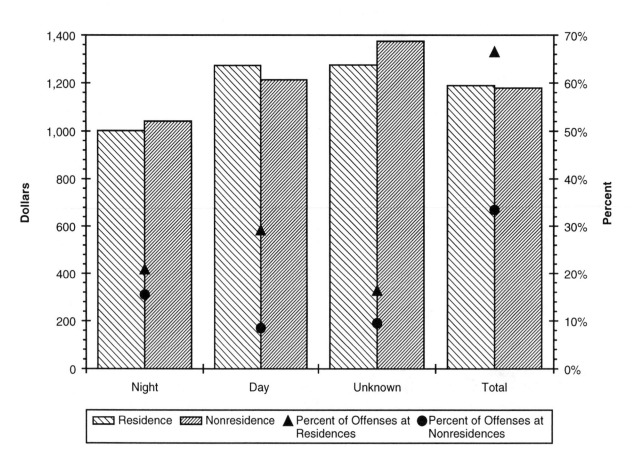

Time of Burglary	Residence		Nonresidence	
	Average Value	Percent of Offenses	Average Value	Percent of Offenses
Night	$1,002	20.9	$1,041	15.5
Day	$1,273	29.2	$1,213	8.5
Unknown	$1,275	16.4	$1,375	9.5
Total	$1,189	66.5	$1,179	33.5

Comments   The average burglary in 1993 resulted in the loss of $1,189 for residences and $1,179 for places other than residences, such as stores and offices. Over 66% of all reported burglaries took place at residences.

Burglaries that occurred at an unknown hour resulted in the greatest loss of cash and property. Places other than residences that were burglarized at an unknown hour on average experienced a loss of $1,375, while residences burglarized lost $1,275 on average.

The popular image of burglary often focuses on crimes that occur at night. However, most residential burglaries are committed during the day (29.2%). Only nonresidential burglaries are performed most often at night (15.5%). A burglar requires secrecy in order to complete the crime. Residential burglaries happen most often during the day because that is when people usually are away from home. In the same manner, most nonresidential burglaries occur at night because that is when businesses usually are closed.

Source   U.S. Department of Justice, Federal Bureau of Investigation, *Crime in the*

United States, 1993 (Washington, D.C.: U.S. Government Printing Office, 1994), p. 205.

Contact   U.S. Department of Justice, Federal Bureau of Investigation, Uniform Crime Reports, Criminal Justice Information

Services Division, Washington, D.C. 20535. Information Dissemination: (202) 324-5015.

How much is stolen in a typical larceny-theft?

Average value of loss from a larceny-theft in the U.S., 1993.

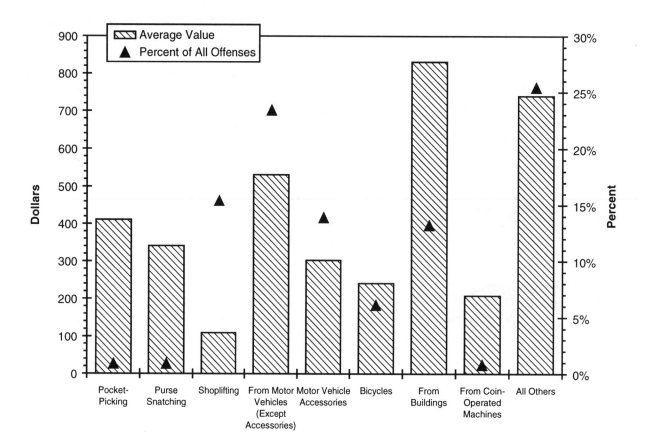

Type of Larceny-Theft	Percent of all Offenses	Average Value
Pocket-picking	0.9	$411
Purse snatching	0.9	$341
Shoplifting	15.4	$109
From motor vehicles (except accessories)	23.4	$531
Motor vehicle accessories	13.9	$303
Bicycles	6.1	$241
From buildings	13.2	$831
From coin-operated machines	0.8	$208
All others	25.4	$740
Total	100.0	$504

Comments In 1993, the average value of cash and property stolen in a larceny-theft was $504. The average value varied significantly depending on the type of crime.

Shoplifting had the lowest average value ($109), while thefts from buildings had the highest average value ($831). Although thefts from shoplifting had the lowest average value, shoplifting accounted for 15.4% of all larceny-thefts, while thefts from buildings made up 13.2%. This means that there were more offenses of shoplifting than thefts from build-ings, even though the latter were much more profitable on average.

Among the crimes classified here, thefts from motor vehicles accounted for the highest percentage of all larceny-thefts. These thefts comprised 23.4% of all larceny-thefts with an average value of $531 per theft. Pocket-picking (0.9%), purse-snatching (0.9%), and thefts from coin-operated machines (0.8%) accounted for the lowest percentages of larceny-thefts and generally resulted in some of the lowest average values.

Source U.S. Department of Justice, Federal Bureau of Investigation, *Crime in the United States, 1993* (Washington, D.C.: U.S. Government Printing Office, 1994), p. 205.

Contact U.S. Department of Justice, Federal Bureau of Investigation, Uniform Crime Reports, Criminal Justice Information Services Division, Washington, D.C. 20535. Information Dissemination: (202) 324-5015.

Property damages from arson

The estimated costs (in millions of dollars) of property damages to structures and vehicles from arson in the U.S., 1978–94.

Year	Structure Fires	Vehicle Fires
1978	1,067	51
1979	1,328	167
1980	1,760	75
1981	1,658	107
1982	1,604	138
1983	1,421	122
1984	1,417	138
1985	1,670	134
1986	1,677	151
1987	1,590	135
1988	1,594	151
1989	1,558	139
1990	1,394	167
1991	1,531	182
1992	1,999	158
1993	2,351	137
1994	1,447	*

* Amount for structure fires includes vehicle fires.

Comments The total amount of property damage caused by arson increased from about $1.1 billion in 1978 to $1.4 billion in 1994. Property damage estimates include the total loss of contents, buildings and other structures, vehicles, machinery, vegetation, and any other property involved in a fire. These figures do not include indirect losses, such as loss of business or temporary shelter costs.

Property damages due to arson increased rapidly from $1.1 billion in 1978 to around $1.8 billion in 1980, and steadily declined until 1984, when property losses totaled approximately $1.5 billion. After rising to over $1.8 billion in 1985 and 1986, annual property damage amounts again fell until 1990, when the total was again around $1.5 billion. Property damages, however, soared during 1991–93, reaching a high of nearly $2.5 billion in 1993.

The reason why property damages from arson rose so rapidly in 1992 was mainly due to the $567 million in damage caused by the Los Angeles Civil Disturbance. The chaos immediately after the Rodney King trial intensified into looting, riots, street violence, and arson.

In 1993, property damages escalated due to two more episodes of large-scale arson. Three wildfires traced to arson caused $809 million in damage to southern California during October and November of that year. In addition, the explosion at the World Trade Center and the resulting fire in New York City caused another $230 million in property damage.

Source Fire Analysis and Research Division, National Fire Protection Association.

Contact National Fire Protection Association, 1 Batterymarch Park, Quincy, MA 02269-9101. (617) 770-3000.

How much has been spent on the justice system in recent years?

Justice system direct expenditures (in millions of dollars), 1982–92.

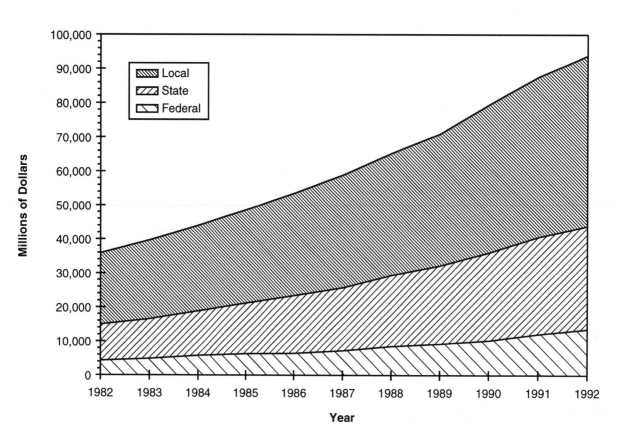

Year	Federal	State	Local	Total
1982	$4,269	$10,651	$20,922	$35,842
1983	4,844	11,709	23,127	39,680
1984	5,787	13,081	25,075	43,943
1985	6,279	14,903	27,381	48,563
1986	6,430	16,978	30,092	53,500
1987	7,231	18,465	33,175	58,871
1988	8,464	20,880	35,887	65,231
1989	9,204	23,009	38,736	70,949
1990	10,219	25,764	43,451	79,434
1991	12,106	28,493	46,968	87,567
1992	13,529	30,271	49,977	93,777

Comments From 1982 to 1992, the amount of money spent on the justice system rose from $35.8 billion to over $93.7 billion, an increase of over 160%. Expenditures include the costs of police protection, judicial and legal costs, and corrections expenses.

Local expenditures accounted for the largest share of justice system costs. Although local expenditures made up the greatest amount in terms of dollars and increased by about 139% during 1982–92, the actual pro-portion of local expenditures to total expenditures fell from 58% in 1982 to 53% in 1992.

State expenditures made up the next highest share of justice system costs. State expenditures increased 184% during 1982–92, and rose from 30% to 32% of the total during those years.

Federal expenditures, the smallest share of the total cost, increased 216% during 1982–92. The money spent at the federal level, however, accounted for only 12% of the total in 1982 and about 15% in 1992.

Source U.S. Department of Justice, Bureau of Justice Statistics, *Sourcebook of Criminal Justice Statistics—1994* (Washing-ton, D.C.: U.S. Government Printing Office, 1995), p. 4, table 1.4.

Contact U.S. Department of Justice, Bureau of Justice Statistics Clearinghouse, Box 6000, Rockville, MD 20850. (800) 732-3277. A World Wide Web server is operated at http://ncjrs.aspensys.com:81/ncjrshome.html. Inquiries can also be sent by e-mail to askncjrs@aspensys.com.

How much is the justice system costing each of us?

Justice system per capita expenditures, 1980–92.

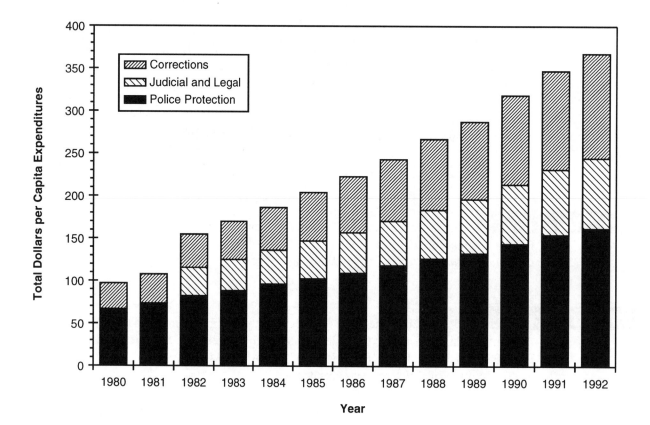

Year	Police Protection	Judicial and Legal	Corrections	Total
1980	$66.73	NA	$30.37	NA
1981	73.30	NA	34.30	NA
1982	82.10	$33.50	39.10	$154.70
1983	88.30	36.90	44.50	169.70
1984	96.20	40.10	50.00	186.30
1985	102.60	44.70	56.90	204.10
1986	109.30	47.80	65.60	222.80
1987	118.70	51.80	72.40	243.00
1988	126.60	57.10	83.00	266.80
1989	132.90	63.20	91.40	287.50
1990	144.00	69.60	104.90	318.50
1991	154.60	76.50	116.20	347.30
1992	162.10	82.30	123.40	367.70

Comments Using population estimates provided by the U.S. Bureau of the Census, the Bureau of Justice Statistics calculated the amount of money that was annually spent on the justice system on a per capita (per person) basis during 1980–92. The expenditures per capita indicate how much money it would have cost under the imaginary concept that every single person in the U.S. paid the same amount into the cost of the justice system. A statistic that uses a per capita measurement is useful in looking at trends while accounting for changes in population size.

From 1982 to 1992, total justice system expenditures increased from $154.70 to $367.70 per person, a rise of 137.7%. Some types of expenditures grew at a faster rate than others. Expenses for corrections grew the fastest, as the number of prison inmates swelled during the 1980s. Corrections expenditures amounted to just $39.10 in 1982, but increased 215.8% by 1992, when the amount was $123.40 per person. Judicial and legal expenditures, although a smaller portion of the total, saw a significant increase during that time. Even though judicial and legal expenses went from $33.50 to $82.30 per person during 1982–92, that rise was an increase of 145.4%. Police protection expenditures went from $82.10 per person in 1982 to $162.10 per person in 1992, a gain of 97.4%.

Source U.S. Department of Justice, Bureau of Justice Statistics, *Sourcebook of Criminal Justice Statistics—1994* (Washington, D.C.: U.S. Government Printing Office, 1995), p. 11, table 1.7.

Contact U.S. Department of Justice, Bureau of Justice Statistics Clearinghouse, Box 6000, Rockville, MD 20850. (800) 732-3277. A World Wide Web server is operated at http://ncjrs.aspensys.com:81/ncjrshome.html. Inquiries can also be sent by e-mail to askncjrs@aspensys.com.

How much does government spend on the criminal justice system?

Criminal justice system public direct expenditures (in thousands of dollars)
by activity and level of government in the U.S., 1992.

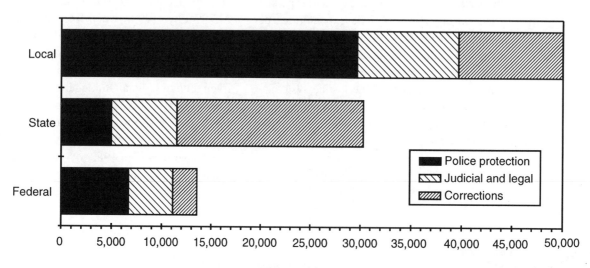

Milllions of Dollars

Activity	Federal	State	Local	All Governments
Police protection	$6,703,000,000	$4,967,069,000	$29,656,462,000	$41,326,531,000
Judicial and legal	4,415,000,000	6,552,687,000	10,021,201,000	20,988,888,000
Corrections	2,411,000,000	18,750,826,000	10,299,607,000	31,461,433,000
Total	$13,529,000,000	$30,270,582,000	$49,977,270,000	$93,776,852,000

Comments In 1992, governmental agencies across the U.S. spent almost $93.8 billion of taxpayers' money in direct expenditures on the criminal justice system. Direct expenditures are measured to avoid the double-counting that would occur through intergovernmental expenditures. Local governments accounted for about 53% of criminal justice system expenditures, state governments, 32%; and the federal government, about 15%.

Local governments had the greatest total direct expenditures, at nearly $50 billion. The amount for state governments was $30.3 billion, while the federal expenditures totaled just over $13.5 billion.

Police protection and corrections together accounted for the majority of all public expenditures on the criminal justice system at each level of government. Together, they comprised about 78% of the total for all levels of government combined.

Local governments spent 59% of their direct criminal justice expenditures on police protection and 21% on corrections. State governments spent 16% on police protection and 62% on corrections; and the federal government spent 50% on police protection and 18% on corrections.

Source U.S. Department of Justice, Bureau of Justice Statistics, *Sourcebook of Criminal Justice Statistics—1994* (Washington, D.C.: U.S. Government Printing Office, 1995), p. 4, table 1.3.

Contact U.S. Department of Justice, Bureau of Justice Statistics Clearinghouse, Box 6000, Rockville, MD 20850. (800) 732-3277. A World Wide Web server is operated at http://ncjrs.aspensys.com:81/ncjrshome.html. Inquiries can also be sent by e-mail to askncjrs@aspensys.com.

How much tax money is spent on police protection and on corrections during a year?

Police protection and corrections expenditures by federal, state, and local government agencies in the U.S. during fiscal year 1992. Percentages are shown in relation to general expenditures.

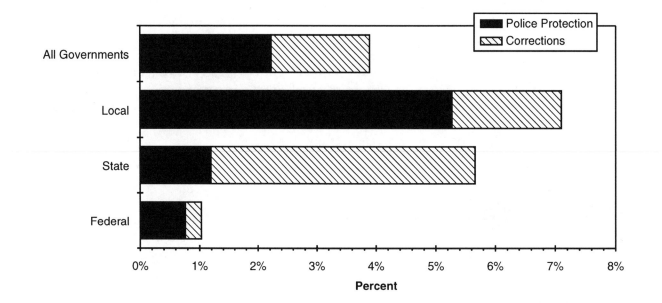

Type of Government	General Expenditures ($ millions)	Police Protection ($ millions)	As a Percent of all General Expenditures	Corrections ($ millions)	As a Percent of all General Expenditures
Federal	$886,545	$6,703	0.76%	$2,411	0.27%
State	409,132	4,863	1.19%	18,306	4.47%
Local	562,842	29,682	5.27%	10,300	1.83%
Total (all governments)	$1,858,519	$41,248	2.22%	$31,017	1.67%

Comments   About 3.9% of all general expenditures by governmental agencies in the U.S. went for police protection and corrections during fiscal year (FY) 1992. The category "general expenditures" also includes public finances spent on education, public welfare, health and hospitals, highways, fire protection, natural resources, sewerage and sanitation, housing and community development, governmental administration, parks and recreation, and interest on the general debt.

The percentage of expenditures on police protection and corrections were lowest for the federal government. Together, the two categories barely accounted for 1% of all federal expenditures.

State governments spent nearly 5.7% of all general expenditures on police protection and corrections in FY 1992. Prisons and other correctional facilities are usually the responsibility of state governments. State governments spent over $18.3 billion on corrections alone in FY 1992, or about 4.5% of expenditures. About 59% of all government expenditures on corrections were made at the state level in FY 1992.

Local governments spent over 7% of their general expenditures on police protection and corrections in FY 1992. However, while states are largely responsible for maintaining correctional facilities, policing is primarily the obligation of local governments. Local governments spent almost $29.7 billion on police protection in FY 1992. Those local payments accounted for about 72% of all governmental expenditures on policing that year.

Expenditures for police protection involve money spent on police patrols, communications, crime prevention activities, detention and custody of persons awaiting trial, traffic safety, and vehicular inspection. Corrections expenditures include those associated with the confinement and correction of adults and minors convicted of offenses, as well as pardon, parole, and probation expenses. These statistics do not include public finances spent on buying, constructing, or renovating any buildings used for police protection or corrections.

Source   U.S. Bureau of the Census, *Government Finances: 1991–92*, series GF, No. 5 (Washington, D.C.: U.S. Government Printing Office) as cited by *The American Almanac 1994–1995: Statistical Abstract of the United States* (Austin, Tex.: The Reference Press, Inc., 1994), p. 298.

Contact   U.S. Department of Commerce, Bureau of the Census, Washington, D.C., 20233. (301) 457-2800. The Bureau of the Census also maintains a World Wide Web server at http://www.census.gov.

Glossary

Aggravated assault: An unlawful attack by one person upon another for the purpose of inflicting severe or serious bodily injury, regardless of whether an injury occurred. Serious injury includes broken bones, lost teeth, internal injuries, loss of consciousness, and any injury requiring two of more days of hospitalization. This type of assault usually is accompanied by the use of a weapon or by means likely to produce death or great bodily harm. It also includes conduct under these statutory names: aggravated assault and battery, assault with intent to kill, assault with intent to commit murder or manslaughter, atrocious assault, attempted murder, felonious assault, and assault with a deadly weapon. Simple assaults are excluded.

Arson: Any willful or malicious burning or attempt to burn, with or without intent to defraud, a dwelling house, public building, motor vehicle or aircraft, or any personal property of another. Also includes intentional destruction by means of explosion.

Assault: An unlawful physical attack or threat of attack. Assaults may be classified as simple or aggravated. Rape and attempted rape are excluded from this category, as well as robbery and attempted robbery. The severity of assaults ranges from minor threat to incidents that are nearly fatal.

Attempted forcible entry: A form of burglary in which force is used in an attempt to gain entry.

Bombing incident: The actual or attempted detonation of an explosive or incendiary devise in violation of state, local, or federal law. Before 1990, the FBI excluded threats to bomb, hoax bomb devices, accidental explosions, recoveries of explosive or incendiary devises, and such misdemeanor offenses as the illegal use of fireworks. Beginning in 1990, only bomb threats and such violations as the illegal use of fireworks were excluded from the tabulations.

Burglary: FBI Uniform Crime Reports definition: The unlawful entry or attempted forcible entry of any fixed structure to commit a felony or theft. Attempted forc-

ible entry is included. Vehicles and vessels used for regular residence, industry, or business are also included as fixed structures.

National Crime Victimization Survey definition: Unlawful or forcible entry or attempted entry of a residence. This crime usually, but not always, involves theft. The illegal entry may be by force, such as breaking a window or slashing a screen, or may be without force by entering through an unlocked door or an open window. As long as the person entering has no legal right to be present in the structure, a burglary has occurred. Furthermore, the structure need not be the house itself for a burglary to take place. Illegal entry of a garage, shed, or any other structure also constitutes household burglary. If breaking and entering occurs in a hotel or vacation residence, it is still classified as a burglary for the household whose member or members were staying there at the time the entry occurred.

Capital punishment: See *death penalty*.

Career criminal: A person who frequently engages in illegal activities as a primary form of income. Many career criminals are repeat offenders and recidivists who carry out illegal activities as part of a parasitic lifestyle.

Carjacking: A type of robbery that involves the theft or attempted theft of a motor vehicle by force or threat of force.

Central city: The largest city (or group of cities) in a Metropolitan Statistical Area. See also *Metropolitan Statistical Area*.

Child: A person less than 18 years of age or considered to be a minor by state law.

Civil case: Civil cases are lawsuits where one individual or group disputes against another, and the government's legal system acts as a referee between the two. Civil cases fall into one of three categories: torts, contracts, or real property. Unlike criminal cases, civil cases do not involve prosecution by a governmental agency.

Community service: A type of sentence requiring the offender to perform a specified amount of public service work, such as collecting trash in parks or other public facilities.

Community-based facilities: Public or privately contracted sites which hold persons for less than 24 hours per day. Such facilities permit the offender limited opportunities for work, school, or community contacts. Community-based facilities are used for a variety of purposes including specialized interventions or assistance (for example, drug or alcohol treatment), graduated release from prison prior to parole, or as a sanction instead of prison or jail confinement.

Conditional release: In corrections, a conditional release occurs when a prisoner is dismissed from prison into community supervision with a set of behavioral conditions for remaining on parole. If these conditions are violated, the inmate can be returned to prison. This incarceration can be for any of the remaining portion of the sentence the inmate may have on the current offense.

Correctional institutions: Prisons, reformatories, jails, houses of correction, penitentiaries, correctional farms, workhouses, reception centers, diagnostic centers, industrial schools, training schools, detention centers, and a variety of other types of institutions for the confinement and correction of convicted adults or juveniles who are judged delinquent or in need of supervision. Also included are facilities for the detention of adults and juveniles accused of a crime and awaiting trial or hearing.

Corrections: The confinement and rehabilitation of adults and juveniles convicted of offenses against the law, and the confinement of persons suspected of a crime awaiting trial and adjudication. Corrections includes costs and employment for jails, prisons, probation, parole, pardon, and correctional administration. Data for lock-ups or "tanks" holding prisoners less than 48 hours are included under "police protection."

Counterfeiting: A type of forgery that involves falsely making, fabricating, or altering any obligation of the United States or a foreign government. This includes U.S. and foreign bank notes and securities, coins or bars stamped at any mint in the U.S., money orders issued by the U.S. Postal Service, domestic or foreign stamps, or the official seal of any department or agency of the U.S. A counterfeiting offense also includes the passing, selling, attempted selling, or importing of such falsely made articles. The making, selling, or possession of plates and engravings used for printing counterfeit articles would also qualify as a counterfeiting offense.

Crimes of violence: Murder, rape, robbery, and assault. The National Crime Victimization Survey only counts rape, robbery, and assault as crimes of violence since it is impossible to survey murder victims.

Criminal homicide: Criminal homicide is a summary category, not a single codified offense. In law, the term applies to all homicides where the perpetrator intentionally killed someone without legal justification, or accidentally killed someone as a consequence of reckless or grossly negligent conduct. Criminal homicide therefore includes murder, nonnegligent (voluntary) manslaughter, negligent (involuntary) manslaughter, and vehicular manslaughter.

Curfew and loitering laws: Offenses relating to violations of local curfew or loitering ordinances where such laws exist.

Death penalty: In most states, the courts may sentence an offender to death for the most serious crimes, such as murder. The execution of the death sentence may be by lethal injection, electrocution, exposure to lethal gas, hanging, firing squad, or other method specified by state law.

Death row: In states with a death penalty, death row specifically refers to a block of prison cells reserved for offenders awaiting a death sentence.

Delinquency: Acts or conduct in violation of criminal law, when such acts or conduct are committed by juveniles.

Delinquent act: An act committed by a juvenile for which an adult could be prosecuted in a criminal court, but when committed by a juvenile is within the jurisdiction of juvenile court. Delinquent acts include crimes against persons, crimes against property, drug offenses, and crimes against public order, when such acts are committed by juveniles.

Detention: The placement of a youth in a restrictive facility between referral to court intake and case disposition.

Disposition: Definite action taken or treatment plan decided upon or initiated regarding a particular case.

Disturbing the peace: Unlawful interruption of the peace, quiet, or order of a community, including offenses called "disorderly conduct," "vagrancy," "loitering," "unlawful assembly," and "riot."

Driving under the influence: Driving or operating any motor vehicle or common carrier while drunk or under the influence of liquor or drugs.

Drug abuse violations: Offenses related to growing, manufacturing, making, possessing, using, selling, or distributing narcotic and dangerous nonnarcotic drugs. A legal distinction is made between trafficking and possession, with trafficking the more serious offense. Drug trafficking includes manufacturing, distributing, selling, smuggling, or possession with the intent to sell. Drug possession only includes ownership of illegal drugs and attempts to acquire them.

Drunkenness: Public intoxication except for driving under the influence.

Economically-motivated crimes: An offense committed for the purpose of stealing or illegally obtaining cash, property, or credit. An economically-motivated crime can be either a violent or a property offense. Examples of such crimes include burglary, theft, motor vehicle theft, robbery, and illegal drug trafficking.

Electronic crimes: A type of fraud that occurs through illegal access or manipulation of electronic transfers. Electronic crimes can be either uncomplicated or intricate. An example of a simple electronic crime is withdrawing funds from a stolen ATM or credit card. Some electronic crimes are more complicated and can involve penetration of computerized financial files and alteration of records.

Embezzlement: Misappropriation or misapplication of money or property entrusted to one's care, custody, or control.

Ethnicity: A person's ancestral heritage. For the surveys and data presented in this volume, ethnicity is distinct from racial status, and is typically indicated by the terms "Hispanic" or "non-Hispanic." See also *Hispanic origin.*

Execution: The act of carrying out a death penalty sentence by legally killing the convicted offender.

Expenditures: External cash payments made from any money source, including all payments financed from borrowing, fund balances, intergovernmental revenue, and other current revenue. It excludes any intergovern-

mental transfers and noncash transactions, such as the provision of meals or housing of employees. Also excluded are retirement of debt, investment in securities, extension of loans, or agency transactions. Total expenditures for government functions related to justice do not include interest payments on the debt. A "direct expenditure" is all expenditure except that classified as intergovernmental.

Family murder: The killing of one relative by another. Victims and offenders can be spouses, common-law spouses, children, step-children, grandchildren, parents, step-parents, grandparents, siblings, step-siblings, cousins, in-laws, and extended family members.

Felony: The legal classification that includes the most severe types of criminal offenses, often ones that involves violence or the threat of violence. Although most states define a felony as an offense punishable by a year or more in prison, not all states distinguish felonies from misdemeanors in the same way. In the criminal justice system, felonies are distinct from misdemeanors, juvenile offenses, and petty offenses.

Financial crime: An offense that involves the fraudulent diverting of funds, credit, or value from the legitimate source. Examples of financial crime include electronic funds transfer crimes, food coupon fraud, access device crimes, telecommunications crimes, and computer fraud.

Firearm: Any pistol, revolver, rifle, or shotgun using explosive powder to propel a projectile or projectiles.

Forcible entry: A form of burglary in which force is used to gain entry to a residence. Some examples include breaking a window or slashing a screen.

Forgery: The offense that involves falsely (and with intent to defraud) making, counterfeiting, altering, or possessing with intent to pass off as genuine any official document, obligation, or security. Forgery can apply to money orders, bank notes, court documents, deeds, military discharge papers, coins, ships' papers, power of attorney documents, customs documents, and so forth. The offense also includes making, selling, possessing, or printing the plates or engravings used to produce false articles. A forgery offense can also involve receiving, possessing, concealing, selling, or disposing of any falsely made securities, tax stamps, or pledges that have crossed a state line or the U.S. border after being stolen or unlawfully converted. See also *counterfeiting.*

Fraud offenses: The crime type comprising offenses sharing the elements of practice of deceit or intentional misrepresentation of fact, with the intent of unlawfully depriving a person of his or her property or legal rights.

Gambling, illegal: Unlawful staking or wagering of money or other thing of value on a game of chance or on an uncertain event.

Gangland killing: A murder committed by a gang member in the line of gang-related activities, except juvenile gang killings.

Good time: When correctional authorities deduct from a prison or jail sentence, often to reward or encourage good behavior, they give "good time." When the good time is applied to a specific action, such as working in a prison industry or performing a meritorious deed, it is called "earned."

Hate crimes: Offenses against persons or property that are motivated by some type of bias. Such bias can be aimed against members of certain racial, ethnic, or religious groups, or against someone who has a particular sexual orientation.

Hispanic origin: A person of Hispanic origin may be of any race. A few states, however, treat the ethnic category as a racial one. Reports usually rely on respondents identifying themselves as someone descended from any Spanish culture or origin. Examples might include self-descriptions such as: Mexican-American, Mexican, Mexicano, Chicano, Puerto Rican, Cuban, Central American, or South American.

Homicide: Causing the death of another person without legal justification or excuse, including the crimes of murder, nonnegligent manslaughter, and negligent manslaughter.

Household: People whose usual place of residence is the same housing unit, or people staying in a housing unit who have no usual place of residence elsewhere.

Household crimes: Attempted and completed crimes that do not involve personal confrontation. Examples of household crimes include burglary, motor vehicle theft, and household larceny.

Household larceny: Theft or attempted theft of property or cash from a residence or in the immediate vicinity of the residence. In order to occur within a house, a thief must have a legal right to be in the house (such as a ser-vant, delivery person, or guest), as unlawful or forcible entry constitutes a burglary.

Incarceration: The confinement of a convicted criminal in a federal or state prison or a local jail to serve a court-imposed sentence. Confinement is usually in a jail (administered locally) or a prison (operated by a state or the federal government). In many states, offenders sentenced to one year or less are held in a jail; those sentenced to longer terms are committed to a state prison.

Incident: A specific criminal act involving one or more victims and offenders. For example, if two people are robbed at the same time and place, this is classified as two robbery victimizations but only one robbery incident.

Income, annual family: The total income of the household head and all relatives living in the same housing unit for the 12 months preceding the interview. Includes wages, salaries, net income from businesses or farms, pensions, interest, dividends, rent, and any other monetary income. The incomes of people who are not related to the head of the household are not included.

Jails: Confinement facilities operated by local governments to hold persons awaiting trail. Jails are also used generally to hold persons sentenced to confinement for less than one year. In Vermont, Rhode Island, Connecticut, Delaware, Alaska, Hawaii, and the District of Columbia, jails are operated by the same authority that administers the state prison system.

Judicial and legal services: All civil and criminal courts and activities associated with courts.

Jurisdiction: A unit of government or the legal authority to exercise governmental power. According to the latter meaning, prisoners under a state's jurisdiction may be in the custody of local jails.

Justifiable homicide: The FBI restricts this definition to the killing of a felon by a law enforcement officer in the line of duty and the killing of a felon by a private citizen during the commission of a felony, based on initial police investigation. Excludes excusable homicides and any homicides ultimately ruled as noncriminal.

Juvenile: Youth at or below the upper age of juvenile court jurisdiction.

Juvenile court: Any court that has jurisdiction over matters involving juveniles.

Juvenile gang killing: A murder committed by a member of a juvenile gang for the promotion or protection of the gang's activities. Most juvenile gang killing victims are also youths, usually from rival gangs. Juvenile gang killings are often caused from feuds over territorial claims, personal disputes, or acts of revenge for previous attacks. Shootings by juvenile gangs (particularly driveby shootings) have often injured or killed bystanders who were caught in the crossfire.

Kidnapping: Transportation or confinement of a person without authority of law and without his or her consent, or without the consent of his or her guardian, if a minor.

Larceny: Theft or attempted theft of property or cash without involving force or illegal entry. This category is subdivided into personal larceny and household larceny.

Larceny-theft (except motor vehicle theft): The FBI definition encompasses the unlawful taking, carrying, leading, or riding away of property from the possession or constructive possession of another. Examples are shoplifting, pocket-picking, thefts of bicycles or automobile accessories, or the stealing of any property or article which is not taken by force and violence or by fraud. Attempted larcenies are included. Embezzlement, "con" games, forgery, worthless checks, etc., are excluded.

Life sentence: Any prison sentence with a fixed or maximum term of life in prison, regardless of the possibility of parole.

Liquor law offenses: State or local liquor law violations, except drunkenness and driving under the influence.

Lynching: The murder of an accused person (usually by hanging) without a legitimate trial. A lynching can be done by either an organized group of people or by a mob.

Mandatory sentencing: A mandatory sentencing law requires the judge to impose a sentence of incarceration, often of specified length, for certain crimes or categories of offenders. There is no option of probation or a suspended sentence.

Manslaughter: The unlawful killing of one person by another, but not as a result of hostility. Manslaughters are often further categorized as one of the following: nonnegligent, negligent, involuntary, or vehicular. In the criminal justice system, a homicide judged as manslaughter is not as severe as a murder.

Manslaughter by negligence: The killing of another person through gross negligence, excluding traffic fatalities. The FBI's crime index does not include manslaughter by negligence.

Maximum sentence lengths: Some jurisdictions sentence prisoners to a range of years; the larger number in that range is the most that a prisoner may serve on the sentence. Often, good time is subtracted from the maximum sentence.

Metropolitan Statistical Area (MSA): The Office of Management and Budget defines this as a population nucleus of 50,000 or more, generally consisting of a city and its immediate suburbs, along with adjacent communities having a high degree of economic and social integration with the nucleus. MSAs are designated by counties, the smallest geographical unit for which a wide range of statistical data can be obtained, except in New England where they are designated by cities and towns.

Minimum time to be served: The jurisdiction's estimate of the shortest time that each admitted prisoner must serve before becoming eligible for release. Factors used in this estimate include sentence length, good-time credits, earned-time credits, parole eligibility requirements, and early release requirements and allowances.

Misdemeanor: The legal classification that includes criminal offenses less severe than felonies. Although most states define a misdemeanor as an offense punishable by less than a year in prison, not all states distinguish misdemeanors from felonies in the same way. In the criminal justice system, misdemeanors are distinct from felonies, juvenile offenses, and petty offenses.

Motor vehicle: An automobile, truck, motorcycle, or any motorized vehicle legally allowed on public roads.

Motor vehicle theft: The stealing or unauthorized taking, including attempted theft, of a self-propelled vehicle that runs on the surface and not on rails. Specifically excluded from this category are motorboats, construction equipment, airplanes, and farming equipment.

Movement: In corrections, the term refers to the admission to or release from a status—prisoner, parolee, or probationer. A transfer between facilities typically does not count as a movement.

Murder and nonnegligent manslaughter: The FBI defines this term as the willful (nonnegligent) killing of one human being by another. Deaths caused by negligence, attempts to kill, suicides, accidental deaths, and justifiable homicides are excluded.

New court commitments: Persons entering prison directly from a sentence by a court and not from an unsuccessful period of community supervision (parole). Includes new court admissions, probation revocations, and admissions after the imposition of a suspended sentence.

Nonfatal violent crimes: All violent crimes except murder and nonnegligent manslaughter.

Nonstranger: A classification of a crime victim's relationship to the offender. An offender who is related to, well known to, or casually acquainted with the victim is a nonstranger. For crimes with more than one offender, if any of the offenders are nonstrangers, then the whole group of offenders is classified as nonstranger. This category only applies to crimes which involve contact between the victim and the offender. The distinction is not made for personal larceny without contact since victims of this offense rarely see the offenders.

Offender: The perpetrator of a crime; this term usually applies to crimes involving contact between the victim and the offender.

Offense: A crime. When referring to personal crimes, the term can be used to refer to both victimizations and incidents.

Offenses against the family and children: Nonsupport, neglect, desertion, or abuse of family and children.

Organized crime: Illegal activities methodically conducted by established groups of associated individuals. These activities can include drug trafficking, prostitution, gambling, embezzlement, extortion, weapons violations, smuggling, counterfeiting and forgery, fraud, usury, and other crimes. The term "organized crime" has traditionally been used to refer to groups such as the Mafia or La Cosa Nostra.

An organized crime operation is often managed much like a legitimate business, consisting of specialized functions. In the legal market, businesses deal with importers, suppliers, and wholesale and retail distributors in order to sell a product to customers. Legitimate businesses also rely on the use of marketing strategies, accounting, credit arrangements, distribution and routing plans, and customer service. These same roles and functions are also present in organized crime, especially when it involves drug trafficking.

Other offenses against persons: This category includes kidnapping, violent sex acts other than forcible rape (e.g., incest, sodomy), custody interference, unlawful restraint, false imprisonment, reckless endangerment, harassment, etc., and any attempts to commit such acts.

Parole: The release of a prisoner by the decision of a parole authority. The offender is placed under the supervision of a parole officer who monitors the offender's compliance with rules of conduct imposed by the paroling authority. Violations of these rules may result in reprisonment for the balance of the unexpired sentence.

Parole revocations: The administrative action of a paroling authority removing a person from parole status in response to a violation of conditions of parole, including commission of a new offense, often resulting in the offender being returned to prison.

Personal crimes: Rape, personal robbery, assault, personal larceny with contact, or personal larceny without contact. This category includes both attempted and completed crimes.

Personal crimes of theft: Personal larceny. The theft or attempted theft of property or cash by stealth, either with contact (but without force or threat of force) or without direct contact between the victim and the offender.

Personal crimes of violence: Rape, personal robbery, or assault. This category includes both attempted and completed crimes, and the crime always involves contact between the victim and the offender.

Personal larceny: Equivalent to the personal crimes of theft. Personal larceny is divided into two subgroups depending on whether or not the crime involved personal contact between the victim and the offender.

Personal larceny with contact: Theft or attempted theft of property or cash directly from the victim by stealth, not force or threat of force. Includes both purse snatching and pocket-picking.

Personal larceny without contact: Theft or attempted theft of property or cash from any place other than the victim's home or its immediate vicinity, without direct contact between the victim and the offender. This crime differs from household larceny only in the location in which the theft occurs. Examples of personal larceny without contact include theft of an umbrella in a restaurant, a radio from the beach, or cash from an automobile parked in a parking lot. Occasionally, the victim may see the offender commit the crime.

Physical injury: The National Crime Victimization Survey measures physical injury in cases of rape, personal robbery, and assault. Completed or attempted robberies that result in injury are classified as involving "serious" or "minor" injuries. Examples of injuries from serious assault include broken bones, loss of teeth, internal injuries, loss of consciousness, and undetermined injuries requiring two or more days of hospitalization. Injuries from minor assault include bruises, black eyes, cuts, scratches, swelling, or undetermined injuries requiring less than two days of hospitalization. Assaults without a deadly weapon are classified as aggravated if the victim's injuries fit the description given for serious assault. All completed rapes are defined as having resulted in physical injury. Attempted rapes are classified as having resulted in injury if the victim reported having suffered some form of physical injury.

Police protection: The function of law enforcement, preserving order, and apprehending those who violate the law. These activities can be performed by a city police department, sheriff's department, state police, or a federal law enforcement agency such as the FBI and the Drug Enforcement Administration.

Prison admission: In corrections, a prison admission occurs when a person is taken into physical custody (regardless of jurisdiction) and is usually held in a state prison facility. A prison admission can also include someone who was supposed to be held in a state facility, but was sent to a local jail because of crowding, safekeeping, or some other reason.

Prison release: In corrections, a prison release occurs when a prisoner is allowed to leave the physical custody of a state facility or a local jail because of overcrowding, safekeeping, or some other reason. A valid prison release includes persons who have left prison because of expiration of sentence, parole, or some other conditional release to community supervision.

Prisons: Confinement facilities operated by state governments or the federal government. Prisons are used to hold persons sentenced to confinement generally for more than one year.

Probation: The sentencing of an offender to community supervision by a probation agency, often as a result of suspending a sentence to confinement. Such supervision normally requires specific rules of conduct while in the community. If the rules are violated, a sentence to confinement may be imposed. Probation is the most widely used correctional method in the United States.

Prostitution and commercialized vice: Sex offenses (including attempts) of a commercialized nature, such as transactions of money in exchange for sexual services. Also includes operating a brothel, hiring, or transporting persons for the purposes of paid sexual services.

Public order offenses: Violations of the peace or order of the community or threats to the public health through unacceptable public conduct, interference with governmental authority, or violation of civil rights or liberties. Weapons offenses, bribery, escape, and tax law violations are included in this general category.

Race: For information based on census data, race is determined by self-declaration. In the criminal justice system, classification by race often depends on the reporting program within the state. Some states may report only two categories: "white" and "nonwhite." A few others may categorize Hispanics as belonging to "other race."

The term "white" generally refers to persons with ancestral origins in any of the indigenous peoples of Europe, North Africa, or the Middle East. The term "black" is commonly used to signify persons with ancestral origins in any of the sub-Saharan racial groups of Africa. "Other" refers to persons having ancestral origins with any of the original peoples of North America and the Arctic region, the Far East, Southeast Asia, the Indian Subcontinent, or the Pacific Islands.

Racketeering: To obtain money or profits illegally, often by means of acquiring, conducting, or maintaining an existing organization or enterprise, which acts as a cover or "front" for the illegal activities. Racketeering activities can include any act or threat involving murder, kidnapping, gambling, arson, robbery, bribery, extortion, dealing in narcotic and dangerous drugs, fraud, and other crimes. See also *organized crime*.

Rape: The National Crime Victimization Survey defines this crime as "carnal knowledge of a female or male through the use of force, including attempts." This category includes all forced sexual intercourse by means of psychological coercion as well as physical force. An incident of forced sexual intercourse refers to vaginal, anal, or oral penetration by the offender or offenders and includes incidents of penetration involving a foreign object. Statutory rape (without force—victim under age of consent) is excluded. Includes both heterosexual and homosexual rape.

Rape, forcible : The FBI's Uniform Crime Reports definition is "carnal knowledge of a female forcibly and against her will." This definition also includes rapes by force and attempts or assaults to rape. Statutory offenses (no force used—victim under age of consent) are not included.

Some states have enacted gender-neutral rape or sexual assault statutes that prohibit forced sexual penetration of either sex. Data reported by such states do not distinguish between forcible rape of females as defined above and other sexual assaults.

Recidivist: A current prisoner with a previous adult criminal record of sentences to probation or prison.

Robbery: Completed or attempted theft, directly from a person, of property or cash by force or threat of force, with or without a weapon.

Robbery with injury: Completed theft or attempted theft from a person, accompanied by an attack, whether with or without a weapon, resulting in injury. An injury is classified as resulting from a serious assault, irrespective of the extent of injury, if a weapon was used in committing the crime, or, if a weapon was not used, when the extent of the injury was either serious (e.g., broken bones, loss of teeth, internal injuries, or loss of consciousness) or undetermined but required two days of hospitalization. An injury is classified as resulting from a minor assault when the extent of the injury was small (e.g., bruises, black eyes, scratches, or swelling) or undetermined but required less than two days of hospitalization.

Robbery without injury: Theft or attempted theft from a person, accompanied by force or the threat of force, either with or without a weapon, but not resulting in injury.

Runaway: A juvenile who deserts his or her guardian. Persons under age 18 charged as runaways may be taken into protective custody under provisions of local statutes.

Rural: A county or group of counties not located inside a metropolitan statistical area. The category includes a variety of localities, including smaller cities with popu-

lations less than 50,000. However, the term primarily refers to sparsely populated areas.

Sentence enhancements: In nearly all states, a judge may lengthen the prison term for an offender with prior felony convictions. The lengths of such sentence enhancements and the criteria for imposing them vary among the states.

Sex offenses: A broad category of varying content, usually consisting of all offenses having a sexual element except for forcible rape and commercial sex offenses, which are defined separately.

Sexual assault: Distinct from rape or attempted rape offenses, sexual assault includes attacks or attempted attacks generally involving unwanted sexual contact between the victim and the offender. Attempted attacks may or may not involve force, such as grabbing or fondling. Attempted attacks also may include verbal threats of sexual assault.

Shoplifting: The theft of merchandise from a retail store. Shoplifting is a type of larceny committed against retail establishments.

Simple assault: Attack without a weapon resulting either in minor injury (e.g., bruises, black eyes, cuts, scratches, or swelling) or in an undetermined injury requiring less than two days of hospitalization. Also includes attempted assault without a weapon.

Stolen property offense: Unlawfully and knowingly receiving, buying, or possessing stolen property, including attempts.

Stranger: A classification of the victim's relationship to the offender for crimes involving direct contact between the two. Incidents are classified as involving strangers if the victim identified the offender as a stranger, did not see or recognize the offender, or knew the offender only by sight. Crimes involving multiple offenders are classified as involving nonstrangers if any of the offenders was a nonstranger. Since victims of personal larceny without contact rarely see the offender, no distinction is made between strangers and nonstrangers for this crime.

Suburban areas: A county or counties containing a central city, plus any contiguous counties that are linked socially and economically to the central city. Suburban areas are categorized as those portions of metropolitan areas situated "outside central cities."

Suspicion: No specific offense; suspect released without formal charges being placed.

Sworn police: Law enforcement personnel that have the authority to place persons under arrest.

Time served in prison: The amount of time spent in prison between the date of admission and the date of release. Time served in prison underestimates the actual time served because it excludes time spent in jail that was credited to the prison sentence for the current offense.

Total sentence length: The longest time that an offender could be required to serve for all offenses.

Truth-in-sentencing: In corrections, truth-in-sentencing describes a close correspondence between the sentence imposed upon those sent to prison and the time actually served prior to prison release.

Unconditional release: In corrections, an unconditional release occurs when a prisoner is dismissed from further correctional supervision and cannot be returned to prison for any remaining portion of the sentence for the current offense.

Unlawful entry: A form of burglary committed by someone having no legal right to be on the premises, even though no force is used.

Upper age of jurisdiction: The oldest age at which a juvenile court has original jurisdiction over an individual for law-violating behavior. This age varies from 15–18 years of age depending on the state's statute, but most states have set the upper age jurisdiction at 17 years of age. Within most states there are exceptions to the age criteria that place or permit youth at or below the state's upper age of jurisdiction to be under the original jurisdiction of the adult criminal court. For example, in most states if a youth of a certain age is charged with one of a defined list of what are commonly labeled "excluded offenses," the case must originate in the adult criminal court. Therefore, while the upper age of jurisdiction is commonly recognized in all states, there are numerous exceptions to this age criterion.

Vagrancy: Includes vagabondage, begging, and loitering.

Vandalism: Destroying or damaging, or attempting to damage, the property of another without his or her consent, or public property. Excludes damage by burning, which is arson.

Victim: The recipient of a criminal act, usually used in relation to personal crimes, but also applicable to households.

Victimization: A crime as it affects one individual or household. For personal crimes, the number of victimizations is equal to the number of victims involved. The number of victimizations may be greater than the number of incidents because more than one person may be victimized during as incident. Each crime against a household is assumed to involve a single victim, the affected household.

Victimize: To commit a crime against a person or household.

Warrant: A legal order that authorizes a law enforcement officer to make an arrest, a search, a seizure, or some other specified act.

Weapons offenses and violations : Unlawful sale, distribution, manufacture, alteration, transportation, possession, or use of a deadly weapon, or accessory, or any attempt to commit any of these acts.

Youth population at risk: For delinquency and status offense matters, this is the number of children from age 10 through the upper age of jurisdiction. For dependency matters, this is the number of children at or below the upper age of court jurisdiction. All states define by statute the upper age of jurisdiction. In most states, individuals are considered adults when they reach their 18th birthday. Therefore, for these states, the delinquency and status offense youth population at risk would equal the number of children 10 through 17 years of age living within the geographical area serviced by the court.

Youthful offender status: State legislators create this status through statutes that provide for special sentencing, commitment, or record sealing procedures for young adult offenders adjudicated in a criminal court (as opposed to a juvenile court). Such offenders may be above the statutory age limit for juveniles but below a specified upper age limit.

Index

A

Alabama
    aggravated assaults 62
    arrests, by type 120
    crimes committed per police officer 2
    jail inmates 160
    motor vehicle theft 76
    prison inmates 154
    prison inmates, growth 156
    probation population 146
    property crime rates 42
    violent crime rates 40
Alaska
    aggravated assaults 62
    arrests, by type 120
    crimes committed per police officer 2
    jail inmates 160
    motor vehicle theft 76
    prison admissions and releases 170
    prison inmates 154
    prison inmates, growth 156
    probation population 146
    property crime rates 42
    violent crime rates 40
Annual Survey of Jails (ASJ) xxiii
Arizona
    aggravated assaults 62
    arrests, by type 120
    crimes committed per police officer 2
    jail inmates 160
    motor vehicle theft 76
    prison admissions and releases 170
    prison inmates 154
    prison inmates, growth 156
    probation population 146
    property crime rates 42
    violent crime rates 40
Arkansas
    aggravated assaults 62
    arrests, by type 120
    crimes committed per police officer 2
    jail inmates 160

motor vehicle theft 76
    prison admissions and releases 170
    prison inmates 154
    prison inmates, growth 156
    prisoner executions 182
    probation population 146
    property crime rates 42
    violent crime rates 40
Arrests
    by offense 118
    by racial diversity 128
    by type of offense 124
    economically-related crimes 134
    juvenile 124
    total, by offense 130, 132
Arson
    arrests 114
    arrests in U.S. 132
    arrests, by age 124
    arrests, by gender 126
    arrests, by racial diversity 128
    arrests, urban vs. rural 118
    civilian deaths from 84
    definition 211
    hate crime victims 98
    juvenile arrests 114, 124
    juvenile offenders 108
    murder committed during 50
    offenses, by property type 82
    sentence length, average 174
    structure fires, trends 84
    time served, average 174
    value of losses, trends 200
    vehicle fires, trends 84
Assault
    age of offenders 106
    defendants, by prior convictions 184
    definition 211
    estimated number of victims 6
    family income of victims 28
    female victimization rates 18
    hate crime victims 98
    juvenile offenders 108
    male victimization rates 18

number reported 6
occurrence, by time of day 12
percentage reported, trends 10
racially-biased incidents 102
rates, by locality 36
sentence length, average 174
time served, average 174
value of losses, total 190
victimization rates, by race 26
victim-offender relationship 32
victims, by age group 20
Assault, aggravated
    age of offenders 106
    arrests in U.S. 132
    arrests, by age 124
    arrests, by gender 126
    arrests, by racial diversity 128
    arrests, by U.S. region 122
    arrests, urban vs. rural 118
    convictions, by type 140
    definition 211
    frequency, by state 40
    hate crime victims 98
    juvenile arrests 124
    juvenile offenders 108
    percentage reported, trends 10
    racially-biased incidents 102
    rates, by locality 36
    reported offenses, by state 62
    reported offenses, trends 60
    victimization rate, trends 60
    victimization rates, by race 26
    victim-offender relationship 32
    victims, by age group 20
Assault, simple
    definition 218
Attempted forcible entry
    definition 211

B

Bombing incident
    definition 211
Bombings
    deaths 86
    incidents, trends 86
    persons injured from 86
    value of property damaged 86
Bureau of Justice Statistics xxi–xxiii
Bureau of the Census xxi

Burglary
    arrests 114, 138
    arrests in U.S. 132
    arrests, by age 124
    arrests, by gender 126
    arrests, by racial diversity 128
    arrests, urban vs. rural 118
    by type, trends 44
    convictions 138
    convictions, by type 140
    crimes reported 138
    defendants, by prior convictions 184
    definition 211
    family income of victims 30
    frequency by state 42
    hate crime victims 98
    household victimization rate 66
    imprisonment 138
    juvenile arrests 114, 124
    juvenile offenders 108
    murder committed during 50
    occurrence, by time of day 12
    offenses, by time of day 196
    rate per population 70
    reported percentage of, trends 8
    reported, trends 70
    sentence length, average 174
    time served, average 174
    value of losses, by incident location 196
    value of losses, total 190
    value of losses, trends 192

C

California
    aggravated assaults 62
    arrests, by type 120
    crimes committed per police officer 2
    jail inmates 160
    motor vehicle theft 76
    prison admissions and releases 170
    prison inmates 154
    prison inmates, growth 156
    probation population 146
    property crime rates 42
    violent crime rates 40
Capital punishment
    definition 211
Career criminal
    definition 211
Carjacking
    definition 211

Central city
    definition 211
Child
    definition 211
Children
    murder 110
Cities
    arrests, by offense 118
    crime rates 34
Civil case
    definition 211
Civil cases
    by type 186
    money awarded 188
Colorado
    aggravated assaults 62
    arrests, by type 120
    crimes committed per police officer 2
    jail inmates 160
    motor vehicle theft 76
    prison admissions and releases 170
    prison inmates 154
    prison inmates, growth 156
    probation population 146
    property crime rates 42
    violent crime rates 40
Commercialized vice
    definition 217
Community service
    definition 212
Community-based facilities
    definition 212
Computer fraud
    arrests and cases closed 96
Conditional release
    definition 212
Connecticut
    aggravated assaults 62
    arrests, by type 120
    crimes committed per police officer 2
    jail inmates 160
    motor vehicle theft 76
    prison admissions and releases 170
    prison inmates 154
    prison inmates, growth 156
    probation population 146
    property crime rates 42
    violent crime rates 40
Convictions, by type 140

Correctional institutions
    definition 212
Correctional population 142, 144
Correctional Populations in the U.S. (CPUS) xxi
Corrections
    definition 212
Corrections costs
    by government level 206, 208
    per capital 204
Counterfeiting
    arrests, trends 134
    arrests, urban vs. rural 118
    by type of operation 92
    definition 212
    trends 92
    value of notes, trends 94
Crime
    arrests, by offense 118
    arrests, by racial diversity 128
    by metropolitan area 38
    convictions 140
    estimated number of victims 6
    family income of victims 28, 30
    frequency, by state 40, 42
    household affected, trends 64, 66
    justice system costs 202, 204
    number committed per police officer 2
    number reported 6
    occurrence, by month 14
    occurrence, by time of day 12
    offenses, known vs. cleared 136
    poverty comparison, trends 16
    rates, by locality 36
    rates, by population group 34
    reported, by state 2
    total arrests, by offense 130, 132
    value of losses, total 190
    value of losses, trends 192
    value of property recovered 68
    value of property stolen 68
    victimization rate, by race 26
    victim-offender relationship 32
    victims, by age group 20
Crimes of violence
    definition 212
Criminal homicide
    definition 212
Cross-tabulation 25
Curfew and loitering laws
    definition 212

D

Death penalty
  definition 212
Death row
  definition 212
Delaware
  aggravated assaults 62
  arrests, by type 120
  crimes committed per police officer 2
  jail inmates 160
  motor vehicle theft 76
  prison admissions and releases 170
  prison inmates 154
  prison inmates, growth 156
  prisoner executions 182
  probation population 146
  property crime rates 42
  violent crime rates 40
Delinquency
  definition 212
Delinquent act
  definition 212
Detention
  definition 212
Disposition
  definition 212
District of Columbia
  aggravated assaults 62
  arrests, by type 120
  crimes committed per police officer 2
  jail inmates 160
  motor vehicle theft 76
  prison admissions and releases 170
  prison inmates 154
  prison inmates, growth 156
  probation population 146
  property crime rates 42
  violent crime rates 40
Disturbing the peace
  definition 212
Driving under the influence
  definition 213
Drug abuse violations
  definition 213
Drug offenses
  sentence length, average 174
  time served, average 174
Drug trafficking
  arrests 138
  convictions 138

convictions, by type 140
crimes reported 138
imprisonment 138
Drugs
  arrests, trends 88
  defendants, by prior convictions 184
  prison inmates, trends 152
Drunkenness
  definition 213

E

Economically-motivated crimes
  definition 213
Electronic crime
  arrests and cases closed, by type 96
  definition 213
Embezzlement
  arrests, trends 134
  definition 213
Ethnicity
  definition 213
Execution
  definition 213
Executions
  legal and illegal, trends 176
  legal, trends 178, 180
  states, most executions 182
Expenditures
  definition 213

F

Family murder
  definition 213
Federal Bureau of Investigation (FBI) xxi, xxiii
Felony
  definition 213
Felony defendants
  with prior convictions 184
Females
  murder victims, by age group 22
  violent crime victims 18
Financial crime
  arrests and cases closed, by type 96
  definition 213
Firearm
  definition 213
Florida
  aggravated assaults 62

arrests, by type 120
crimes committed per police officer 2
jail inmates 160
motor vehicle theft 76
prison admissions and releases 170
prison inmates 154
prison inmates, growth 156
prisoner executions 182
probation population 146
property crime rates 42
violent crime rates 40
Forcible entry
definition 213
Forgery
arrests, trends 134
definition 213
Fraud
arrests and cases closed 96
arrests, trends 134
arrests, urban vs. rural 118
convictions, by type 140
definition 214
sentence length, average 174
time served, average 174

G

Gambling, illegal
definition 214
Gangland killing
definition 214
Gang-related killings 112
Georgia
aggravated assaults 62
arrests, by type 120
crimes committed per police officer 2
jail inmates 160
motor vehicle theft 76
prison admissions and releases 170
prison inmates 154
prison inmates, growth 156
prisoner executions 182
probation population 146
property crime rates 42
violent crime rates 40
Good time
definition 214

H

Hate crimes
definition 214
number of, by type 98
racially-biased 100
violent incidents, by offense 102
Hawaii
aggravated assaults 62
arrests, by type 120
crimes committed per police officer 2
jail inmates 160
motor vehicle theft 76
prison admissions and releases 170
prison inmates 154
prison inmates, growth 156
probation population 146
property crime rates 42
violent crime rates 40
Hispanic origin
definition 214
Homicide
arson-related deaths 84
bombing-related deaths 86
convictions, by sentence imposed 164
convictions, by type 162, 164
definition 214
hate crime murders 98
juvenile offenders 108
murder defendants, by prior convictions 184
murder victims, by age group 22
murder victims, by race 24
murder, by circumstance of occurrence 50
sentence length, average 174
Household
definition 214
value of losses, total 190
Household burglary
estimated number of victims 6
number reported 6
Household crimes
definition 214
Household larceny
definition 214
Households
affected by crime, trends 64, 66
income vs. crime rates 30
reported crimes against, trends 8
value of property recovered 68
value of property stolen 68

I

Idaho
    aggravated assaults 62
    arrests, by type 120
    crimes committed per police officer 2
    jail inmates 160
    motor vehicle theft 76
    prison admissions and releases 170
    prison inmates 154
    prison inmates, growth 156
    prisoner executions 182
    probation population 146
    property crime rates 42
    violent crime rates 40
Illinois
    aggravated assaults 62
    arrests, by type 120
    crimes committed per police officer 2
    jail inmates 160
    motor vehicle theft 76
    prison admissions and releases 170
    prison inmates 154
    prison inmates, growth 156
    prisoner executions 182
    probation population 146
    property crime rates 42
    violent crime rates 40
Incarceration
    definition 214
Incident
    definition 214
Income levels vs. crime rates 28
Income vs. crime rates 30
Income, annual family
    definition 214
Indiana
    aggravated assaults 62
    arrests, by type 120
    crimes committed per police officer 2
    jail inmates 160
    motor vehicle theft 76
    prison inmates 154
    prison inmates, growth 156
    prisoner executions 182
    probation population 146
    property crime rates 42
    violent crime rates 40
Intimidation
    hate crime victims 98
    racially-biased incidents 102

Iowa
    aggravated assaults 62
    arrests, by type 120
    crimes committed per police officer 2
    jail inmates 160
    motor vehicle theft 76
    prison admissions and releases 170
    prison inmates 154
    prison inmates, growth 156
    probation population 146
    property crime rates 42
    violent crime rates 40

J

Jail inmates
    number of, by state 160
    number of, trends 158
Jails
    adults in 142, 144
    definition 214
Judicial and legal services
    definition 214
Jurisdiction
    definition 214
Justice system
    direct expenditures 202
    per capita expenditures 204
    total costs, by government level 206
Justifiable homicide
    definition 214
Juvenile
    definition 214
Juvenile court
    definition 214
Juvenile Court Statistics (JCS) xxii
Juvenile delinquency
    reason for referral 108
    trends 108
Juvenile gang killing
    definition 215
Juveniles
    arrests, by type of crime 114
    arrests, by type of offense 124
    gang-related killings 112

K

Kansas
    aggravated assaults 62

arrests, by type 120
crimes committed per police officer 2
jail inmates 160
motor vehicle theft 76
prison admissions and releases 170
prison inmates 154
prison inmates, growth 156
probation population 146
property crime rates 42
violent crime rates 40
Kentucky
  aggravated assaults 62
  arrests, by type 120
  crimes committed per police officer 2
  jail inmates 160
  motor vehicle theft 76
  prison admissions and releases 170
  prison inmates 154
  prison inmates, growth 156
  probation population 146
  property crime rates 42
  violent crime rates 40
Kidnapping
  definition 215

L

Larceny
  convictions, by type 140
  definition 215
  frequency by state 42
  household victimization rate 66
  juvenile offenders 108
  occurrence, by time of day 12
  reported percentage of, trends 8
  value of losses, by offense type 198
  value of losses, trends 192
Larceny-theft
  definition 215
Life sentence
  definition 215
Liquor law offenses
  definition 215
Louisiana
  aggravated assaults 62
  arrests, by type 120
  crimes committed per police officer 2
  jail inmates 160
  motor vehicle theft 76
  prison admissions and releases 170
  prison inmates 154
  prison inmates, growth 156

probation population 146
property crime rates 42
violent crime rates 40
Lynching
  definition 215

M

Maine
  aggravated assaults 62
  arrests, by type 120
  crimes committed per police officer 2
  jail inmates 160
  motor vehicle theft 76
  prison admissions and releases 170
  prison inmates 154
  prison inmates, growth 156
  probation population 146
  property crime rates 42
  violent crime rates 40
Males
  murder victims, by age group 22
  violent crime victims 18
Mandatory sentencing
  definition 215
Manslaughter
  definition 215
Manslaughter by negligence
  definition 215
Maryland
  aggravated assaults 62
  arrests, by type 120
  crimes committed per police officer 2
  jail inmates 160
  motor vehicle theft 76
  prison admissions and releases 170
  prison inmates 154
  prison inmates, growth 156
  prisoner executions 182
  probation population 146
  property crime rates 42
  violent crime rates 40
Massachusetts
  aggravated assaults 62
  arrests, by type 120
  crimes committed per police officer 2
  jail inmates 160
  motor vehicle theft 76
  prison admissions and releases 170
  prison inmates 154
  prison inmates, growth 156

probation population 146
property crime rates 42
violent crime rates 40
Maximum sentence lengths
    definition 215
Metropolitan areas
    crime index 38
Metropolitan Statistical Area (MSA)
    definition 215
Michigan
    aggravated assaults 62
    arrests, by type 120
    crimes committed per police officer 2
    jail inmates 160
    motor vehicle theft 76
    prison admissions and releases 170
    prison inmates 154
    prison inmates, growth 156
    probation population 146
    property crime rates 42
    violent crime rates 40
Minimum time to be served
    definition 215
Minnesota
    aggravated assaults 62
    arrests, by type 120
    crimes committed per police officer 2
    jail inmates 160
    motor vehicle theft 76
    prison admissions and releases 170
    prison inmates 154
    prison inmates, growth 156
    probation population 146
    property crime rates 42
    violent crime rates 40
Misdemeanor
    definition 215
Mississippi
    aggravated assaults 62
    arrests, by type 120
    crimes committed per police officer 2
    jail inmates 160
    motor vehicle theft 76
    prison admissions and releases 170
    prison inmates 154
    prison inmates, growth 156
    probation population 146
    property crime rates 42
    violent crime rates 40
Missouri
    aggravated assaults 62
    arrests, by type 120

crimes committed per police officer 2
jail inmates 160
motor vehicle theft 76
prison admissions and releases 170
prison inmates 154
prison inmates, growth 156
probation population 146
property crime rates 42
violent crime rates 40
Montana
    aggravated assaults 62
    arrests, by type 120
    crimes committed per police officer 2
    jail inmates 160
    motor vehicle theft 76
    prison admissions and releases 170
    prison inmates 154
    prison inmates, growth 156
    probation population 146
    property crime rates 42
    violent crime rates 40
Motor vehicle
    definition 215
Motor vehicle theft
    arrests 114, 132, 138
    arrests, by age 124
    arrests, by gender 126
    arrests, by racial diversity 128
    arrests, urban vs. rural 118
    convictions 138
    crimes reported 138
    definition 215
    estimated number of victims 6
    family income of victims 30
    frequency by state 42
    hate crime victims 98
    household victimization rate 66
    imprisonment 138
    juvenile arrests 114, 124
    juvenile offenders 108
    murder committed during 50
    number reported 6
    occurrence, by time of day 12
    rate per population 76
    rate per registered vehicle 76
    reported percentage of, trends 8
    reported, by state 76
    reported, trends 78
    sentence length, average 174
    time served, average 174
    value of losses, total 190
    value of losses, trends 192

value of property recovered 68
value of property stolen 68
Movement
    definition 215
Murder
    arrests in U.S. 132
    arrests, by age 124
    arrests, by gender 126
    arrests, by racial diversity 128
    arrests, urban vs. rural 118
    children 110
    circumstance of occurrence 50
    committed per year, trends 48
    convictions, by sentence imposed 164
    convictions, by type 140, 162, 164
    defendants, by prior convictions 184
    definition 216
    frequency, by state 40
    hate crime victims 98
    juvenile arrests 124
    juvenile offenders 108
    racial diversity 24
    racially-biased incidents 102
    sentence length, average 174
    time served, average 174
    victims, by age group 22
Murders
    gang-related 112

N

National Center for Juvenile Justice xxii
National Corrections Reporting Program (NCRP) xxii
National Crime Victimization Survey (NCVS) xxi, xxii
National Jail Census (NJC) xxiii
National Judicial Reporting Program (NJRP) xxiii
National Pretrial Reporting Program (NPRP) xxiii
National Prisoner Statistics (NPS) xxiii
Nebraska
    aggravated assaults 62
    arrests, by type 120
    crimes committed per police officer 2
    jail inmates 160
    motor vehicle theft 76
    prison admissions and releases 170
    prison inmates 154
    prison inmates, growth 156
    prisoner executions 182
    probation population 146

property crime rates 42
violent crime rates 40
Nevada
    aggravated assaults 62
    arrests, by type 120
    crimes committed per police officer 2
    jail inmates 160
    motor vehicle theft 76
    prison inmates 154
    prison inmates, growth 156
    probation population 146
    property crime rates 42
    violent crime rates 40
New court commitments
    definition 216
New Hampshire
    aggravated assaults 62
    arrests, by type 120
    crimes committed per police officer 2
    jail inmates 160
    motor vehicle theft 76
    prison admissions and releases 170
    prison inmates 154
    prison inmates, growth 156
    probation population 146
    property crime rates 42
    violent crime rates 40
New Jersey
    aggravated assaults 62
    arrests, by type 120
    crimes committed per police officer 2
    jail inmates 160
    motor vehicle theft 76
    prison admissions and releases 170
    prison inmates 154
    prison inmates, growth 156
    probation population 146
    property crime rates 42
    violent crime rates 40
New Mexico
    aggravated assaults 62
    arrests, by type 120
    crimes committed per police officer 2
    jail inmates 160
    motor vehicle theft 76
    prison inmates 154
    prison inmates, growth 156
    probation population 146
    property crime rates 42
    violent crime rates 40
New York
    aggravated assaults 62

arrests, by type 120
crimes committed per police officer 2
jail inmates 160
motor vehicle theft 76
prison admissions and releases 170
prison inmates 154
prison inmates, growth 156
probation population 146
property crime rates 42
violent crime rates 40

Nonfatal violent crimes
definition 216
Nonnegligent manslaughter
definition 216
Nonstranger
definition 216
North Carolina
aggravated assaults 62
arrests, by type 120
crimes committed per police officer 2
jail inmates 160
motor vehicle theft 76
prison admissions and releases 170
prison inmates 154
prison inmates, growth 156
prisoner executions 182
probation population 146
property crime rates 42
violent crime rates 40
North Dakota
aggravated assaults 62
crimes committed per police officer 2
jail inmates 160
motor vehicle theft 76
prison admissions and releases 170
prison inmates 154
prison inmates, growth 156
probation population 146
property crime rates 42
violent crime rates 40

O

Offender
definition 216
Offense
definition 216
Offenses against the family and children
definition 216
Office of Juvenile Justice and Delinquency
Prevention (OJJDP) xxii

Ohio
aggravated assaults 62
arrests, by type 121
crimes committed per police officer 2
jail inmates 160
motor vehicle theft 76
prison admissions and releases 170
prison inmates 154
prison inmates, growth 156
probation population 146
property crime rates 42
violent crime rates 40
Oklahoma
aggravated assaults 62
arrests, by type 121
crimes committed per police officer 2
jail inmates 160
motor vehicle theft 77
prison admissions and releases 170
prison inmates 154
prison inmates, growth 156
probation population 146
property crime rates 42
violent crime rates 40
Oregon
aggravated assaults 62
arrests, by type 121
crimes committed per police officer 3
jail inmates 161
motor vehicle theft 77
prison admissions and releases 170
prison inmates 155
prison inmates, growth 157
probation population 147
property crime rates 43
violent crime rates 40
Organized crime
definition 216
Other offenses against persons
definition 216

P

Parole
adults on 142, 144
adults on, by status 172
definition 216
sentence length prior to, by offense 174
Parole revocations
definition 216

Pennsylvania
aggravated assaults 63
arrests, by type 121
crimes committed per police officer 3
jail inmates 161
motor vehicle theft 77
prison admissions and releases 170
prison inmates 155
prison inmates, growth 157
probation population 147
property crime rates 43
violent crime rates 40
Personal crimes
definition 216
Personal crimes of theft
definition 216
Personal crimes of violence
definition 216
Personal larceny
definition 216
Personal larceny with contact
definition 216
Personal larceny without contact
definition 216
Physical injury
definition 217
Police officers
number per population, trends 4
reported crimes per 2
Police protection
cost per capita 204
definition 217
expenditures, by government level 208
total costs, by government level 206
Poverty
comparison to crime, trends 16
Prison admission
definition 217
Prison release
definition 217
Prisons
admissions, by type 166
admissions, trends 168
admissions, violent offenders 170
adults in 142, 144
definition 217
federal inmate growth 157
federal inmates 155
inmate growth, by state 156
inmate population, by type 152
inmates with death sentence, trends 180

inmates, by state 154
population proportion, trends 150
releases, by type 166
releases, violent offenders 170
state inmate growth 157
state inmates 155
turnover rates, trends 168
Probation
adults on 142, 144
adults on, by state 146
characteristics of adults 148
definition 217
Property crime
arrests in U.S. 132
arrests in U.S., trends 130
arrests, by age 124
arrests, by gender 126
arrests, by state 120
by metropolitan area 38
frequency, by state 42
juvenile arrests 124
occurrence, by month 14
offenses, by state 120
offenses, known vs. cleared 136
prison inmates, trends 152
rates, by population group 34
sentence length, average 174
time served, average 174
Property value
stolen or recovered 68
Prostitution
arrests, by age group 90
arrests, trends 90
arrests, urban vs. rural 118
definition 217
murder committed during 50
Public order offenses
definition 217
Puerto Rico
crimes committed per police officer 3

R

Race
definition 217
Racketeering
definition 217
Rape
age of offenders 106
arrests in U.S. 132
arrests, by age 124

arrests, by gender 126
arrests, by racial diversity 128
arrests, urban vs. rural 118
convictions, by type 140
defendants, by prior convictions 184
definition 217
estimated number of victims 6
female victimization rates 18
frequency, by state 40
hate crime victims 98
juvenile arrests 124
juvenile offenders 108
male victimization rates 18
murder committed during 50
number reported 6
occurrence, by time of day 12
percentage reported, trends 10
racially-biased incidents 102
rates, by locality 36
reported to police, trends 54
sentence length, average 174
time served, average 174
value of losses, total 190
victimization rates, by race 26
victimization, trends 54
victim-offender relationship 32
victims, by age group 20
Rape, forcible
    definition 218
Recidivist
    definition 218
Rhode Island
    aggravated assaults 63
    arrests, by type 121
    crimes committed per police officer 3
    jail inmates 161
    motor vehicle theft 77
    prison inmates 155
    prison inmates, growth 157
    probation population 147
    property crime rates 43
    violent crime rates 40
Robbery
    age of offenders 106
    arrests 114, 138
    arrests in U.S. 132
    arrests, by age 124
    arrests, by gender 126
    arrests, by race 104
    arrests, by racial diversity 128
    arrests, urban vs. rural 118
    by site of offense, trends 46

convictions 138
convictions, by type 140
crimes reported 138
defendants, by prior convictions 184
definition 218
estimated number of victims 6
family income of victims 28
female victimization rates 18
frequency, by state 40
hate crime victims 98
imprisonment 138
juvenile arrests 114, 124
juvenile offenders 108
male victimization rates 18
murder committed during 50
number reported 6
occurrence, by time of day 12
percentage reported, trends 10
racial composition 104
racially-biased incidents 102
rates, by locality 36
reported, by type 56
reported, trends 58
sentence length, average 174
time served, average 174
value of losses, by incident location 194
value of losses, total 190
value of losses, trends 192
victimization rates, by race 26
victimization, by type 56
victimization, estimated 104
victimization, trends 58
victim-offender relationship 32
victims, by age group 20
Robbery with injury
    definition 218
Runaway
    definition 218
Rural
    definition 218
Rural counties
    crime rates 34

S

Sentence enhancements
    definition 218
Sex offenses
    definition 218
Sexual assault
    definition 218
    estimated number of victims 6

number reported 6
rates, by locality 36
reported to police 52
time served, average 174
victimization rates by race 26
victimization, estimated 52
victims, by age group 20
Shoplifting
definition 218
reported incidents, trends 80
South Carolina
aggravated assaults 63
arrests, by type 121
crimes committed per police officer 3
jail inmates 161
motor vehicle theft 77
prison admissions and releases 170
prison inmates 155
prison inmates, growth 157
probation population 147
property crime rates 43
violent crime rates 41
South Dakota
aggravated assaults 63
arrests, by type 121
crimes committed per police officer 3
jail inmates 161
motor vehicle theft 77
prison admissions and releases 170
prison inmates 155
prison inmates, growth 157
probation population 147
property crime rates 43
violent crime rates 41
Stolen property offense
definition 218
Stranger
definition 218
Suburban areas
definition 218
Suburban counties
crime rates 34
Suspicion
definition 219
Sworn police
definition 219

T

Telecommunications
arrests and cases closed 96

Tennessee
aggravated assaults 63
arrests, by type 121
crimes committed per police officer 3
jail inmates 161
motor vehicle theft 77
prison admissions and releases 171
prison inmates 155
prison inmates, growth 157
probation population 147
property crime rates 43
violent crime rates 41
Texas
aggravated assaults 63
arrests, by type 121
crimes committed per police officer 3
jail inmates 161
motor vehicle theft 77
prison admissions and releases 171
prison inmates 155
prison inmates, growth 157
prisoner executions 182
probation population 147
property crime rates 43
violent crime rates 41
Theft
arrests 114, 132
arrests, by age 124
arrests, by gender 126
arrests, by racial diversity 128
arrests, urban vs. rural 118
defendants, by prior convictions 184
estimated number of victims 6
family income of victims 28, 30
frequency by state 42
hate crime victims 98
juvenile arrests 114, 124
murder committed during 50
number reported 6
rate per population 72
rates, by locality 36
reported percentage of, trends 8
reported, by type 74
reported, trends 72
sentence length, average 174
time served, average 174
value of losses, by offense type 198
value of losses, trends 192
victimization rates, by race 26
victims, by age group 20
Time served in prison
definition 219

Total sentence length
    definition 219
Truth-in-sentencing
    definition 219

U

U.S. Department of Justice (USDJ) xxi, xxiii
Unconditional release
    definition 219
Uniform Crime Reports (UCR) xxi, xxiii
United States Secret Service (USSS) xxiv
Unlawful entry
    definition 219
Upper age of jurisdiction
    definition 219
Utah
    aggravated assaults 63
    arrests, by type 121
    crimes committed per police officer 3
    jail inmates 161
    motor vehicle theft 77
    prison admissions and releases 171
    prison inmates 155
    prison inmates, growth 157
    probation population 147
    property crime rates 43
    violent crime rates 41

V

Vagrancy
    arrests, urban vs. rural 118
    definition 219
Vandalism
    arrests 114
    arrests, urban vs. rural 118
    definition 219
    hate crime victims 98
    juvenile arrests 114
    juvenile offenders 108
Vermont
    aggravated assaults 63
    arrests, by type 121
    crimes committed per police officer 3
    jail inmates 161
    motor vehicle theft 77
    prison admissions and releases 171
    prison inmates 155
    prison inmates, growth 157
    probation population 147

property crime rates 43
    violent crime rates 41
Victim
    definition 219
Victimization
    definition 219
    rates, by age group 20
Victimize
    definition 219
Violent crime
    age of offenders 106
    arrests in U.S. 132
    arrests in U.S., trends 130
    arrests, by age 124
    arrests, by gender 126
    arrests, by state 120
    by metropolitan area 38
    child murder 110
    frequency, by state 40
    juvenile arrests 124
    occurrence, by month 14
    offenses, by state 120
    offenses, known vs. cleared 136
    percentage reported, trends 10
    prison inmates, trends 152
    rates, by population group 34
    sentence length, average 174
    time served, average 174
    value of losses, total 190
    victim-offender relationship 32
Virginia
    aggravated assaults 63
    arrests, by type 121
    crimes committed per police officer 3
    jail inmates 161
    motor vehicle theft 77
    prison inmates 155
    prison inmates, growth 157
    prisoner executions 182
    probation population 147
    property crime rates 43
    violent crime rates 41

W

Warrant
    definition 219
Washington
    aggravated assaults 63
    arrests, by type 121
    crimes committed per police officer 3
    jail inmates 161

motor vehicle theft 77
prison admissions and releases 171
prison inmates 155
prison inmates, growth 157
prisoner executions 182
probation population 147
property crime rates 43
violent crime rates 41
Weapons offenses and violations
definition 219
West Virginia
aggravated assaults 63
arrests, by type 121
crimes committed per police officer 3
jail inmates 161
motor vehicle theft 77
prison admissions and releases 171
prison inmates 155
prison inmates, growth 157
probation population 147
property crime rates 43
violent crime rates 41
Wisconsin
aggravated assaults 63
arrests, by type 121
crimes committed per police officer 3
jail inmates 161

motor vehicle theft 77
prison admissions and releases 171
prison inmates 155
prison inmates, growth 157
probation population 147
property crime rates 43
violent crime rates 41
Wyoming
aggravated assaults 63
arrests, by type 121
crimes committed per police officer 3
jail inmates 161
motor vehicle theft 77
prison admissions and releases 171
prison inmates 155
prison inmates, growth 157
probation population 147
property crime rates 43
violent crime rates 41

Y

Youth population at risk
definition 219
Youthful offender status
definition 219